OTHER MAGE TITLES BY WILLEM FLOOR

THE PERSIAN GULF SERIES

A Political and Economic History of 5 Port Cities, 1500–1750

The Rise of the Gulf Arabs, The Politics of Trade on the Persian Littoral, 1747–1792

The Rise and Fall of Bandar-e Lengeh, The Distribution Center for the Arabian Coast, 1750–1930

Bandar Abbas: The Natural Trade Gateway of Southeast Iran

Links with the Hinterland: Bushehr, Borazjan, Kazerun, Banu Ka'b, & Bandar Abbas

The Hula Arabs of the Shibkuh Coast of Iran

IRANIAN HISTORY

Agriculture in Qajar Iran

Public Health in Qajar Iran

The History of Theater in Iran

A Social History of Sexual Relations in Iran

Guilds, Merchants, and Ulama in Nineteenth-Century Iran

Labor & Industry in Iran 1850 -1941

The Rise and Fall of Nader Shah: Dutch East India Company Reports 1730-1747

Games Persians Play: A History of Games and Pastimes in Iran from Hide-and-Seek to Hunting

ANNOTATED TRANSLATIONS

A Man of Two Worlds: Pedros Bedik in Iran, 1670–1675
Pedros Bedik
translated with Colette Ouahes from the Latin

Astrakhan Anno 1770
Samuel Gottlieb Gmelin

Travels Through Northern Persia 1770–1774
Samuel Gottlieb Gmelin

Titles and Emoluments in Safavid Iran: A Third Manual of Safavid Administration
Mirza Naqi Nasiri

IN COLLABORATION WITH HASAN JAVADI

The Heavenly Rose-Garden: A History of Shirvan & Daghestan
Abbas Qoli Aqa Bakikhanov

Travels in Iran and the Caucasus, 1652 and 1655
Evliya Chelebi

THE PERSIAN GULF

MUSCAT
CITY, SOCIETY & TRADE

WILLEM FLOOR

MAGE
PUBLISHERS

Library of Congress Cataloging-in-Publication Data
Available in detail at the Library of Congress

ISBN
1-933823-76-3
978-1-933823-76-8

Printed and Manufactured in the United States

MAGE PUBLISHERS
Washington DC
202-342-1642 • as@mage.com
Visit Mage Publishers online at
www.mage.com

Contents

T a b l e s

Illustrations

Foreword

Muscat has played an important role for seafarers and trade for more than one thousand years. However, its socio-economic history has been neglected and is overshadowed by studies on its dynastic and political history. Therefore, I don't discuss the political history of the twin-cities during this period, as this has already been adequately covered in existing publications. Of course, where necessary, reference is made to political events to clarify certain socio-economic developments.[1]

Peterson's recent book *Historical Muscat*, only offers a very cursory glance of its history. In this study, however, the city and its people are not relegated to the back-seat, but in fact, are the main focus of historical inquiry. In it, an overview is given about the morphology and the amenities of the cities of Muscat and Matrah as well as what kind of people lived there and how, and in what way they amused and dressed themselves, their living conditions and how they made a living. The reason that these two cities are dealt with together rather than separately is that politically and commercially Muscat included Matrah as well as the neighboring villages and hamlets such as Kalbuh, Riyam, and Sidab, which by 1900 had grown into small towns.

The Introduction presents what is known about Muscat's role prior to 1500, which, unfortunately is very little. In the first chapter, Muscat position under the kingdom of Hormuz is discussed during its period as a Portuguese protectorate. The chapter starts with the year 1500, because, even though Muscat was part of this kingdom since about 1300 if not earlier, nothing is known about the city during this early period. The second chapter focuses on Muscat under direct Portuguese rule, in particular how the Portuguese tried to carve out a commercial role for the port after the fall of Hormuz in 1622. The third chapter details the socio-economic vicissitudes of Muscat and its population during the rule of the Ya`ariba dynasty, which lasted about one century. This study closes with chapter four, which analyses in great detail the city, society and trade of Muscat during the first 150 years of the rule by the Al Bu Sa`id dynasty. The cut-off date of 1900 is arbitrary and basically was mostly imposed by the available published data.

As usual, great thanks are due to my friend Keith Openshaw who, once again, was kind enough to edit my effort to express myself in English. Finally, also many thanks to João Teles e Cunha (Lisbon) and Larry Potter (New York) for their comments on the draft text.

---

1 For Muscat's political history, see Miles, *The Countries*; Risso, *Oman & Muscat*; Landen, *Oman*; Bhacker, *Trade and Empire*; Floor, *Political and Economical*; and Idem, *The Rise of the Gulf Arabs*.

Introduction

The etymology of the name Muscat is unknown and it may be a bastardization of an Arabic or Persian word. It is unlikely that Muscat actually means 'anchorage' or 'place of letting fall the anchor,' which is the usual explanation of its name.[1] There is little known about Muscat/Matrah before 1500. There is no archeological evidence concerning its early habitation. Ptolemy's mention of the 'hidden port' or *kryptos limen* (κρυπτόσ λιμήν) may have referred to Muscat, because its harbor is indeed concealed from sight by the island at its entrance. The harbor only becomes visible when a ship rounds the entrance.[2] The suggested establishment of the city by Anushirvan or by Himyarite traders is not supported by any archeological or other evidence.[3] The fact that, according to later sources, allegedly in 700 CE the bay of Muscat could easily accommodate the mooring of 300 ships, of course, indicates that it may have been already an attractive place to call on.[4] There are two tenth century sources, Ibn Khordadhbih and an anonymous one, that mention Muscat, where ships took in water drawn from wells and where they also bought cattle. Another reason to call on Muscat, according to Albuquerque, was that because the harbor was sheltered "all ships that navigate these parts must of necessity enter, to avoid the opposite coast, which contains many shallows."[5]

There was at least one town on the Arabian Coast that was a well known trade emporium. In the tenth century Persian *Hudud al-'Alam* or *Geography of the World* it is referred to as Omman, i.e. ancient Ommana, "a large town on the sea-coast. Merchants are numerous in it. It is the emporium (*barkadha*) of the whole world. There is no town in the world where the merchants are wealthier than here, and all the commodities of East, West, South, and North are brought to this town and from there carried to different places." The merchants of this town also traded with Abyssinia.[6] However, it is unlikely that this 'Omman was Muscat, although some have suggested that it might be Sohar. However, Potts has convincingly shown that Ommana most likely was al-Dur, situated near Umm al-Qaiwain, which was an important emporium in Achaemenid and later times.[7]

---

1 Peterson, *Historical*, p. 3; on the name Muscat, see Smith, "Muscat," pp. 146-47; Miles, *The Countries*, p. 468.

2 Miles, *The Countries*, p. 462; Geary, *Through*, vol. 1, pp. 11-12.

3 Qudamah b. Ja'far cited by al-Naboodah, "The commercial activity," p. 81; Boussac and Salles, *Athens*, p. 122. North-west and south-east of Muscat there is archeological evidence of early BCE habitation, Ratnagar, *Trading Encounters*, pp. 40, 225

4 Badger, *History*, vol. 1, p. 5.

5 Albuquerque, *Commentaries*, vol. 1/24, p. 83.

6 Minorsky, *Hudud al-Alam*, pp. 148, 164.

7 Boussac and Salles, *Athens*, pp. 123-24, 132-39; Potts, *The Arabian Gulf*, vol. 2, pp. 305-17. At Ommana also boats were 'sewn together.' Ratnagar, *Trading Encounters*, p. 223 (quoting *De Pleribus*).

Muscat continued to be known, but only for its traditional function as supplier of water and provisions to ships from or going to India and Yemen, which is a recurrent fact mentioned in medieval Arab sources.[8] In 1330, Ibn Battuttah only refers to Muscat in passing as "a small town in which there is a great abundance of the fish called *qulb al-mas*."[9] However, this marginal role of Muscat changed in the fifteenth century. Shahrokh Mirza's ambassador Samarqandi called on Muscat both on his way to and when he returned from India. The Russian merchant Nikitine also stopped twice in Muscat, both on his outward and inward journey. Around 1500, Ibn Majid wrote about his hometown: "Muscat is a port unequalled in the world." It had become the commercial center of the Batinah Coast, where "boats take on cargoes of fresh and dried dates and horses and sell cloth, oil, slaves, and cereals."[10]

The sudden rise of Muscat as a port is somewhat of a puzzle. João Teles e Cunha argues that this development was connected with the rise of the Hormuz thalassocracy and Muscat's integration in the Hormuzian trade and political system, especially as a way station to and from India, for which was better positioned than the old emporia situated to its southeast, like Quryat, Qalhat and Sur. This may all be true, but it does not really explain why it did not happen earlier. The pros and cons of Muscat as a port had not changed, to wit: it has a large natural harbor and defenses, but it offers no protection against the north-western wind or *shomal*, which blows "directly into it; yet the undertow prevent ships from riding with a heavy strain on their cables."[11] It had little to offer apart from water and provisions. Moreover, because of Muscat's isolation from its hinterland it had to rely on nearby Matrah for its supplies, both food and merchandise, which town has an even more spacious natural harbor and a good connection with the hinterland. However, Matrah always played and continued to play a subordinate role to Muscat, its twin.

---

8   Smith, "Muscat," p. 147; Wilkinson, "Maskat," (both citing al-Muqaddasi; al-Hamadhani, Ibn al-Faqih; Yaqut; Ibn al-Mujawir, *Akhbar-Sin wa 'l-Hind*).

9   Ibn Battutta, *Travels*, p. 303.

10   Ibn Majid, *Arab Navigation*, p. 213.

11   Bombay Records, p. 10.

1

The Hormuz Kingdom Period
1500-1622

Around 1500, Muscat was a large and very populous city, larger than Qalhat, "wherein dwell many persons of standing." It may have had as many as 7,000 inhabitants. Many of its residents were Banyan Bhatias from Thatta, who were already in Muscat in since the fifteenth century. The city had several quarters and straight but narrow streets. In fact, they were so narrow that during the attack of the city in 1507 Albuquerque's men had trouble using their long spears during their pursuit of the city's residents. This was due to the fact that space came at a premium, as there was so little of it, and therefore, houses were built close together. Other reasons were that this made the town easy to defend, since all the defenders had to do was barricade the narrow streets. Besides the high houses and narrow lanes provided shade and coolness in its merciless climate. The Portuguese admired the many multi-storied houses, which were built of sandstone and lime. The city had many mosques, the largest of which was partly constructed of carved timber with stone vaults and wooden pillars and an adobe dome. It was topped by a roof terrace, similar to a mosque in Hormuz. During the sack of the city this mosque was destroyed. More than a century later a church was built in its place.[1]

Although there was regular exchange between the urban and rural population, both sedentary and transhumant as well as between the city and sea-faring ships, the town's people were nevertheless on their guard *vis à vis* their trading partners. According to the *Commentaries* of Albuquerque, people in these ports "feared both the land and the sea."[2] Therefore, the ports on the Batinah coast, had defensive structures built against possible attacks emanating from their hinterland such as rock walls or a strong fort with eight towers, such as at Sohar that required 1,000 people to defend it. In Muscat, there were stockades on the land side to protect against attacks from the interior.[3] It is likely that there

---

1 Albuquerque, *Commentaries*, vol. 1/21, p. 71 (Qoryat had more than 5,000 inhabitants), 1/23, p. 78, 1/24, pp. 82-83; Correia, *Lendas da India*, I, p. 802 (Muscat has 700 inhabitants; mosque with wooden pillars), 806; Castanheda, *História*, II/55, p. 330 (Muscat is more populous than Qoryat), II/56, p. 334; Barbosa, *The Book*, vol. 1, p. 71; Aubin, "Le Royaume," p. 115, n. 236 has rightly argued that Correia's number of 700 inhabitants cannot be correct and given that it was more populous than Qalhat a zero must have been omitted in Correia's text.

2 Albuquerque, *Commentaries*, vol. 1/27, p. 100.

3 Albuquerque, *Commentaries*, vol. 1/20, p. 66, 1/23, p. 79, 1/27, p. 95, 97; 1/58, p. 219; Correia, *Lendas da India*, vol. 1, pp. 808, 811; Castanheda, *História*, II/56, p. 332, II/57, p. 333, 335; Barbosa, *The Book*, vol. 1, p. 72, 74; Barros, *Ásia*, 2ª-II-i, pp. 94-95.

were already towers guarding the small passes to the interior, because Castaneda writes that in 1507 the Muscatis had a gate at the passes to the interior guarded with cannon. These towers are shown on drawings a century later, but it is not clear whether the Portuguese improved existing defenses or introduced these guard-towers, because in 1625, della Valle reported that the Portuguese were building such a protective wall across the hills.[4]

At the same time, some ports (Qoryat, Muscat) had some kind of wooden palisade built at the entrance to their bay. This served as a protection against sea attack, such as those by the feared Nautaques pitates, which were a constant problem for Hormuz. despite the attempts to eradicate them and the annual bribes (*moqarrariyeh*) paid to their chiefs.[5] At Muscat this wall of timber was "ten palms broad and twenty high, packed with earth, very strong, and on either side it had been carried into two very high mountain ranges, which ran down into the sea, and made the whole very strong; and in this wall they had made some defenses, like bulwarks, with many mortars of the size of our camelos [a heavy gun] mounted on them." Despite the presence of these guns, the Muscatis defended themselves against the Portuguese attack with arrows and stones from behind the protection of the wall. The naval bombardment by Albuquerque's ships had little effect on this wall, because it was closely packed with earth.[6] Furthermore, in case the city was taken, people had built a secret storage space inside their houses. Albuquerque observed that the inhabitants of Muscat "fearing lest the inhabitants of the interior should come and rob them, had each built a compartment inside his house, without door or windows, and filled it with merchandise."[7] These compartments were so well hidden that Albuquerque's ships' crews initially were very frustrated that they did not find any loot in the city. It was only by chance, when a soldier hacked into a wall out of frustration that the existence of these compartments was revealed.[8]

At the time of Albuquerque's attack of the city, there were 34 ships lying in the harbor. These ships were both large and small, many of which were fishing barks. Muscat also had facilities to build and repair ships, because Albuquerque found an arsenal full of every requisite for shipbuilding, which he set fire to when departing from the city.[9]

> Towards the interior, there is a plain as large as the square of Lisbon, all
> covered with salt pans, not that the tide reaches there, but the water which
> is produced therein is saltish, and converts itself into salt. Hard by there are
> many pools of fresh water, of which the inhabitants make use; and there are
> orchards, gardens and palm-groves, with pools for watering them by means of
> wooden engines.[10]

These palm groves, located in the Tuyan (i.e. wells) valley, are depicted in Bocarro's *Livro das Plantas*, which shows three walled gardens in an area he called *orta do cabaço*

---

4 Castanheda, *História*, II/55, p. 330.

5 Floor, *Political and Economic*, p. 43.

6 Albuquerque, *Commentaries*, vol. 1/22, p. 73, 76.

7 Albuquerque, *Commentaries*, vol. 1/23, p. 80.

8 Albuquerque, *Commentaries*, vol. 1/23, p. 80.

9 Albuquerque, *Commentaries*, vol. 1/24, p. 82.

10 Albuquerque, *Commentaries*, vol. 1/23, p. 83.

Figure 1, Nautaques pirates, from *Imagens do Oriente*

or 'garden of gourds,' (see fig. 5). However, Muscat was very much depending on food imports from neighboring ports, which made a living from it. Although in general supplies were ample, in May 1553, when some 30 to 40 Indian ships calling on Muscat, these could only procure two dozen of chickens in total.[11] West of Muscat harbor is the small cove of Makallah, where native vessels could find shelter. Barros and Couto mention that this cove continued to be called Moculla Chini, suggesting that Chinese vessels dropped anchor in this place in the past, a memory of the Zheng He expeditions in the early 1400s.[12]

Qalhat had been an important port and the second capital of the Hormuz kingdom. However, it lost its importance in the 1400s, well before the earthquake of 1482-83, which usually is credited with its reduced role. Its role as runner-up to Hormuz was taken over by Muscat. Aubin has suggested another possible reason, viz. that Muscat could accommodate larger vessels than Qalhat, which moreover only could accommodate vessels during the monsoon.[13] Although Qalhat still served as the supplier of Oman's hinterland, had an important merchant community and in 1514 paid more taxes than Muscat, this

---

11 Albuquerque, *Commentaries*, vol. 1/23, p. 83; Figueroa, *Comentarios*, vol. 1, p. 174; Wicki, *Documenta Indica*, III, p. 21; Rego, *Documentação*, vol. 5, p. 324.

12 Miles, *The Countries*, p. 462.

13 Barros, *Ásia*, 2ª-II-i, p. 94; Samarqandi, *Matla` al-Sa`deyn*, vol. 2, pp. 769, 844; Castanheda, *História*, V/33, p. 59; Albuquerque, *Commentaries*, vol. 1/24, p. 83.

reflected the former, but not the actual situation. All contemporary authors class Muscat ahead of Qalhat after 1500, and it was already known as the port of Oman at that time.[14]

Around 1500, Muscat was the main commercial center for the entire Batinah coast. In fact, Albuquerque called it "the principal entrepôt of the kingdom of Ormuz." It received many supplies from the interior (wheat, barley, and dates) and from abroad many Indian products (textiles, oil, slaves, grains, rice, and sugar), while it exported horses, dates and salted fish.[15] Although Oman exported grains, it imported rice from India, which the Bedouins came to buy at Muscat and probably at other ports as well.[16] According to Ibn Majid, Muscat "was the most well-known port in the world ... a port the like of which cannot be found in the whole world. There can be found business and good things which cannot be found elsewhere."[17] Muscat was also the only location on the Batinah coast where vessels could obtain coir fiber, ropes, and wooden water barrels, which brought the governor of Muscat large profits. It also had a shipyard with the necessary accessories.[18] It is likely that Oman already cultivated sugar cane, because during the sack of Muscat in 1507, large stocks of oil and molasses (a typical sugar cane product) added to the vehemence of the fire.[19] The bay of Muscat was rich in fish, many of which were exported to India and other countries in salted and dried form.[20] When Albuquerque sailed into the Persian Gulf he burnt many fishing and other vessels at all the various ports, although most at Muscat, indicating the importance of the fishing industry.[21] Membré reported that "in the said Muscat they catch so many fish that even the animals eat them. I have even seen houses and walls built of dried fish."[22] The latter observation clearly refers to the drying installations of Muscat that used a salty marsh, "as large as the Rossio of Lisbon" that were the most productive.[23] Not only the coastal population benefited from this regional and Indian Ocean trade, but also the nomads from the interior of Oman who came to sell their products (horses, poultry, goats, dates)[24] as well as some of their women who came to prostitute themselves with the sailors.[25] Muscat was not the only port on the Batinah coast (e.g., Qalhat, Qoryat) that exported hundreds of horses; in particular Khur Fakkan,

---

14 Barbosa, *The Book*, vol. 1, p. 69; Aubin, "Documents," p. 233; (Qalhat: 11,000 *ashrafis*); Correia, *Lendas da India*, I, p. 803 (Muscat: 5,000 *ashrafis*); Ibn Majid, *Arab Navigation*, p. 213; Albuquerque, *Commentaries*, vol. 1/22, p. 72, 1/24, p. 83; Barros, *Ásia*, 2ª-III-ii, p. 237; Markovits, *The Global World*, p. 11.

15 Ibn Majid, *Arab Navigation*, p. 213; Albuquerque, *Commentaries*, vol. 1/24, p. 83; Correia, *Lendas da India*, I, pp. 802-04; Castanheda, *História*, II/55, p. 331; Barros, *Ásia*, 2ª-II-i, p. 99f.

16 Figueroa, *Comentarios*, vol. 1, p. 239-40.

17 Ibn Majid, *Arab Navigation*," p. 213.

18 Correia, *Lendas da India*, I, p. 806; Albuquerque, *Commentaries*, vol. 1/23, p. 82-83.

19 Albuquerque, *Commentaries*, vol. 1/23, p. 83; Membré, *Mission*, p. 52 ("in the said Muscat there is a river and near the river are sugar"); Bocarro, *O Livro das Plantas*, vol. 2, p. 52 (large amounts of very white sugar cane, some of it powdered). Because molasses was not a traded commodity, only sugar, it must be an Omani local product; see also below in the Ya`ariba chapter.

20 Barbosa, *The Book*, vol. 1, p. 71; Teixeira, *Travels*, pp. 222-23.

21 Albuquerque, *Commentaries*, vol. 1/19, pp. 60-61; Castanheda, *História*, II/54, p. 328; Barros, *Ásia*, 2ª-II-i, p. 100; Membré, *Mission*, p. 60 (houses and walls made of dried fish; animals were fed with fish).

22 Membré, *Mission*, p. 53.

23 Albuquerque, *Commentaries*, vol. 1/24, p. 83; Barbosa, *The Book*, vol. 1, p. 71; Correia, *Lendas da India*, I, p. 792 (Qalhat), 802.

24 Pires, *The Suma*; Figueroa, *Comentarios*, vol. 1, p. 174; Wicki, *Documenta Indica*, vol. 3, p. 21; Rego, *Documentação*, vol. 5, p. 324.

25 Figueroa, *Comentarios*, vol. 1, p. 239; see also Ibn Battuta, *The Travels*, vol. 2, pp. 398, 400; Wicki, *Documenta Indica*, vol. 1, p. 604 (01/12/1549), vol. 3, pp. 21-22 (24/09/1553).

Figure 2, Bathing in Muscat, from *Imagens do Oriente*

which was the major horse fair of North Oman.[26] However, then as later, Matrah was the real source of supply of goods from the interior.

Muscat was governed by a vizier (*goazil*) appointed by the king of Hormuz. In 1507, this vizier was a eunuch.[27] The appointment of officials to revenue bearing or salaried posts gave the king of Hormuz some measure of influence over his leading subjects, because the local elite remained a powerful political force and had an economic stake in Muscat's maritime economy. Every year, the king used to send to Qalhat a noble to be vizier, who administered justice and made war and peace as he chose. As to the taxes and duties paid to the king, no one interfered except the vizier of Hormuz, during his tenure of office. In 1523, the king of Hormuz decided, under Portuguese pressure, to discontinue this long-standing practice and to employ members of local families instead.[28] This meant that Sheikh Rabi`ah Masqati became vizier or governor of Muscat. Sheikh Rabi`ah Masqati had gained in influence, due to his support of the Portuguese during the 1521 Hormuz rebellion. He further gained in influence, because from 1529 until 1546, two family

---

26   Albuquerque, *Commentaries*, vol. 1/21, p. 71, 1/25, p. 87, 1/26, p. 92, 1/27, p. 100; Barbosa, *The Book*, I, p. 70; Correia, *Lendas da India*, I, p. 800; Barros, *Ásia*, 3ª-VII-v, p. 164; Membré, *Mission*, p. 52.

27   Albuquerque, *Commentaries*, vol. 1/23, p. 83; Castanheda, *História*, II/55, p. 330.

28   On the previous practice see Albuquerque, *Commentaries*, vol. 1/21, p. 67. In 1545 the vizier of Qalhat, Sheikh Rabi`ah (Xeque Rabea) was a member of the clan of the Sheikh of Muscat. Castro, *Obras*, vol. 3-105, pp. 104-05 (18/11/1545).

members, Sheikh Rashed b. Ahmad Masqati (1529-34) and his son Sheikh Ahmad, held the function of vizier of the kingdom of Hormuz. In 1528, the Portuguese had come to the conclusion that their interests would be better served by a change of the old 'Persian' guard, which had been basically running the affairs of Hormuz for the last five decades. That group also had been responsible for the uprising of 1521 on Hormuz. Therefore, in 1529, the king's representative Nuno da Cunha placed a representative of the Arab elite in charge of the Hormuz bureaucracy as a counterbalance to both the king of Hormuz and the 'Persian' elite. The man chosen for that job, Rashed b. Ahmad, was the son of Sheikh Ahmad who had shown his loyalty to the Portuguese cause in 1521. The latter's murder by Mohammad Shah II in early 1528 was used by Nuno da Cunha as a stick to browbeat any Hormuzian opposition against the appointment Rashed b. Ahmad.[29]

The two Muscati viziers entrusted many important functions to their fellow Arabs and in particular favored their family members. Furthermore, in recognition of his siding with the Portuguese in 1523, the governor of India acknowledged and confirmed Sheikh Rabi`ah's traditional commercial rights such as to remain the farmer of the ports of Muscat, Qalhat and Qoryat after 1523.[30] This may have contributed to the 'rebellion' of Qalhat in 1526, although commercial rivalry with Muscat and also, the latter's increasing importance at the expense of Qalhat may have played a role.[31] Sheikh Rabi`ah controlled trade in his home town. He and his family held the monopoly of the sale of fresh water and cordage to passing ships. They also controlled the customs-house, the weigh-house (*qappan*), and the office of the customs' judge until 1591.[32]

In addition to its advantageous location as a port-of-call for long-haul voyages from Bengal and beyond, Muscat appears to have benefited from the fact that members among its elite were financially interested in maritime trade. These interests were important enough to secure their continued support, reason why the Muscati elite was willing to cooperate with the Portuguese without yielding local control. The vizier of Muscat was also independent enough, for example in 1552, to totally frustrate Gonçalo da Cunha, who complained to the governor of the *Estado* that Sheikh Rabi`ah did whatever he pleased and he therefore, demanded authority to impose himself on the vizier.[33] This underlines the marginal role of Muscat in particular and Oman in general in Portuguese commercial strategy, which, moreover did not cause them any problem. Therefore, the Portuguese preferred to leave the local power structure unchanged.

Sheikh Rabi`ah remained loyal to the Portuguese when in 1546, four Ottoman ships came to Qalhat where they demanded the local vizier to hand over the Portuguese, which he refused. Then the ships sailed to Muscat, which they bombarded and set fire to on 10 October 1546, but Sheikh Rabi`ah (Xeque Rabia) and his brother Sheikh Ali (Xeque Alii) assisted by some 28 Portuguese beat them off. Having lost a dozen men the Ottoman ships

---

29   Couto, *Década* 4ª-III-xii, pp. 322-23; Botelho, *O Tombo*, p. 85.

30   "Memorandum about the government of India and the rents of Hormuz", n. p., n.d. [before 11/06/1527], in Farinha, "Os portugueses," p. 94.

31   According to Couto, *Década*, 4ª, I-iv, p. 29, the riots, rather than a rebellion it would seem, were due to orders given by Mohammad Shah II and his vizier Ra'is Sharaf al-Din to draw attention to the abuses by Diogo de Melo, Captain of Hormuz.

32   Correia, *Lendas*, vol. I, p. 806; *APO* 5/3-936, pp. 1247-1251 (22/05/1591).

33   Schurhammer, *Die zeitgenössischen Quellen*, p. 240, n. 3663 (28/01/1548).

Figure 3, Arab sailor and coastal dweller, from *Imagens do Oriente*

went to Qoryat and then disappeared.[34] As more Ottoman vessels were expected to return in 1547, the captain of Hormuz had ships lie in wait at Muscat, just in case. Also, one vessel was lying at Ra's al-Hadd to warn the fleet when the Ottomans came.[35] The next and bigger attack failed to materialize until five years later, because in the 1540's the Ottomans had their hands full with suppressing anti-Ottoman uprisings in Yemen and along the Arabian coast. These were sometimes fueled by Portuguese incentives and promises of help, which led the Porte to secure its hold of the region before launching a new attack against the Estado da Índia.

A much bigger Ottoman attack, both in size and objective followed the one of 1546. In 1552, Piri Reis left Suez with 25 galleys, four galleons, and one ship with 850 soldiers to take Hormuz, and if possible, Bahrain. In August 1552 the Ottoman fleet arrived before Muscat. At that time João de Lisboa and 70 men defended the fort that just had been

---

34 Castro, *Obras*, vol. 3-367, p. 252 (30/10/1546); 3-373, p. 257 (04/11/1546); Schurhammer, *Zeitgenössische Quellen*, p. 165, no. 2475 (31/10/1546), no. 2481 (04/11/1546); 166, no. 2486-87 (11/11/1546)

35 Özbaran, *The Ottoman Response*, pp. 147-48; Castro, *Obras*, vol. 3-367, pp. 252-54 (30/10/1546), 3-373, p. 257 (04/11/1546), 3-559, p. 414f. (23/06/1547). Ships also arrived from the Red Sea in Hormuz to trade. The Portuguese were kept informed by their agents in Qalhat (the vizier, Sheikh Rabi`ah, and the factor), for example, about Ottoman naval activities. Already in 1536 and later in 1545, the Portuguese had been warned about naval preparations at Suez and a possible attack of Hormuz. *Gavetas*, vol. I-583, pp. 915-16 (20/11/1545); Castro, *Obras*, vol. 3-71, p. 77 (21/09/1545).

completed to provide better protection for the Portuguese.[36] Muscat was easily taken after a one month's siege. Piri Reis, in the words of Faria y Souza "broke the Articles, putting the captain and sixty men to the oar; some of them were afterwards ransomed." Together with their Portuguese prisoners, who were put to use as galley slaves, the Ottoman fleet sailed to Hormuz, where it arrived on 19 September 1552.

Given the fact that the Portuguese promoted the commercial well-being of Hormuz over that of the other kingdom's ports they did not appoint any Captains to the two main ports on the coast of Oman, where they had small factories, of which Muscat was one. In three years, the factor of Muscat collected 3,000-4,000 *cruzados* in place of a salary; the post was usually given to a loyal and meritorious soldier who has served many times in the Estado da Índia. The factor of Qalhat had no salary either and collected 1,500-2,000 *cruzados* in fees during his three years in office.[37] Despite the limited Portuguese role and interest in Muscat (and the coast of Oman in general), in 1552, there was nevertheless a significant number of 60 *casados* living in Muscat, some of whom lived with Moslem women. This relatively large number of *casados* was incidental and temporary, however, and was due to the defensive operations that were undertaken by the Portuguese in that year under João de Lisboa (see above).[38] Before and after that date the number of Portuguese in Muscat and Qalhat was in the single digits.[39]

Muscat was not considered to be of great importance in Portuguese strategic policy until the late 1580s. This attitude was due to the fact that Portuguese strategists believed it was less expensive and militarily more effective to only have a strong naval presence in the Persian Gulf when needed rather than having one or more permanent strong forts outside Hormuz.[40] This policy may explain why even the battle for the Persian Gulf with the Ottomans in the 1550s did not result in greater Portuguese interest in Muscat in particular and the Omani coast in general. In all haste a fort was built in Muscat to oppose the Ottoman onslaught, but it had been built so shoddily and with too small a garrison that Piri Reis had no problem taking it in 1552. Strangely enough, the Ottomans did not put

---

36　Couto, *Década* 6ª-X-i, pp. 405-08. João de Lisboa had been sent there to build, repair and modernize the existing fortifications, because the Portuguese feared that the Ottomans wanted to conquer Muscat. Schurhammer, *Zeitgenössische Quellen*, p. 328, no. 4746 (27/01/1552); Ibid, p. 348, no. 4923 (01/12/1552) (70 Portuguese and 150 slaves were taken prisoner; also captured were all artillery and 15,000 *pardaus*); Wicki, *Documenta Indica*, vol. 2, pp. 486-87. The fort built by de Lisboa was Fort Capitan or as it was later called, Qal`at Mirani.

37　Aubin, "Le <Orçamento do estado da Índia>, pp. 172-79; Luz, *Livro*, f. 36r; Botelho, *O Tombo*, pp. 95-104; Rego, *Documentação*, vol. 9, pp. 583-85. The Portuguese factory in Qalhat was established in 1520, see Aubin, "<<Mercês>>", p. 577. Often the function of factor of both Muscat and Qalhat was held by one person, who combined it with other functions such as that of *vedor* and *alcaide mór*. APO 5/2-487, p. 552 (02/1564); APO 5/2-599, p. 634 (21/03/1567); APO 5/2-618, pp. 653-54 (13/01/1568); APO 5/2-651, p. 680 (11/03/1658); APO 5/2-660, p. 686 (30/03/1568); BFUP 15, no. 32, p. 362 (27/02/1617). It was only in 1588 that Muscat became a captaincy. Anonymous, *Relãçao das plantas*, p. 11; BFUP 15, no. 161, pp. 580-81 (04/07/1588). For defensive purposes the Captain of Muscat was subordinate to the Captain of Hormuz. BFUP 3, no. 11, p. 530 (25/01/1601).

38　Couto, *Décadas*, 6ª, X-i, p. 408; Wicki, *Documenta Indica*, vol. I, p. 604. Rafael Lobo wrote he needed many men in Masaqt. Schurhammer, *Zeitgenössische Quellen*, p. 175, no. 2623 (22/12/1546). A Portuguese soldier begged Gaspar Barzaeus S.J. for a job in the Paul College to be gone "from this hell hole." (i.e. Muscat), Schurhammer, *Zeitgenössische Quellen*, p. 304, no. 4513 (08/09/1550). At that time many Portuguese merchants visited Muscat. Anonymous, *Epistolae Indicae*, p. 22.

39　Although in mid-1547 it is reported that there were 40-50 Portuguese in Muscat, I believe that their presence was due to military operations against the imminent Ottoman threat, which also is mentioned, see Castro, *Obras*, III, p. 417 (23/06/1547) and Floor, *Political and Economic*, pp. 172-74.

40　Sanceau, *Cartas*, p. 24 ("Letter of D. João de Castro to king D. João III", [Goa], non-dated [1539]).

any garrison in Muscat to secure it. Thus, they failed to establish a bridgehead in Oman from which they might have launched future operations. This disastrous experience did not result in a change of Portuguese policy, for Muscat was not reinforced thereafter. The Portuguese continued to rely on their naval strength, which indeed was able to defeat the Ottoman fleet in 1554 at Muscat. This policy of benign disinterest in Muscat and other Omani ports continued in the decades thereafter. When news reached Hormuz at the end of 1580 about the possibility of an imminent attack of Muscat by Ali Beg, the Captain of Hormuz, D. Gonçalo de Meneses was unable to convince his colleagues to send a military force there to deal with this eventuality. As a result, Ali Beg was able to sack Muscat in 1581.[41] The Portuguese in the town fled to Matrah, but not feeling safe there continued to Bruxel, "a Fort four leagues up the Inland, belonging to the Catani, Head of a Hord of Arabs." There the refugees were kindly treated, despite suggestions by some of the chief's followers to take advantage of the situation.[42]

This attack worked as a kind of wake-up call for the Portuguese, although it took several years before they acted. It was only under viceroy D. Duarte de Meneses (1584-1588) that Muscat's fortifications were vastly improved and completed by the early 1590s.[43] This decision was in line with King Filipe I's Asian policy of reinforcing existing possessions rather than initiating new expensive conquests.[44] To pay for the new fortifications of Muscat and its military garrison of some 50 soldiers, on 6 October 1591, under Portuguese pressure, Sheikh Qays b. Rashed b. Rabi`ah al-Masqati, the vizier of Muscat and scion of the local vizier family, relinquished half of the fort's customs revenue to King Filipe I of Portugal in the act of vassalage.[45] Sheikh Qays b. Rashed b. Rabi`ah al-Masqati kept jurisdiction over non-Portuguese traders. Also, the customs officials continued to be Muscatis, although they were supervised by a Portuguese factor and clerk who recorded the Portuguese share of the customs. The share of the local Sheikhs in the customs revenues was later reduced to 30%. As of that moment, Portuguese residents at Muscat paid 3.5% as they had paid before. Portuguese non-residents paid 5%, all others (Moslems, Jews, Hindus) paid 7.5% *ad valorem*. All international trade goods such as Indian textiles, indigo, spices, drugs and sugar had to pass through Hormuz, however, where they paid 11%. In case they came to Muscat anyway the same rate applied.[46] The new regulation was aimed to better control trade in strategic goods. Muscat then became the center of Portuguese operations on the coast of Oman. Despite these measures that were aimed, amongst others, to promote trade the viceroy Rui Lourenço de Távora noted 20 years

---

41 Couto, *Décadas*, 10ª, I-xi/xii, pp. 84-99. Nevertheless the construction of a fort at Muscat on an impregnable location had already been considered in 1580 to be the answer to Ottoman attacks. *BFUP* 15, no. 49, p. 575 (01/12/1580).

42 Couto, *Década* 10ª-I-xi-xii, pp. 84f.; Faria e Sousa, *Portuguese Asia*, vol. 2, pt. 3, ch. 2, 8-12.

43 *APO* 3-26, p. 95 (13/02/1587); *APO* 3-76, p. 268 (12/01/1591); *APO* 3-117, p. 377 (15/02/1593); *APO* 3-162, p. 475 (18/02/1595); Matos, *Das relações*, p. 344 (Descriçao das terras do Oriente); Scholz, *Muscat*, vol. 1, 33; Stiffe, "Ancient," pp. 608-18; Serjeant, *The Portuguese*, pp. 163-66. Nothing was done about the defense of the other ports on the coast of Oman, which were considered to be of no importance.

44 *APO* 3-33, pp. 119-120 (21/01/1588).

45 "Donation of half of Muscat's customs" (Hormuz, 22/05/1591), in *APO* 5/3-936, pp. 1247-1251. This family had held the vizierate of Muscat for decades and supplied two viziers to Hormuz between 1528-46.

46 *APO* 5/3-936, pp. 1247-51 (22/04/1589); *ANTT* LM XLIX f. 364 vs. (*casados* and *moradores* at Muscat paid 8.5% on imports).

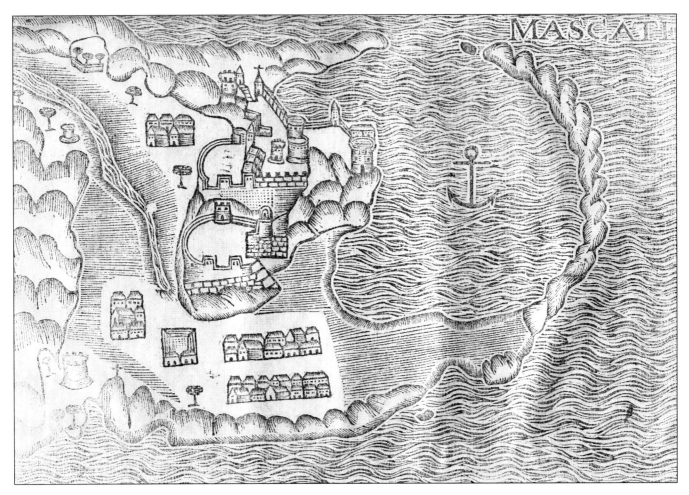

Figure 4, Plan of Muscat, Faria y Souza, *The Portuguese Asia*

later the oppressive and counterproductive measures taken by the Captains of Muscat against merchants.[47]

The annual expenditure (captain, garrison, military supplies) of Muscat in 1590 was 10,000 *cruzados*, which had to be paid out of the customs revenues of Hormuz.[48] This situation has not changed by 1607, when Muscat's revenues amounted to 400 *xerafins* and its expenditures to 5,740 *xerafins*, resulting in a deficit of 5,340 *xerafins* that had to be paid for by the Hormuz factory.[49] It was for this reason that the wisdom to spend so much money on such a small and insignificant fortress continued to be debated in Lisbon in years thereafter.[50] A similar discussion also took place in Muscat, but here the emphasis was on the 'hostile takeover' of Muscat and its revenues by the Portuguese. This led to resentment and even an outburst of public discontent in Muscat, which was serious enough in size and scope for viceroy Matias de Albuquerque (1591-1597) to report to Lisbon in 1595 that the situation had calmed down and become normal again.[51]

---

47 Matos, *Das relações*, p. 262 (10/12/1609) quoting BNL-FG 1975, f. 364r-65vs.
48 "Estado da India" *DUP*, vol. 1, p. 214.
49 "Budget of the *Estado da Índia* ca. 1607", in da Silva, "Une image," p. 271.
50 *APO* 3-365, pp. 927-928 (21/11/1598).
51 *APO* 3-206, p. 586 (28/01/1596); *DRI* III-514, p. 212 (14/02/1615).

Around 1610, one of the sheikhs of Muscat was interested to sell three-fifth's of his share in Muscat's customs. The negotiations were not successful, however, because Garcia de Melo, the Captain of Hormuz, wanted the Muscati sheikhs to be involved in protecting the port's interests (no smuggling, stimulating of trade) and thus protect it against attacks from outside such as by the Ottomans. The Portuguese also wanted to neutralize the effect of the anti-Portuguese unrest in 1595 under Sheikh Rashed (xeque Raxete), with whom they had come to an agreement a few years earlier.[52] The Sheikh's interest to sell his share in the customs may have been influenced by the fact that Muscat was not a very thriving place.

Of course, there was trade with India and the Red Sea, but that did not necessarily mean that this trade was very important and remunerative. Unfortunately, data are lacking on this subject. One may not draw the conclusion that the trade of Muscat was important, because in 1553 there were 30-40 vessels from India in the bay of Muscat. However, their presence did not necessarily mean that they traded with Muscat, given Hormuz's monopoly. It only meant that the ships stopped at Muscat to get water and provisions after crossing the Arabian Sea, because that was what the city was, a way station between India and Hormuz.[53] The fact that the fort built by João de Lisboa in 1552 was financed out of the rents of Qalhat and Muscat indicates that it was not a very wealthy port. In fact, it remained a deficit settlement that had to be financially supported by Hormuz. Therefore, it comes as little surprise that the Portuguese living in Muscat were engaged in smuggling. Governor-general Castro wrote in 1546 that the old custom that an official ordered ships calling on Muscat to go to Hormuz, after having collected a fee, was no longer respected. Instead a servant of the senior Portuguese official in Muscat charged one *pardau* per ship as self-styled factor, a totally illegal activity and assumption of function. This was such an attractive alternative to living in Hormuz that several Portuguese deserted from Hormuz and went to Muscat where they engaged in smuggling.[54]

In 1611, Antonio de Gouveia described the city as "the poorest I have seen in any place that I have been to, because most people do not have more than a small hut made of mats, without anything more than a sleeping mat (*cambullim*), and in such miserable quarters, they are exposed to the elements, even suffering excessive cold. ... their usual sustenance consists of only dates, without anything else, and when they manage to eat rice, it is an occasion for festivities."[55] In 1617, Figueroa gave a similar assessment. He wrote that Muscat had but 300 houses, most of which were small and dilapidated. The poor, mostly Arabs, lived in so-called *barasti* huts made of palm fronds. Around the base of these huts its residents had made a circle of stones as protection against the rain. The huts were built so close together that there was hardly room to pass between them. The Portuguese *casados* and some soldiers lived in three or four terraced stone houses in the small quarter around the church. The adjacent Augustinian convent, built in 1607, had room for 12 men of the cloth. It had a nice garden with fruit trees, but above all date-palms, which were very productive and had very good dates. In the back of the convent

---

52 *APO* 6-1082, pp. 910-11 (09/02/1613); *APO* 6-1230, pp. 1037-38 (29/01/1610); *DRI* II-224, pp. 142-43 (26/01/1612); *DRI* II-226, pp. 148-49 (31/01/1612); *DRI* III-514, p. 212 (14/02/1615).

53 *Documentaçao*, vol. 5, p. 324

54 Castro, *Obras*, vol. 3. 130-131, pp. 121-22 (02 and 03/02/1546), vol. 3. 705, p. 523 (07/02/1548), vol. 3.738, 546 (09/04/1548).

55 Gouveia, *Relaçam*, IV. p. 14.

there was a sweet water well, where the Augustinians had built a water tank in which they sought relief during the hot summer months. In this quarter were also the shops of the Banyans and Jews, while the streets were also wider. Because of the heat, in summer people slept on the roofs of their houses.[56]

Apart from the Portuguese *casados* and soldiers who lived in 3-4 houses, the rest of the population of Muscat consisted of Arabs, Banyans and Jews. The Portuguese, Banyans and some Moslems from Hormuz and Sind traded with Arabia and Persia. The Jews who lived in 15 to 20 houses were very poor. They lived by selling foodstuffs and spoke Arabic. They also lodged low-life Moslems who came from neighboring areas to Muscat. According to Figueroa, "the rest of the people are very poor; they only eat dates and milk, and a little rice on occasion of a festivity." They also were poorly dressed in white long camel hair robes with wide sleeves and white or black headdress; the latter is very much respected among them. Women were dressed similarly.[57]

Because King Filipe II suspected that Shah Abbas I wanted to conquer Hormuz, defensive works were started there in 1609; similar works were undertaken in Muscat in 1611.[58] The viceroy and his council in Goa, however, did not support their king's political-commercial overtures to Shah Abbas, which they considered to be detrimental to the trade and revenues of Hormuz and Muscat and the increase of their customs revenues.[59] The Captains of Hormuz and other Portuguese officials rather than promoting their king's interests promoted their own. They increasingly smuggled strategic goods to those ports competing with Hormuz.[60] Even Portuguese vessels from Goa avoided Hormuz and Muscat and viceroy Ruy Lourençou de Távora (1609-1612) issued an order in 1609 that all Portuguese ships had to pass via Hormuz. In 1612 Filipe II renewed the same order for Portuguese ships and those with Portuguese passes to call on Hormuz.[61] One of those smuggling ports was Sohar. Since 1610, the sheikh of Sohar offered the governor of Shiraz goods at the same price offered by Shirazi merchants at Hormuz. This offer of merchandise (textiles, spices and other Indian products) was detrimental to the position of Hormuz and Muscat.[62] As a result, many Portuguese smugglers went there and it happened often that in one day 20 vessels unloaded their cargo of iron, pepper and other illegal goods, and the more so after the Portuguese had lost Comorão (Bandar Abbas). The increased smuggling activity caused a significant loss to the customs revenues of Hormuz and not a little to those of Muscat. In May 1616, therefore, the Portuguese attacked the port and destroyed it.[63] This had a temporary and positive effect on Hormuz and Muscat, but six years later the fall of Hormuz totally changed the political and commercial power structure in the Persian Gulf.

---

56 Figueroa, *Comentarios*, vol. 1, pp. 171, 174-75.

57 Figueroa, *Comentarios*, vol. 1, pp. 174-75.

58 *DRI* II-2-5, pp. 103-04 (05/03/1612); *DRI* II-224, pp. 142-44 (26/01/1612).

59 Matos, *Das relações*, p. 263, quoting BNL: FG 7144, f. 27r-29vs and Ibid., f. 55r-56vs.

60 Teles, *Economia*, p. 24 quoting *AHU* cx3-12 (20/01/1615); BNL-FG 1975, f. 362-65vs (n.d.; 1610); BNL-FG 2702, f. 59vs-60vs (26/09/1609); *DRI* I-110, p. 323 (13/02/1610); *BFUP* 3, p. 594 (08/03/1609).

61 *DRI* II-236, pp. 170-71 (27/02/1612).

62 Bocarro, *Década 13*, vol. 2, chap. CLVII, pp. 641-642; *BFUP* 4, p. 851 (29/12/1616).

63 Bocarro, *Década 13*, vol. 2, pp. 641-48; Cordeiro, *Questões*, pp. 306-08; Badger, *History*, vol. 1, pp. 43-44 (for the cause of the attack and a description thereof); Lorimer, *Gazetteer*, p. 399; Ross. *Annals*, pp. 42-44; *BFUP*, nº 4, p. 851 (29/12/1616). For a discussion of the importance of Wadi Sama'il see Lorimer, *Gazetteer*, pp. 1414 (hub of the road system), 1663-72 (most important valley in Oman).

2

Direct Portuguese Rule 1622-1650

After the Safavid conquest of Hormuz in April 1622, the Portuguese regrouped at Muscat temporarily allying themselves with the Imam of Nizwah, who gathered a total force of 15,000 men to oppose the expected Persian invasion. These forces later met at Rostaq (Rastagua) and then at Sohar waiting for the arrival of a Portuguese naval flotilla. After Easter 1623 a Portuguese flotilla left Muscat under da Silveira and met the Persian fleet at *Khur Fakkan*. The Portuguese were about to win the ensuing battle when an accident happened aboard their commander's ship. This allowed the Persian ships to withdraw. In May 1623, Rui Freire returned to Muscat to resume his attacks of Persian shipping and coastal areas. Safavid forces immediately abandoned a few forts near Muscat and concentrated their forces in Khur Fukkan, Diba, Lima, Khasab, Rams and Jolfar.[1]

In 1625, della Valle visited Muscat and wrote that the city was small, but contained many inhabitants, in particular after the fall of Hormuz. There were Portuguese, Arabs, Indians, heathens (presumably Banyans), and Jews. There were two churches; the oldest built on or near the destroyed Friday mosque and the other in the Augustinian convent. The latter, of which construction began in 1597, formed part of a large official Portuguese precinct that comprised the governor's city residence, the factory and the barracks. This precinct became later known as *gharayzah*, most likely a corruption of the Portuguese word for church (*igreza or igreja*). In 1625, the customs house was built and a boat dock under Ft. Mirani. Because the heat was insufferable, Afonso de Mielo, the Captain of Muscat lived in this precinct during the summer and only during the cold season returned to the Capitan citadel. The nephew of the king of Hormuz, who also called himself Mohammad Shah just like his uncle (who was imprisoned in Shiraz), stayed with him. The Portuguese continued to maintain the fiction that the king in Muscat was their vassal in continuation of their protectorate of Hormuz.[2] His official title was 'governor of the Arab Lands belonging to the Kingdom of Hormuz'.

---

1 Boxer, *Commentaries*, p. 181; Cordeiro, *Questões*, vol. 3, pp. 303-17; Teles, *Economia*, pp. 45-46; *DRI* IX-191, p. 148 (28/12/1622).

2 Della Valle, *Voyages*, vol. 4, p. 409; Le Gouz, *Voyages*, p. 121; Miles, *The Countries*, pp. 163-64, 464.

Figure 5, Bocarro manuscript *Plantas das fortalezas*, Biblioteca Nacional de Espana

After 1622, the center of Portuguese power in the Gulf was the port of Muscat, which, at that time, was a small town of maybe 5,000 inhabitants. Although small, it was densely populated, in particular for a while after the fall of Hormuz, when 2,500 Portuguese and other refugees arrived from that town.[3] The majority of the population was Moslem, although there are no data available on either their number or the number of mosques.[4] The bay of Muscat was 20 to 25 *braças* (one *braça* equals 2.2 meters) deep and had a capacity to receive 20 galleons and 20 to 30 frigates. Ships had to enter via an opening in a barrier erected at the entry of the bay, which was guarded by eight lascars as well as by the artillery of the two forts that overlooked the bay.[5] The houses were partly built in stone,

---

3   Della Valle, *Voyages*, vol. 4, p. 409; Monnox, "History," pp. 293, 296, 303.

4   Although the Omanis were Ibadi Moslems, they also still believed in older superstitions. Close to Muscat, at a distance of two leagues, at the mouth of the "rio das Duas Bocas" there was a village with Arabs, who were all practicing sorcerers (*feiticeiros*). For details see "Estado da India" *DUP*, vol. 1, p. 216.

5   Anonymous, *Livro das Plantas*, p. 11.

partly with date-palm fronds in the form of huts. In 1625, the Portuguese had just started to build a simple and weak earth wall, with some towers rather far away from one another. According to della Valle, in this way all their houses were believed to be secure, because on one side they had this wall, while the sea also served as protection. Later they reinforced this sea wall (*sikkat al-madfa'*).[6] On the other side were the steep inaccessible mountains. The principal fort and the governor's residence was Fort Boqueirão or Quelbúque (also called Capitan, later called Qal'at Mirani). It was built at the port, some distance from the houses, on top of the mountains that surround them and at the right side of the port. That fort was considered to be practically impregnable, for only famine could force it to yield. On the other side of the port there was another hardly less formidable fort, which was the so-called old fort or Fort Santo António; it also had some artillery. At the top of the pass leading to Kalbuh, the Portuguese had built a rampart, defended by cannons, to prevent attacks on the town from that side.[7] Rui Freire further reinforced the defenses of Muscat by "strengthening the batteries at Quilbu and the gardens near Cabaço, whilst he erected towers on the tops of the hills up which the enemy might climb, placing guards in them, whereby the place was rendered impregnable."[8] In 1634, both forts in Muscat were repaired and in 1640 they were considered impregnable.[9] According to Portuguese prisoners, there were not many military forces in Muscat, which seems unlikely.[10] Improvements that were undertaken included rebuilding of the town wall from Buma Salih to Bab Methaib and the excavation of the moat, the construction of a new customs house, landing place and dock at the creek as well as the establishment of a hospital. Also, towers were erected at the passes of Kalbuh, Riyam and Sidab.[11]

The town of Matrah (Matara) was situated in Matrah Bay, 4 km from Muscat. Its harbor offered little protection against the winds, save in the north-western part. Rui Freire had built a fort there to house the factors who came from the mountains and could not reach Muscat, because of the lack of roads. Its garrison consisted of one Portuguese captain and 30 lascars. The captain, like all other captains of forts on the Batinah coast, received 40 *pardaus de larins* every three months, paid by Muscat and its neighboring forts. The lascars, like all the others on the coast, were paid 8.5 of the same *larins* per month, which amount was paid in Muscat.[12] Furthermore, it was Barkah's task to assist Muscat, because it was said that Muscat "could not breathe without Sib and Barka," which were its major food suppliers.[13]

With the fall of Hormuz in May 1622, the *Estado* was forced to reorganize its operations in the Persian Gulf and therefore it concentrated its forces in Muscat, the only port where it had a fortified factory. The existing administrative structure was remodeled on

---

6 Miles, *The Countries*, pp. 463-64.

7 Della Valle, *Voyages*, vol. 4, p. 408; Bocarro, *Livro das plantas*, p. 47; Anonymous, *Relãçao das plantas*, p. 11; Figuero 2011, vol. 1, p. 173.

8 Boxer, *Commentaries*, p. 207.

9 Lorimer, *Gazetteer*, p. 401. For their armament and ammunition in 1634 see Bocarro, *Livro das plantas*, pp. 47-48.

10 Dunlop, *Bronnen*, p. 578 (06/04/1636).

11 Administration Report 1884-85, p. 39; Bocarro, *Livro das Plantas*, p. 48. For the hospital regulations, see ANTT, DRI, 45, fol. 309-333v (12/02/1636).

12 Anonymous, *Relãçao das plantas*, p. 11; Bocarro, *Livro das plantas*, p. 54, which also has a drawing of the fort (fig. vi).

13 Anonymous, *Relãçao das plantas*, p. 13.

that of Hormuz (see Table 1) and a basic tariff, varying between 3.5 to 7.5%, was applied between 1623 and 1633. Through alliances with neighboring sheikhs the Portuguese had been able to expel the Safavid forces from the Omani coast. They further established a chain of fortified factories and customs-houses along the Omani littoral, took control over the Jolfar pearl trade, the horse and dried fruit trade of the interior Oman, and re-established the trade links between Muscat-Basra as well as with W. India and exerted themselves to make Muscat a competitive port. However, Muscat never acquired the distributive or financial role of Hormuz, because it was not the point of transshipment for the caravan trade to major markets. One of those markets, Persia was off-limits to the Portuguese, because they were at war. Even after 1629, when the Portuguese obtained the right to establish a factory in Bandar-e Kong,[14] which meant access to the Persian market, Muscat never thrived because the 'cáfila' or convoy from Sind had no interest in trading in Oman. Moreover, Muscat had no hinterland with a sizable market of consumers with sufficient purchasing power. Nevertheless, the export of horses, dried fruits and other food supplies were important enough to turn Muscat into a port of some local importance. It became a regular stop for ships with Portuguese passes on their route to Bandar-e Kong and Basra. However, Muscat continued to be a drain on the finances of the *Estado* for it was a money-losing operation.[15]

Table 1: Staff of the Portuguese Factory at Muscat ca. 1634

Rank	Remuneration
Captain-general of the war at sea and on land	600,000 *res*/year
Captain of the fort	10 *larins*/day
Vedor da fazenda (inspector of the exchequer)	4 *xerafins*/year
Ouvidor (magistrate)	100,000 *res*
Clerk of the factory	80,000 *res*
Clerk of the customs-house	50,000 *res*
Bailiff (*meirinho*) of the Captain-General	24,000 *res*
One of his men (*pião*)	4 *laris*, 2 *parras*/month + 16 units of rice
Bailiff of the *fazenda*	60 *pardaus*/year
Bailiff of the *ouvidor*	60 *pardaus*/year
Chief of the watch (*sobresolda*)	24,000 *res*/year

14 Earlier (Floor, *Political and Economical*, p. 430), I had written that this took place in 1631. However, João Teles e Cunha rightly pointed out to me that after September until late November 1627 Rui Freire made a raid on the pearl fisheries near Bahrain with the help of Qatif, after which the governor of Bandar Abbas proposed a truce for a year and offered the Portuguese half of the costum revenues of a Persian port of Rui Freire's choosing; he chose Bandar-e Kong. In April 1628, Rui Freire dispatched the favorable answer given by the Safavid authorities to Goa. Apparently the truce was only signed in September or October 1628, or even later, after receiving approval from Goa, which meant that the agreement was fully operational by 1629. Boxer, *Commentaries*, pp. 200-07. In fact, the first commercial Portuguese voyage to Kong took place in 1629. TT-Graça, cx. 2-3.°, fls. 401-402.

15 Teles, *Economia*, pp. 137-39 quoting BNL-FG 1983 (Assento 09/09/1623), f. 24v-25; *ACE* vol. 1-2, pp. 4-7 (04/06/1624); Della Valle, *Voyages*, vol. 4, pp. 442-43. Muscat also exported a local Omani woolen fabric, which the Portuguese called *cambolin* or cloak. Anonymous, *Livro das Plantas*, p. 12; for the word *cambolin* see Hobson-Jobson, q.v. "Cumly."

Rank	Remuneration
Captain of Fort Boqueirão	100,000 *res*/year
Captain of Fort Santo Antonio	120,000 *res*/year
Army surgeon	120 *pardaus*/year
Chief of the naval yard	2 *laris*/day
Master cooper	37,000 *res*/year – normal pay + bonus
Surgeon and apothecary of the *fazenda*	200 *pardaus*/year
Master smith	37,000 *res*/year– normal pay + bonus
Hospital (managed by Augustinian fathers)	380 *pardaus*/month
Augustinian fathers	1,200 *pardaus*/year

Source: Bocarro, *Livro das Plantas*, p. 48. (singular *real*, plural *réis*).

The successful Portuguese offensive against Persian shipping and its coastal settlements had not solved the real problem, viz. how to get access to the Persian market, which was now being supplied by Asian, Dutch and English merchants. Much of the import of Indian goods into Safavid Persia during the second decade of the seventeenth century had been channeled via Makran, in particular the ports of Gwadar and Jask, thus avoiding Portuguese controlled shipping lanes. This was facilitated by the English East India Company shipping from Surat and a new alternative maritime route became more important once the English moved to Bandar Abbas, followed by the Dutch shortly thereafter. Goa therefore had to act. The revenues of Muscat between November 1623 and May 25, 1624 were 37,500 *xerafins*, while the expenses for March 1623-December 1624 were 176,576 *xerafins*, mainly for the upkeep of the 727 troops.[16] To finance its forces in the Hormuz Straits Goa sent 100 *bahar* of cinnamon in April 1623 to be sold in Basra.[17]

The low revenues of Muscat may be ascribed to the lack of linkage with the international commercial networks as well as the lack of funds to invest in local trade (whose resources were limited) and few foreign markets, horses and dates excepted, in which there was a thriving trade for Omani products. This and the uncertainty about the future forced merchants to sell their goods at low prices in 1623-34. The customs rates at Muscat were nevertheless very attractive, 3.5 % to 7.5 % instead of 11-15 % at Hormuz, which underlines the failed attempt to develop Muscat as an emporium. The last *vedor* of Hormuz had refused, in fact, to pay 2,400 *xerafins* for the farming of Muscat's customs-house, which indicates its marginal commercial importance at that time. There was not enough ready money in Muscat (and at Goa) and the Portuguese soldiers were paid in rice, which therefore, flooded the market depressing prices. As of September 1623, Goa therefore, changed its strategy and allowed, without royal approval, the trade in food supplies in Muscat and other Omani ports with a view to reanimate coastal shipping and thus increase customs revenues. The jurisdictional conflict between the Captain-General of the Straits of Hormuz and the Captain of Muscat, (both were under Goa, i.e. the viceroy's jurisdiction, but Rui Freire had more 'influence' in Lisbon and was seen as keystone to develop and execute Portuguese strategy in the Persian Gulf area rather than the Captain of Muscat,

16 Teles, *Economia*, p. 138 quoting *AHU* cx8-101 (31/01/1625). For the budgetary deficit in ca. 1634 see Bocarro, *Livro das Plantas*, p. 50.
17 Teles, *Economia*, p. 46 quoting YY-SV (08/06/1623), f. 263f and (20/06/1623), f. 265f.

whose power and influence was more limited), did not facilitate matters. Rui Freire, the Captain-General, wanted to make everything subordinate to his war on the Safavids, while the Captain and other officials, depending on Goa, had other priorities. Also, there was a conflict between Martim Afonso de Melo the Captain of Muscat and Rui Freire about the passes. The former wanted to stimulate trade with Sind and allowed his factor therefore, to issue these passes, which right Rui Freire claimed for himself. As a result, in November 1623 a group of Armenian and Persian merchants were arrested and their goods confiscated with a value of 20,000 *pardaus*, despite the fact that they had received a verbal safe-conduct in Lahari-Bandar, the port of Sind.[18] Goa ordered the merchants to be released and their goods returned. The *Estado* wanted Muscat to prosper and that required attracting merchants and reducing military expenditures. It had no major market for local consumption, no important exports, and thus it was only a port of call between two other ports. It nevertheless benefited from increased Portuguese trade with Basra as of 1624. Della Valle described the trade route connecting Muscat with Basra via the small islands in the Persian Gulf.[19]

Portuguese private traders from Diu and the Hormuz *casados* had already been engaged in semi-legal trade with Basra since the mid-sixteenth century. In August 1623, the viceroy sent Nicolau da Silva to Basra with seven barks to discuss the initiation of trade relations. The beginning of official Portuguese trade with Basra was not a major success. The cinnamon sold there by the Portuguese factor lost money, because the caravans could not go to Baghdad which had fallen in Persian hands. This led to the re-opening of the desert route to Aleppo as an alternative to the river route via Baghdad.[20] Nevertheless, the Portuguese had no alternative but to develop trade with Basra, where the *Estado* kept a royal factor while the viceroy also had his agent there.[21] Therefore, the Portuguese developed good relations with Afrasiyab Pasha, the ruler of Basra. Moreover, the Portuguese organized an anti-Safavid alliance that included Omani Arabs and the rulers of Qatif and Basra.[22]

The friendship between Basra and the Portuguese was beneficial to both sides. Muscat bought timber from Anatolia, although it was cheaper to obtain from India; Basra grain from Qeshm, Kish and Rig, and the Portuguese could interrupt that trade.[23] The Portuguese continued to escort their vessels coming from Sind on their annual voyage via Muscat to Basra usually with only one warship. More was not needed, because the English and the Dutch did not sail to Basra respectively prior to respectively 1636 and

---

18 Teles, *Economia*, p. 47 quoting BNL-FG 1983 (Assentos 09/03/1623, f. 8v-9 and 06/04/1612, f. 13r-v.); *ACE*, vol. 1-2, p. 5 (14/06/1624). Filipe III had granted the prizes taken, in particular *pimenteros*, to the captain and the crew of the ship that seized them, which provided a powerful incentive to ignore passes. *DRI* VIII-193, pp. 303-05 (18/03/1622).

19 Della Valle, *Voyages*, vol. 4, pp. 413-33.

20 Teles, *Economia*, pp. 138-41 quoting TT-SV, letters to Filipe III (08/06/1623), f. 263 f.; (20/06/1623), f. 265f.; (25/05/1624), f. 362f.; Gune, *Assentos*, vol. 1-2 (14/06/1624), pp. 5-7; Ibid., vol. 1-19 (04/04/1625), p. 35; *ACE*, vol. 1-2, pp. 5-6 (01/06/1624 and 14/06/1624).

21 Teles, *Economia*, p. 59 quoting TT-LM 26 Filipe III to vice-roy (20/04/1628), f. 364-67vs; *ACE* vol. 1-153, p. 104 (24/09/1626).

22 *DRI* IX-151, pp. 437-38 (07/03/1623).

23 Teixeira, *Travels*, pp. 24, 29; Anonymous, *Chronicle*, vol. 2, p. 1125-27; Boxer, "Anglo-Portuguese Rivalry," p. 126; Della Valle, *Voyages*, vol. 4, p. 445; *AHU*, India, Cx 19, 5; *ANTT*, DRI, 35 and *ANTT*, DRI 55 (11/04/1645), f. 290, 294. According to Anonymous, *Relãçao das plantas*, p. 17 only favorable customs conditions were given.

1645, while the heavily armed Portuguese galliots outgunned Persian Gulf pirates such as the Hulas from Nakhilu.[24] In 1631 allegedly as many as 25 Portuguese vessels called on Basra,[25] which brought the highly coveted coffee from Mokha via Muscat.[26] After the fall of Hormuz in 1622, Basra was supplied "by barkes from Goombrone and Congo within the Gulph, but principally from the Portugasses Muscatt fleet, which usually setts fourth in June for Congo and arrives here some tyme in July."[27] Also, Basra-bound ships rather than calling on Muscat, where the *Estado* applied a strict customs regime, preferred to call on Bandar-e Kong.[28] As a consequence, Bandar-e Kong became a regular port-of-call for vessels bearing Portuguese passes around 1640. In that year, Duarte Lobo, the Captain-General of the Straits, considered moving from Kong to Rishar. He wanted to protect Muscat's revenues from dwindling even further, something that would happen if Basra's "Cáfila" could not make its round trip and end its journey in Sind; thus enabling the Portuguese authorities in Muscat to collect customs duties twice. Back in Goa, the State Council decided to maintain the *status quo ante*, that is, D. Duarte had to find a way to resolve the present dispute without changing ports in Persia, and to keep the trade route open to Basra.[29]

Meanwhile Rui Freire attacked Persian ports such as Jask and Bandar Abbas, while other captains attacked Bandar-e Kong and Brukht (Borco) on the island of Qeshm.[30] Therefore, coastal trade became difficult and in Makran transit trade became almost impossible. Trade links between Muscat and Goa were re-established as is clear from the capture by the English of a vessel going from Muscat to Goa.[31] Although these attacks on the Persian coast had the desired result, they negatively affected the Muscat-Sind trade which, as a result, had no longer access to the Persian market (it had informal access through 'neutral' ports in the Gulf and after 1629 offcially to Bandar-e Kong). The governor of Sind and its traders complained to the *feitor* of Muscat and the Portuguese officials all the way up the hierarchical ladder pressured Goa to resolve this issue. Most of the Sindi trade had been with Persia and the merchants wanted to continue that trade. The route to Basra alone was not profitable enough for the Sind traders, because the extra protection cost for the route to Aleppo after the Safavid conquest of Baghdad in 1623 had increased expenditures for the merchants making this destination less attractive.[32] As of 1627, more Banyans had started to use the Muscat-Basra route, which was very encouraging.[33] Trade relations between Sind and Muscat further developed by Thatta Banyans,

24 Boxer, "Anglo-Portuguese Rivalry," p. 125.
25 Filippo della S. Trinita, *Viaggi Orientali*, p. 56.
26 On the Basra-Sind trade see also Foster, *English Factories* 1634-1636, pp. 130-31, 243; and pp. 168, 255, 713 for Surat junks sailing to Basra; Muscat (re-)exported coffee, incense and azebre (from Yemen) and horses. Bocarro, *Livro das Plantas*, vol. 2, pp. 51-52.
27 Foster, *English Factories* 1637-1641, p. 247, 249 ("the Portugas Muscatt fleet, with juncks from Sinda and Cambaya"); Ibid., *English Factories* 1646-1650, p. 45.
28 Foster, *English Factories*, vol. 6, p. 243 (05/06/1640); NA, VOC 1134, van Oostende to Batavia (08/05/1640), f. 222.
29 *ACE*, vol. 2-135, pp. 377-78 (19/11/1642).
30 Boxer, *Commentaries*, pp. 195-97; ACE I-I-19 (17/03/1625), p. 25
31 Bocarro, *Livro das Plantas*, p. 77; Foster, *English Factories* vol. 3, pp. 61 (14/02/1625), 84-85 (27/04/1625)
32 *ACE* vol. 1-19, p. 35 (17/03/1625).
33 Teles, *Economia*, p. 64, quoting *BFUP* 7, Provisao de Linhares to Diu (11/09/1630), p. 605.

mostly consisting of textiles and food supplies such as wheat, rice, and flour.[34] In the 1630s, the Portuguese Muscat fleet brought "great store of Cambaya and Sinda goods, as cloath, indico, conserves, etc., with store of pepper, cardamom, ginger, cinnamon, and some Dican cloath."[35] Moghul officials in Sind also sent their ships to Muscat and Bandar-e Kong. So important was this trade that they refused a Dutch offer of naval escort, fearing that they would lose the trade to Muscat and other Portuguese controlled ports.[36]

However, despite its continued military support for Muscat, it was trade not war that the *Estado* wanted and needed. As of 1627, more Banyans had started to use the Muscat-Basra route, which was very encouraging.[37] For the same reason, in 1629 Goa signed a commercial agreement-cum-armistice with the Safavid local and provincial authorities concerning the port of Bandar-e Kong and immediately sent a factor to claim its moiety of the customs revenues. At odds with this development was the viceroy's acceptance of Rui Freire's proposal to build forts between Jolfar (now Ras al-Khaimah) and Gwadar. Lisbon vetoed the proposal immediately, because there was no money.[38] There was no time either to spend money on such plans, because there were so many immediate threats that had to be taken care of. The rumor of a new Safavid attack on Basra and an attack by the Ya`ariba Imam of Nizwah in 1631 immediately required Rui Freire's attention. Goa had neither ships nor troops to spare, which it needed for the defense of its settlements in Asia and Mombassa.[39] All this showed how weak the Portuguese position in the Persian Gulf had become; the *Estado* barely could defend its existing positions let alone create and sustain new ones. Because of the war with the Safavids, the threat of the Ya`ariba Imam, the competition of the Dutch and the English, exports to Muscat consisted almost exclusively of food supplies, weapons and soldiers. The resulting deficit of the Muscat factory had to be paid by Goa. Therefore, there was little Portuguese interest in the Persian Gulf trade. The commercial navigation between Muscat and Goa and other Indian destinations had to be protected by military might when the ships had no arms themselves. In fact, the government of Goa each year sent two to three frigates to escort vessels of Portuguese traders from Sind and Diu to Muscat and Basra.[40] Often use was made of the armed ships that were sent with food supplies for Muscat.[41] Goa hoped that that the Sind trade with Muscat would increase as if offered a secure shipping route, and after having brought some order to the confused state of affairs of the Muscat factory. According to the new rules, on arrival the merchandise was opened by the superintendent of the exchequer (*vedor da fazenda*), who verified whether they were in agreement with the list submitted by the merchant. In case there was a difference the non-registered

34   Dunlop, *Bronnen*, pp. 650 (20/04/1638), 655 (10/08/1638). The Dutch also took a Portuguese ship coming from Sind going to Muscat; it was sold at Bandar Abbas and a present was given to the grand-vizier and *shahbandar*. Coolhaas, *Generale Missieven*, vol. 2, p. 35 (18/12/1639); Mandelslo, *Journal*, p. 10 (20/03/1638).

35   Foster, *English Factories* 1637-1641, p. 252.

36   NA, VOC 1103, Schriftelyck verbael ... Cornelis 1631/32, f. 70; Floor, "The First Dutch Voyage," p. 401.

37   Teles, *Economia*, p. 64, quoting *BFUP* 7, Provisao de Linhares to Diu (11/09/1630), p. 605.

38   Teles, *Economia*, p. 64-65, quoting TT-LM 28 Filipe III to Linhares (31/03/1631), f. 172; idem to idem (31/04/1631), f. 244; TM-LM 29 Linhares to Filipe III (18/08/1631); TT-LM 30, Filipe III to de Linhares (03/04/1632), f. 162r-v.

39   *ACE* vol. 1-125, pp. 385-88 (26/10/1631).

40   NA, VOC 1143 (04/06/1635), f. 684-85; *ACE*, vol. 1-26, p. 101 (03/12/1619); *Diario de Linhares*, vol. 2, p. 177.

41   Teles, *Economia*, p. 67 quoting TT-LM 30 de Linhares to Filipe III (03/02/1633), f. 263vs-264.

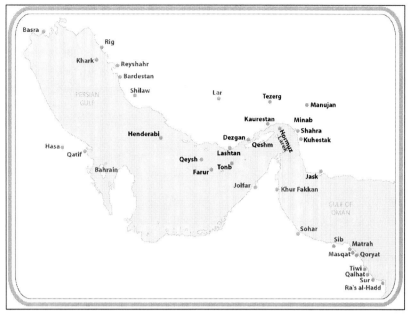

Figure 6, Maps of the Persian Gulf

merchandise was confiscated by the *vedor* for the royal exchequer. The merchants, after having paid imposts, were allowed to trade anywhere in the Persian Gulf, including at Bandar-e Kong, but with the exception of Hormuz and Bandar Abbas. The sheikhs of Muscat, who had a share in the customs revenues were informed that they would not receive this share on anything imported from Hormuz.[42] Apart from the security offered by the convoy, this route was made more attractive to Sindi merchants by the fact that the Portuguese gave loans to Sindi merchants. These loans were given on condition that

---

42   *BFUP* 5, no. 321, p. 143 (25/01/1630); *BFUP* 7, no. 283, p. 551 (08?/11/1630).

the merchants shipped their merchandise with the armed Portuguese escort vessels, who charged more than Asian vessels did.[43]

How close the relations were between Thatta and Masqat is clear from the following entry in the Diary of the Dutch merchant Cornelis Corneliszn, who was in Thatta in 1631 to make a market assessment. This entry shows that Thatta was an important source of intelligence for the Dutch.

> 9 December 1631. I sent for the interpreter who was lofting in our house
> (as he had left his wife and children in Lari Bandar (Bandeer) and asked him
> about the situation of Muscat (Muscatte), whether he had been there. He
> replied, 'yes' and that he had left there more than 9 months ago. It had three
> forts or strongholds, one towards the land, one at the seaside with yet another
> small one, which did not amount to much. The garrison that was there
> nowadays consisted in 50 to 60 Portuguese, the remainder were mostly Moors
> and were [blank] in number.[44] Rui Freire (Roij Frero) commanded them as
> governor, who had the abovementioned *armada de remos* there and was at war
> with the Arabs. I asked him why the forts of Muscatte were manned by so few
> Portuguese to which he replied that Rui Freire (Roijfrero) no longer trusted
> that many Portuguese, because they had so easily lost and surrendered the fort
> of Ormus, while the Moors and Caffers[45] were brave warriors, both at sea and
> at land, and therefore were greatly honored by them if they did something of
> note. He had chosen many officers from among them who were treated like
> Portuguese and in case of a notable succes they were given a liberal donation.[46]

Following their agreement with the Safavids about Bandar-e Kong in 1629, the Portuguese kept a large force at Muscat.[47] The management of the Portuguese factory at Bandar-e Kong, including the receipt of half of the customs, remained in the hands of the superintendent of the exchequer of Portuguese Muscat, who also appointed its factor, "because all these seas are tributary to the generality of Muscat."[48] Most of the

---

43   NA, VOC 1103, Schriftelyck verbael ... Cornelis, f. 82vs.

44   This information does not seem to be correct. In 1633, the Portuguese had a military presence of 1,223 soldiers in the various forts in the Straits of Hormuz consisting in 22 captains (of which five were laskars), 456 soldiers and 745 laskars, in addition to 515 naval personnel. Teles, *Economia*, p. 139.

45   From the Arabic word *kafir*, or infidel, by which term, Arabs traders referred, among others, to Africans. Europeans adopted the same term in one or another bastardized form, in the meaning of black African.

46   Floor, "The First Dutch Voyage," p. 405.

47   Dunlop, *Bronnen*, p. 433 (18/07/1633).

48   *ANTT*, DRI XXIX, f. 84r; see also *HAG*, LM XIVB, no. 28 (8:1); *BFUP* 9 (08/02/1633); *AHU* C.I. 16/35; Boxer, *Commentaries*, p. 206; Portuguese have the moiety of the customs, and give passes to barks to sail after payment, "because all these seas are tributary to the generality of Muscat." Le Gouz, *Les Voyages*, p. 267; Godinho, *Relação*, p. 102.

Bandar-e Kong trade consisted of transshipment of Sindi textiles and South-East Asian spices coming directly and/or via Muscat and forwarding them to Basra.[49]

Table 2: Portuguese military and navy personnel in the Straits of Hormuz 1623-1633

Category/Year		1623	1633
Military	Captains	-.-#	22*
	Soldiers	500	456
	Lascars	167	745
Navy	Captains	-.-	12
	Skippers (*mocadões*) and sailors	-.-	504
Total		627	1,739

Source: Teles, *Economia*, p. 139 quoting TT-S. Vincente f. 226f; BNL-FG 1783, f. 5v-10.

★ of which five were lascars. # not separately indicated.

Not only had Goa to pay for Muscat's deficit, but it continued growing. This was mainly due to the growing cost of military expenditures as is indicated by the increased number of soldiers and navy personnel active in the Hormuz Straits. This number increased by 261% between 1623 and 1633. Most of the growth was in the number of so-called lascars, who represented some 70% of the military personnel in 1633 (see Table 2). In 1625, or thereabouts, Muscat yielded revenues of 7,000 or 8,000 *cruzados*.[50] In 1634, the gross profit of the Muscat factory was less than 60,000 *xerafins*, which did not even cover its expenses amounting to 120,952 *xerafins*, yielding a deficit of 53,827 *xerafins*. Muscat's income represented 5.9% of the *Estado's* total revenues, while its expenses were 10.5% of total expenses in 1634. The revenues of Muscat in 1634 consisted of mostly of customs duties (89.4%), the remainder was a number of minor taxes (tobacco revenues [3.4%], *arequim* [fishing] revenues [6.7%] and duties on horses [0.6%]). An indication of the importance of the fishing industry to Muscat is the fact that its revenues (*renda do arequim*) were the most important source of non-customs related income during the

---

49 For the 1630s see Bocarro, *Livro das plantas*, p. 60 (textiles from Sind, Cambaya, Dahbol; spices, curuma, indigo, Sindi and Bengal sugar, and coffee [*caoa*]) and Dunlop, *Bronnen*, p. 479 (van der Trille, June 1634), who mentioned that there was much import of spices by the Portuguese at Bandar-e Kong. van der Chijs, *Dagh Register* vol. 30, pp. 487-89; Ibid. vol. 31, p. 1324f.; Boxer, "Anglo-Portuguese Rivalry," p. 125. For the situation after 1670 see NA, VOC 1304, Bent to Batavia (4/9/1674), f. 508f; NA, VOC 1354, Casembroot to Batavia (14/6/1682), f. 365vs; (thirteen vessels at Bandar-e Kong); NA, VOC 1379, van den Heuvel to Batavia (7/9/1682), f. 580 (twenty-three vessels at Bandar-e Kong).

50 Matos, *Das relações*, p. 298 quoting BNL: FG 917, f. 167vs-168r. (ca. 1625). For a detailed assessment of military and naval personnel in the Straits in 1634, including their pay and schedule of payment see Bocarro, *Livro das Plantas*, p. 49. The lascars were recruited among the population of Moghestan and Baluchistan. They served mainly on land, because they did not function well aboard ships. Ibid., pp. 49, 52-53. According to Anonymous, *Relãçao das plantas*, p. 11, in 1630 or thereabouts, there was a garrison of 500 soldiers at Muscat, who never stayed all the time in the forts and more when the fleet was in the Straits. There also were about 40 vessels at Muscat as well as 30 lascars under 12 captains.

Portuguese period.[51] According to the Dutch, there was a 10% customs duty on freight goods in case of non-Portuguese ships.[52] Muscat's customs revenues were mainly dependent on the trade between Basra and the West Coast of India. In the past, the Portuguese therefore had only given passes to those sailing to the Persian Gulf and Red Sea, unless they went to Hormuz. After 1622, all ships had to go either to Muscat and/or, after 1630, to Bandar-e Kong. Not the English and Dutch, of course, who were enemies and too strong to be forced to follow Portuguese orders.[53] The Portuguese system of passes was instrumental in directing trade to Muscat and other ports such as Bandar-e Kong. To enforce their pass system Portuguese ships cruised between Hormuz and Muscat.[54] Indian ships after having paid customs duties at Muscat or Bandar-e Kong continued from there to Basra in convoy and under Portuguese protection, for which they also had to buy a pass. The price of such a pass issued at Muscat was only 650 *dinar*s or 105 *reis*.[55] The income of these passes were assigned to a detachment of 20 to 30 small ships guarded by two or three Portuguese frigates and armed *terranquins*, which were mustered locally and crewed by Baluchis. It was a hazardous trade because of the risk of shipwreck and the attacks from the pirates of Nakhilu.[56] Supervising whether pass holders respected its terms sometimes led to political problems. According to the treaty signed with Bijapur, subjects of Adel Shah were entitled to receive six passes (*cartazes*) yearly, as long as their ships would call on Muscat if they were bound for the Persian Gulf. In 1632, Rui Freire caught three Bijapuri ships near Bandar-e Kong that allegedly had not respected the full letter of treaty and were consequently towed to Muscat where their goods were seized, and considered the property of the Portuguese Crown. In Goa, Viceroy Linhares had to make some arrangements to please and appease Bijapur.[57]

There had been talk of abolishing the Captaincy of Muscat, but the death of Rui Freire in December 1632 put an end to that discussion. His death allowed the Captain to try and promote Muscat as an emporium rather than a port-of-call. This meant that the entire defensive system that Rui Freire had built fell apart. Some forts between Suwadi and Jolfar were evacuated at the end 1633 and the beginning 1634 to reinforce Muscat and the defenses of the southern coast.[58] This consolidation coincided with the discontinuation of trade with the interior due to the war with the Imam, which limited Portuguese commercial operations and forced their merchants to stay in Muscat. The *casados* mainly dealt in local trade, supplying the forts and the area around it. Therefore, the *provedor-mor*

---

51 Teles, *Economia*, p. 144, quoting BNL-FG Orçamento de 1634, f. 5vs-10; Bocarro, *Livro das Plantas*, p. 50. Given the fact that fishing was a major economic activity of Muscat, the term *arequim* may refer to the large fish species of the *Alopias vulpinus* or the Thresher shark, variously known in Portugal as: *Arequim*, *Peixe alecrim*, *Peixe raposo*, and *Peixezorra*. This type of shark occurs in the waters of Oman and is worldwide valued for its meat, liver, hide, and fins. It is utilized fresh, dried-salted, or smoked and nowdays also frozen. [http://www.fishbase.org/Summary/SpeciesSummary.php?id=2535]

52 NA, VOC 1134, van Oostende to Batavia (08/05/1640), f. 222r.

53 Le Gouz, *Voyages* p. 121.

54 Dunlop, *Bronnen*, pp. 516 (31/12/1634), 522 (01/01/1635).

55 *Diario do Conde de Linhares*, vol. 2, pp. 179-80 (22/09/1634). It was an emolument for the issuing official.

56 NA, Collectie Sweers/Manis 9, f. 122; NA, VOC 1106, Schriftelijcke Relatie," unfoliated (frigates and small vessels); NA, VOC 1135, Geleynsz to Batavia (24/03/1641), f. 647-668 (mentions 6-10 armed frigates); *ACE*, vol. 2-53, p. 180 (06/08/1637); AHU, India, Cx 19, 5; Linhares, *Diario*, vol. 2, p. 180; *ANTT*, DRI, 32, f. 35 and *ANTT*, DRI 33 (03/02/1635), f. 35; Bocarro, *Livro das plantas*, p. 62.

57 *ACE*, vol. 1-137, p. 426 (21/05/1632).

58 *Diario do Conde de Linhares*, vol. 1, p. 177 (21/09/1634); Bocarro, *Livro das Plantas*, pp. 74-75.

wanted to hold on to these positions, but the captain, because of the cost, did not. At the proposal of the *vedor* of Muscat, Antonio de Fonseca, the forts at Sib and Barkah were maintained by the Portuguese with lascars, while the *casados* were withdrawn to Muscat to shore up the *Estado*'s prestige.[59] Other restrictions and development also constrained the development of Muscat into an emporium, despite the increased use of Muscat as a port-of-call on the Sind-Basra route. For example, the link Muscat-India had to go via Goa, although Chaul was interested in direct voyages.[60] More importantly, the Portuguese establishment at Bandar-e Kong changed Muscat's competitive position so that it became less important. Although it started to loose market share to Bandar-e Kong, the latter continued to contribute to Muscat's revenues. The pilgrim 'trade' was one important aspect of the Sind-Muscat link, for Sindi pilgrims going and returning to/from Mecca usually traveled via Muscat. In 1644, for example, the Mir of Sind asked for passes for five pilgrim ships, which carried pilgrims traveling to Mecca via Muscat.[61]

Initially most trade at Muscat was carried on by the small *casado* community of about 150 persons many of whom were refugees from Hormuz, as well as Banyan and Jewish traders. They traded with Malabar, East Africa, Yemen, Sind and Basra. This was done in small boats built at Shihr and Muscat and manned by black slaves, Arabs, and lascars.[62] As a result of the contraction of trade at Muscat, the share of the *casados* in the market was diminished to not more than two-fifth's of the merchants the rest were Banyans, Jews or Moslems having common interests with the Captain. Given the importance of the trade with Thatta, Sindi Bhatias had offices and warehouses in Muscat. In 1635 the debate about the status of Muscat flamed up again; one party wanting to replace the Captain by a castellan-merchant, the other wanted to have things remain as they were. The former party won. The change did not solve the problem, however and the mercantile branch seems to have prevailed over the military, at least in 1633-34.[63]

By 1640 Muscat had become a full integrated part of the Persian Gulf trading network. The ships from India that supplied the Basra market first called on Muscat, for they were "principally from the Portugasses' Muscat fleet, which usually setts fourth in June for Congo, and arrives here [Basra] sometime in July."[64] This meant an increase in revenues for Muscat, which was reflected in the value of Muscat to its Portuguese commander, which was estimated at 50,000 ducats per year in 1640.[65] However, it was all too late and too little to make a difference for the continued presence of the Portuguese on the Arab littoral. The immediate result of the fall of Muscat in December 1649 was that Portuguese trade in the Persian Gulf was reduced to almost nothing.[66]

---

59 *Diario do Conde de Linhares*, vol. 1, pp. 177-78 (21/09/1634); Bocarro, *Livro das Plantas*, pp. 178-78.

60 *Diario do Conde de Linhares*, vol. 1, p. 168 (Provisão dated 08/09/1634).

61 *ACE*, vol. 3-13, p. 21 (20/05/1644).

62 *APO* 6-564, p. 1252 (25/08/1630); Barendse, *The Arabian Seas*, p. 343; NA, VOC 1113, Report Carstenz, f. 218-20; Coolhaas, *Generale Missieven*, vol. 2, p. 5 (12/01/1639), 111 (30/11/1640) (vessels from Muscat at Goa); Idem, vol. 2, p. 36 (18/12/1639) (Danish ship went to Muscat.)

63 *ACE* II-12 (04/01/1636), pp. 41-46; Idem, II-41 (10/10/1636), p. 111; Foster, *English Factories* (1634-36), p. 135. For the trade of Thatta, see Floor, "The First Dutch Voyage."

64 Baladouni and Makepeace, *Armenian Merchants*, p. 39 (22/06/1640).

65 Lorimer, *Gazetteer*, p. 38.

66 Anonymous, *Chronicle*, vol. 1, p. 359.

LAST PORTUGUESE STAND AT MUSCAT

In addition to the need to contain, if not eliminate, the danger of Dutch, English, and Safavid operations in the Persian Gulf, the Portuguese also needed to cover their back, i.e. to contain if not control the increasing attacks by the growing Ya`ariba forces on Muscat and other fortified ports on the Batinah coast. Until 1624, the Portuguese were more interested in ousting the Safavids, than in consolidating their power and presence on coastal Oman. They broke a few agreements with Omani rulers and clan chiefs to secure the interior, and, if necessary by using their trump card, or so they thought, Mohammad Shah. However, all this military and political effort, as well as their increasing presence, was used by Sheikh Naser b. Morshed al-Ya`ariba, the Sheikh of Nizwah to unite the scattered Omani clans under his guidance to oust the Portuguese. As yet, the Portuguese were not much worried about this problem, because the civil strife was mostly limited to the interior of Oman. In 1624, Sheikh Naser b. Morshed al-Ya`ariba was elected as Imam of the Ibadi sect. He wanted to oust the Portuguese from Oman. He made his center of operations at Nizwah. From there he launched his attacks against the Portuguese and dissenter tribes.[67] In mid–1633, or thereabouts, the Imam's forces attacked Sohar and Jolfar, but failed to seize the former.[68] The Portuguese, fearing an attack on the center of their power in Oman, repaired the fortifications of Muscat.[69] Thereafter, the Ya`ariba forces took Sur from the Portuguese.[70] On August 8, 1640 Naser b. Morshed died. That same day his second-cousin Soltan b. Sayf (r. 1640-1679) succeeded him as Imam.[71] In that year the new Imam learnt that the defenses of Muscat were undermanned and he therefore launched an attack to take the forts, which was unsuccessful and he was repulsed with considerable losses. On November 7, 1643, the Imam was able to take Sohar making 37 Portuguese prisoners, after having killed the rest of the garrison. This success soon was followed by the capture Qoryat and other forts.[72] In 1648, the Imam mounted a new attack of Muscat, which forced the Portuguese, who had become short of ammunition, to come to an agreement that greatly limited their powers. The Arab demands were considered to be outrageous and the war continued. The Portuguese only agreed to talk once the hills above Makallah had fallen into the hands of the Imam, and the plague was reigning in the town (50 dead per day). Peace was agreed as follows:

> that the Portuguese should raze to the ground certain forts which they
> possessed at Matrah, Quryat and Sur; that the Imam should demolish a fort
> which he had built at Matrah, that the place for the future to be considered

---

67 Bocarro, *Livro das plantas*, p. 3; also *ANTT*, DRI XLIV, f. 262 (06/03/1639), which mentions Sur, Qoryat, Badiya, Khur Fakkan, Diba, Rams, and Jolfar; Floor, "A description," p. 33; Miles, *The Countries*, pp. 203-04.

68 Ross, *Annals*, pp. 51-52; Badger, *History*, vol. 1, pp. 66-68 (with a short account of the attack on Jolfar and Sohar); Dunlop, *Bronnen*, p. 500 (15/08/1634); *ACE*, vol. 1-158 (21/09/1633), p. 487; *BFUP* 12, no. 85, p. 450 (n.d. 1634); *BFUP* 9, no. 36 (02/02/1634) (acknowledges loss of Sohar).

69 Badger, *History*, vol. 1, pp. 68-69; Lorimer, *Gazetteer*, p. 37. Reinforcement of the fort by engineer Toral. *BFUP* 8, no. 66 (02?/03/1632)

70 Badger, *History*, vol. 1, p. 69.

71 Ross, *Annals*, p. 55. For the origin and rise of the Ya`ariba dynasty see Bathhurst, *The Ya`rubi Dynasty*; Wilkinson, *Water*; al-Ashban, "The Foundation," pp. 354-71; Bathhurst, "Maritime Trade," pp. 89-106.

72 Badger, *History*, vol. 1, p. 69; Anonymous, *Chronicle*, vol. 1, p. 358; *ACE* vol. 3-2, p. 2 (19/01/1644); Ross, *Annals*, p. 53; Lorimer, *Gazetteer*, pp. 38, 401.

neutral; that `Omani vessels should go abroad unchecked, but should take
Portuguese passes for the return voyage; that subjects of the Imam should
pay no duties, either personal or commercial, on entering or leaving Muscat;
that trade should be in every respect free; and that the Arabs should destroy
all fortifications erected during the siege, while the Portuguese should not
build anything upon the site of their demolished works. These terms clearly
involved the financial ruin of the Portuguese settlement; but there was no
alternative to acceptance.[73]

The special position of Matrah as well as the distinction of two categories of Arabs,
those who were followers of the Imam and those who were not, created by the peace
agreement caused the Portuguese problems. The Arabs of Matrah now could export dates
and horses without fear of Portuguese reprisal, while at Muscat, the Banyans immediately
used the major loophole of two categories of Arabs to import their goods under the name
of an 'Imami' Arab.[74]

Since the agreement was a truce, not a peace treaty, both sides knew that hostilities
would resume sooner rather than later.[75] In the fall of 1649 the peace was broken, and by
October Imam Soltan b. Sayf was besieging Muscat. The town fell on 2 December 1649
followed by the surrender of the impregnable forts on 20 January 1650 in exchange for the
garrison's freedom.[76] Before the fall of Muscat some 700 refugees had fled by sea.[77] Most of
the Portuguese and Baluchi lascars were killed after the capture of the town, although one
year later there were still some black renegade Portuguese in town. However, the majority of
the population was Arab, many of whom had come from the mountains and the interior of

---

73 Lorimer, *Gazetteer*, p. 401. During the four-months' siege of Muscat in 1648 at least 110 Christians had
    died, and many of the large Indian (Sindi and Cambaya) population more than 300. *ANTT*, DRI LIX, f. 82-
    84vs (24/10/1648); Foster, *English Factories* 1646-1650, p. 223; *ACE* vol. 3-24, 25, p. 507-09 (Capitulaçoes
    de pazes 15/12/1648). For a slightly different version see Badger, *History*, vol. 1, p. 69, who has the date
    wrong. Signatories of the peace agreement included the second Ya`ariba Imam, Soltan b. Sayf b. Malek
    al-Ya`aribi (Soltão Bensefo ben Maleque Aleyorly), Rashed b. Salem `Ali (Raxete ben Salemo Ali), and
    Sayf b. `Ali b. Saleh al-Qasemi? (Sefoben Ali ben Sale el Casmy), while also involved was Sa`id b. Khalfan
    (Said Bencalfão). For the identification of two of these persons see Badger, *History*, vol. 1, pp. 73, 90.
74 *ANTT*, DRI LIX, f. 70-r-vs (Assento 12/09/1648); *ACE* vol. 3-18, p. 488f. (15/12/1648); Ibid., vol. 3-27, p.
    509-15 (Regimento for Francisco de Távora de Ataíde; 11/02/1649).
75 *ACE* 3-80, p. 122 (23/09/1648).
76 NA, KA 1071 bis, Sarcerius to Batavia (29/03/1650), f. 696vs; NA, KA 1071, Sarcerius to van Teylingen
    (Surat) (01/01/1650), f. 647r; Lorimer, *Gazetteer*, p. 38 (in 1649, the king of Portugal had given orders to
    keep Muscat and Khasab at all cost; no Sheikhs and Moslems were allowed to remain in the town, and
    had to be transferred to Band Ali, near Bandar Abbas), 401-03 (Lorimer gives the date of surrender of
    the fort as 23 January 1650 and of the factory on 26); Anonymous, *Chronicle*, vol. 1, pp. 358-59; Badger,
    History, vol. 1, pp. 79-81 (for a description of the drawn-out battle), 86-87 (the taking and destruction
    of the two ships). For a sensational story about the events leading to the attack on Muscat in 1649 see
    Hamilton, *A New Account*, vol. 1, pp. 43-44. According to Portuguese sources, the large fort fell on 20
    January and the smaller fort on 26 January 1650. *ACE* vol. 3-29, p. 517 (18/12/1650).
77 *AHU* C.I. 21/12 (18/12/1650); *ACE* vol. 3-29, p. 517 (18/12/1650). On 29 December 1649 the Dutch
    received information from Bandar-e Kong that four barks filled with Banyan and Moslem refugees
    from Muscat had arrived, two of which arrived in Bandar Abbas on 30 December 1649 very destitute
    and famished, who confirmed the fall of the town of Muscat. The Omani attackers had killed most of
    the defenders and had enslaved some, including 200 Portuguese whose wives had already been sent
    ahead to Goa. It was not expected that the two forts would hold out very long the more so, since the
    defenders of one of them had already asked for quarter. NA, KA 1071, Sarcerius to van Teylingen (Surat)
    (01/01/1650), f. 647r.

Oman.[78] In early 1650, Bandar-e Kong received an influx of Banyans and Moslems who had fled in four fully-packed barks from Muscat; they had left on 29 December 1649. On 13 January 1650 two additional barks arrived with similar destitute and hungry refugees.[79]

78   NA, VOC 1188, E. Boudaens, "Schriftelijck relaes," (Surat 29/11/1651), f. 546-vs.
79   NA, KA 1071, Sarcerius to van Teylingen (01/15/1650), f. 647r.

3

Ya`ariba Muscat
(1650-1725)

Muscat Town

Buildings and Walls

The city did not change much after the Omani takeover. Only the buildings that had a Catholic religious function were given a secular function after the fall of Muscat in 1650. In 1651, Muscat was becoming dilapidated, "as is the custom of the Arabs," a visiting Dutch merchant observed. There was not one house that was undamaged, and most of them were in ruins, a result of the siege of and battle for Muscat. The only construction activity that was ongoing was the repairs of the two forts. Many survivors of the Omani capture of Muscat had left and the town's population therefore, was much smaller in size than before.[1] The streets were irregular and so narrow that two men could barely walk abreast.[2] In 1672, Robert Padbrugge, a Dutch merchant described Muscat as follows:

> All Portuguese buildings have been destroyed. The Arabs, because of their great hate for the Portuguese, appear even to have taken revenge on the buildings and did not want to leave one stone on the other. However, there still remain a church, a chapel, and a monastery, which is the Imam's court at present. Further there are some other almost dilapidated buildings. Among them are a few which are partly destroyed in which Sheikh Abdollah (Chegh

---

1   NA, VOC 1188, Boudaens, f. 545vs.
2   Lockyer, *An Account*, p. 208.

Abdul) and the chief of the soldiers live. There are a few other [buildings] which are even more dilapidated. For the rest their dwellings are huts and holes (*moortkuylen*), which nevertheless are so full of people, that one is very much amazed and wondering where all these people, who gush forth from such a small dwelling, are coming from. The more so, since the greater part of the town is filled with merchandise. The streets are so narrow and winding that the town almost looks like a maze. Only in the widest street a wool bale can pass. A very lively wool trade is carried on here.[3]

Figure 7, Muscat from Kaempfer, *Ameoemitatum*, 467

In 1684, Kaempfer noted that in the city itself, most of the houses were made of stone and were pleasing and spacious. There also were many ruined houses and buildings. Moreover, many houses were huts made of date-palm fronds, but they were much neater, cleaner and larger, for they even had a courtyard, than those on the Persian littoral. In the green valley, there were *barasti* huts in which fishermen lived, whose boats were lying on the beach. To the south of the city was an uncultivated plain with some Acacia trees and wells to give water to the animals, a ropeway, and some huts. From a distance of 3.5 km from the city gate, after the first hill, was a fresh-water well. Its water was conducted to the city by canals and led to two water cellars, from which ships were supplied with drinking water. This water was excellent and ships were charged one rupee of four *mahmudi*s per *half-legger*, a cask of 291 liters.[4] Georg Wilmson, a Dutch merchant who resided in Muscat in 1672-73, reported that the Omanis also built large houses, but this was exceptional. A certain Esma`il, a fugitive Arab from Basra, had built a very large house, which served as a kind of hotel for

3 Floor, "A description," pp. 24-25.
4 Kaempfer, *Die Reisetagebücher*, p. 148. One *legger* is 582 liters.

his compatriots indicating regular trade relations with Basra. Another Esma`il, nicknamed "Benderie" (i.e. Bandari), owned five 'hotels', but these were made of date-palm fronds and mats, which he rented out per night at rates of two to three *abbasi*s, depending on their size.[5] Inside the houses people had few if any household effects. "The rich sit on a simple mat woven from date reeds, or what also happens on small pebbles, which serves them an actual carpet. Their night goods consist of a coarse woolen horse-blanket [filled] with flock-wol during winter. They mostly cover themselves with their mantles."[6]

According to Kaempfer, the Augustinian convent, a nice Italianate building, was being used as storage and arsenal, and when the Imam was in town as his residence. There was still the former Catholic church, a white building with high roofs that was also used as storage space. However, it was transformed into the Imam's palace, when he resided in Muscat, which was one to two months per year. The bazaar covered a large space and consisted of covered and partly vaulted alleys that ran parallel to one another and crossed one another regularly in a quadrate pattern. The shops were well-stocked with all kinds of goods.[7] Around 1700, according to Lockyer, the houses were mean two-storied buildings and contained nothing worthwhile inside. The *suq* was in mid-town and well provisioned.[8] Around that same period Hamilton described the *suq* as follows:

> Their Bazaars or Markets are all covered with Date Tree Leaves, spread on Beams of the Same Tree, that reach from House to House-top' and the Houses being all flat on their Tops, terassed with Clay and Straw mixt, in the aforesaid Months every Body lodges on them in the Nights; and the Nights afford plentiful Dews, that sometimes weet them thro' their thick Cotton Quilts.[9]

Kaempfer noted that towers and bulwarks that the Portuguese had built in the hills to provide protection against attacks from the interior. They were white-washed and all-around decorated.[10] According to Hamilton, some two decades later, the town was very strong, although the buildings remained very mean.

> The Wall of the Town that faces the Harbour, has a Battery of large Cannon, about 60 in Number, and there are 8 to 10 small Forts built on the adjacent Rocks or Mountains, which guard all the Avenues to the Town, both by Sea and Land; and there are none permitted to come in or go out of the Harbour between Sun-set and Rising.[11]

---

5   Floor 1985, "A description," p. 60, n. 94; NA, VOC 1304, Report Wilmson, f. 483vs.

6   Floor 1985, "A description," p. 35.

7   There was no Jesuit college; it was the former Augustinian convent. Kaempfer, *Die Reisetagebücher*, pp. 148-49 (he lists many of the products for sale). The Imam spent one third of the year in Muscat, according to Kaempfer.

8   Lockyer, *An Account*, p. 208.

9   Hamilton, *A New Account*, vol. 1, p. 45.

10   Kaempfer, *Die Reisetagebücher*, pp. 147-48.

11   Hamilton, *A New Account*, vol. 1, pp. 44-45 (this is the old sea wall or *Sikkat al-Madfa`*); Kaempfer, *Die Reisetagebücher*, pp. 147-48; Ovington 1696, p. 422; Bafqi, *Jame`-ye Mofidi*, vol. 3/2, p. 810 (At night nobody was allowed to pass the barrier.)

Muscat had a Persian Gulf climate, which meant that from May to September it was excessively hot and humid.[12] In 1672, the Dutchman Jan Struys, found that "it was so hot there that if I had not experienced it myself I would not have believed it. In the evening the wind from the land was so hot that it seemed as if scalding hot water was showered over your body. I have seen myself that people fled into the sea to find relief."[13] Likewise, Lockyer found Muscat terribly hot in summer.[14] According to Ovington it was so hot that when you placed a fish "in the hollow part of a Rock, where the Sunbeams reflect from every side, in the heat of the day, and when the Sun is in the Zenith, will be half roasted in a little time by the Heat."[15]

POPULATION

In addition to mostly Arabs,[16] Indians (Sindis, Banyans), probably the largest minority group, Baluchis and Jews were living in Muscat. There is some evidence that in the mid-1660s a community of Portuguese renegades (Portuguese or Asian Catholics with Portuguese names) still existed in Muscat, some of them former slaves who were not liable for ransom. There also lived Christians in Muscat, because in 1684, Kaempfer was the guest of an Armenian merchant in his stone house, in which other Armenians lived.[17] In the 1670s, many people fled from Kich-Makran to Muscat due to the military operations of Safavid troops in that region, increasing the size of the Baluchi population of Muscat.[18]

There are no data available on the total number of people living in Muscat or the breakdown by religious group. Despite the fact that the Omanis showed tolerance for other ethnic groups and religions they, nevertheless, did not entirely trust them or like them. For example, the Indians in large numbers mainly lived in a kind of suburb on the south side in the western part of the city, because "they are not trusted to be allowed to live inside the town."[19] This despite the fact that one Banyan merchant was rumored to have provided essential information to Imam Sultan b. Sayf, which enabled him to take Muscat.[20] The

---

12 Della Valle, *Voyages*, vol. 4, p. 409; Hamilton, *A New Account*, vol. 1, p. 45.

13 Straussens, *Reisen*, p. 200; see also Kaempfer, *Die Reisetagebücher*, p. 150.

14 Lockyer, *An Account*, p. 208.

15 Ovington, *A Voyage*, p. 422.

16 Both the Dutch and English did not use the term Omanis to refer to the inhabitants of Muscat and Oman, but rather that of Muscat Arabs or Muscateers or some variant thereof, see, e.g., Lorimer, *Gazetteer*, pp. 62-67, 1186.

17 *ACE*, vol. 4-54, p. 154 (26/03/1666); NA, VOC 1188, E. Boudaens, "Schriftelijck relaes," (Surat 29/11/1651), f. 546-vs' Kaempfer, *Die Reisetagebücher*, pp. 147-48.

18 Floor, *Political and Economical*, p. 275; Bardsiri, *Tadhkereh-ye Safavi*, pp. 400-01, 405-07, 412, 662.

19 Floor, "A description," p. 24. According to Padbrugge, the Omanis wanted to get rid of the Banyans. NA, VOC 1288, Report Padbrugge, f. 436.

20 Allen, "The Indian Merchant," p. 40, n. 19; Floor, "A description," p. 33. According to Niebuhr, *Beschreibung*, p. 207 the Portuguese Captain had taken the daughter of a Banyan by force, who then betrayed the castle to the Omanis. According to *ACE* vol. 3-29, p. 517 (18/12/1650), the Captain of Muscat had stored all the gunpowder, ammunition and arms in the factory rather than in the fort as he should have as per his instructions. Allegedly Narutem was able to convince him to disregard his orders in this respect. Narutem's story is also found in Badger, *History*, vol. 1, pp. 81-84.

Banyan merchant Narutem had revealed Portuguese weaknesses to the Imam in 1649. As a reward, his family, but not the Banyan community, received tax exemption for his services.[21]

Although many Indians had left with the Portuguese in 1650 and despite Omani distrust, the Banyan community was large and was increasing after 1650.[22] In 1651, Banyan merchants were the main source of information to the Dutch merchant Elias Boudaens who visited Muscat at that time.[23] Those who had remained were mostly Kaphol Banyans from Diu (who were the wealthiest), while the newcomers were mostly Mappilas, i.e. Moslems from Kerala. The former were granted various exemptions from taxation.[24] In the 1670s, the Banyan merchants owned houses and shops in and outside Muscat and were involved in trade with the interior. Given their importance to the economy, the Bhattias were allowed to build a temple in Muscat.[25] Indians were not only traders, but also craftsmen such as builders, carpenters, and maybe there were some shipbuilders among them. In 1668, some 3,000 captives were taken in a raid of Diu who in 1672 still squatted on the overcrowded beach of Makallah.[26] Around 1700, Omanis had ships built in Surat. Their colors were red which "they display in streamers and pennants on every yardarm and masthead."[27]

The Arab population wore a hairy long robe, girded with a leather (sword) belt, which had wide and rather long sleeves, the whole made a somewhat slovenly impression on Kaempfer. Over it they wore a wide, unlined, thin, similar second hairy robe or mantle. On their feet they wore sandals with leather straps. They wound their head with a long and white fabric, of which the ends hung down their back. Their long saber, which was seldom curved, they wore on their shoulder or back and on the side a falchion. Their muskets were long, as in Persia, which they wore on a belt over the mantle.[28] The clothes were of inferior quality; the Sultan was dressed in a similar manner and walked either with shoes or barefeet. In 1672, the Sultan was dressed as follows during an official audience:

> His Highness the Imam was wearing a turban of fine fabric with a dropping slip at the back of about three-quarter of one ell. However, this was rather unusual for it had a golden end, while others only have [a turban of] common fabrics. His Highness' robe was not very different from that [worn] by the commoners; it was of a light-grey [color[with white stripes running from top to bottom at about a hand's distance from each other. Under it he wore some shirts of fine fabrics with wide long sleeves, which like the mantle, reached as far as his ankles. He had a

21 Badger, *History*, vol. 1, p. 87.

22 NA, VOC 1259, f. 3375; Allen, "The Indian Merchant," pp. 40-41.

23 NA, VOC 1188, Boudaens, "Schriftelijck relaes," (Surat 29/11/1651), f. 546.

24 Allen, "The Indian Merchant," p. 41; Barendse, *The Arabian Seas*, p. 344.

25 Floor, "A Description," pp. 22, 37 (for the payment of poll-tax and other imposts see Ibid., p. 37); Lorimer, *Gazetteer*, p. 1182; Allen, "The Indian Merchant," p. 41, n. 21 (with details about the temple).

26 NA, VOC 1273, Goske to XVII (28/02/1669), f. 1940; Floor, "A Description," pp. 2, 25.

27 Lockyer, *An Account*, p. 207.

28 Kaempfer, *Die Reisetagebücher*, p. 150. For a description of the arms (swords and muskets), see Floor, "A Description," pp. 26-27.

belt around his middle, in which he wore a dagger, which was crosswise
covered with silk yarns. His shoes were in the Persian fashion and yellow.[29]

Whereas the men wore simple neutral clothes, the women wore clothes made of all
kinds of silken fabrics and gold jewelry.[30]

RELIGION

Most people in Muscat were Moslems of the Ibadi sect. They prayed five times a day, but
those who wanted to be considered very devout prayed seven times per day. Not only
boys were circumcised, but so were girls. The consumption of any intoxicant (alcohol,
coffee, bhang, hemp, or tobacco) was strictly forbidden; nevertheless there were ten to
twelve *araq* (liquor) shops in the town. The lure of high profits outweighed the possibility of being sentenced to long-term imprisonment, the statuary sentence for both seller
and buyer. All games to amuse the spirit were banned as well as sodomy, although most
notables engaged in this practice. Magic and astrology were much used and believed in.[31]

    Although Jews and Banyans were permanent inhabitants of Muscat, in addition to the
occasional Christians, they could not exercise their religion in temples and synagogues.
Georg Wilmson, a Dutch merchant and resident of Muscat in 1672-63, observed that
"We have neither seen big temples nor churches or mosques. They all do their religious
duties by themselves and everywhere. The Jewish church was in that quarter of the Sindi
and Banyan prisoners at the foot of the mountains and [its construction] had nicely
begun. However, the great hate these Arabs bear the Jews has prevented its continuation
and completion, so that its construction has been stopped halfway and can still be seen
in that stage."[32] It thus would seem that the Omanis did not like to have special religious
buildings, but it is more likely that this applied to Moslems, as is clear in the case of the
synagogue. The absence of mosques in Muscat may have been due to the limited time
that the Ya`ariba Imam had held the town as well as that most Omanis belonged to the
Ibadi sect.[33] There was no *madraseh* or theological school either, for Wilmson noted that
theological discussions were held in a covered space near the Dutch factory.

        Aside to it [the weigh-house] is a secluded place with banks and covered with
        mats, which is a kind of exchange or gathering place for the important mer-
        chants. Here one also usually sees some jurists, important moolhaas (mullahs)
        or master exegetes of the Alcoran. Although they hold different opinions, they

29   Floor "A description," pp. 26-27, 35 (people wear learthern belts with an iron or copper buckle).
30   Floor, "A description," p. 35.
31   Floor, "A description," pp. 28, 34-36. According to Ovington, *A Voyage*, pp. 427-28 drinking tea and
     coffee was looked upon as vile contempt for the Ibadi religion; the same held for the smoking of
     tobacco and Indian hemp. They drank sherbets and in all matters abstained from anything that might
     inebriate their minds. Kaempfer, *Die Reisetagebücher*, p. 149 reported that the Imam during an audience
     had coffee, sweets and fruit served. For the Ibadi sect, see T. Lewicki, "al-Ibadiyya," *Encyclopedy of Islam*[2];
     Valerie Jon Hoffman, *The Essentials of Ibadi Islam*. Syracuse UP, 2010.
32   Floor, "A description," pp. 24-25.
33   On some of the Ibadi religious practices, see Floor, "A description," p. 36.

do not hate one another or dispute among themselves as we have observed
when Galiel (Khalil) took us there once and with great respect pointed out
two exegetes. The one was of the old and Omers (Omar's) religion [i.e. Sunni
Islam] and the other of Halys (Ali's) religion and persuasion [i.e. Shi`a Islam],
but we were not able at all to see something of that expressed in their faces.
There were also a few books lying pell-mell and open, out of which, so it
seemed, each in his turn read something more to edify than to cause dispute.[34]

Although the Omanis did not permit temples and the like they allowed non-Moslems
to practice their religion and even have sexual relations with Moslem women, as discussed
above. They also allowed cemeteries for non-Moslems.

The empty area (*yacht*) between the city walls and the gaps of the mountains is very wide. Moreover, it is intersected with many indentations in
between the mountains. Some of which represent the best lands of the
farmers. However, most of it lay unused (*ledich*) and covered with rocks. Their
cemetery is also to be found there, likewise that of the Benjaanen (Banyans),
the other Indians and that of the Europeans, which is closest to the town. ...
The area between that quarter and our [i.e. European] cemetery is mostly
covered with horse stables, both of the Imam and the governor as well as of
others, in addition to two rope-walks.[35]

FOOD SUPPLIES

There was no important agricultural activity in or immediately around the town of Muscat
itself, while its population after 1650 was growing. In pre-Ya`riba times, food supplies had to
be brought in by sea. The main towns that supplied Muscat with food were Sib and Barkah.[36]
Under the Ya`riba dynasty, Muscat continued to be "unable to feed itself. For the greater
part of its wheat and other grains it expects each year from Persia and other parts of the
Indies, just as the rice from the Kanara coast."[37] Muscat had no real road to the interior,
because the narrow passes were difficult to traverse by pack animals. Nevertheless, Muscat
was "very well supplied with food of all varieties" by sea, although the staple was dates.[38]
Kaempfer made purchases for his sea voyage in 1685, and commented that only butter, milk
and chickens were in short supply. He found that surprising, because the country did neither
lack in these products nor in sheep, goats and cattle, which peasants brought to the city by

34 Floor, "A description," p. 25. See, however, Hamilton, *A New Account*, vol. 1, p. 46 who states "their
    Molahs or Priests often preach themselves into violent passions, especially if the Subject of their
    Sermon be about the Verity of their Religion; and they challenge the Priests of any other Religion
    whatever, to confirm theirs with as good Evidences as they can."
35 Floor, "A description," pp. 23-24.
36 Anonymous, *Relãçao das plantas*, pp. 12-13.
37 Floor, "A description," p. 30.
38 Hamilton, *A New Account*, vol. 1, p. 45; Ovington, *A Voyage*, p. 423 ("oranges, lemons, citrons, grapes,
    apricocks [sic], and peaches, and most sorts of roots and green herbs"); Lockyer, *An Account*, p. 208.

boat.[39] However, "in general, both rich and poor live very frugal, their food mostly consists of sun dried whey, which is beaten tender between two stones. They eat it with some dates or some rice and salt or fresh fish. Sometimes also a little meat, as it may happen."[40]

Muscat had only one important economic resource, viz. fish, of which it had plenty. Hamilton noted the rich fishing grounds of Muscat.

> And the Reason why Fishes are so plentiful and cheap in the Market, is by the easy and odd Way they have in catching them, or rather conjuring of them; for I have seen a Man and two Boys catch a Tun Weight in an Hour or two. The Man stands on a Rock, where the Sea is pretty deep near it, and calls *Tall*, *tall*, for a Minute or two, and the Fish come swarming about the Rock. The two Boys, in a little Bot, shut them in with a Net about 20 or 30 Yards long, and 3 or 4 deep, and drawing te Net near the Rock, keep all in; and, when People come for Fish, he asks them was Sorts they want, and puts an Hoop-net, fixed to the End of a Pole, into the Water, and serves every Body with what Kind they ask for; and when he has done, he hales out his Net, and gives the rest their Liberty.

Hamilton further noted that on the naked rocks slaves roasted fish, which were also eaten by cattle and horses.[41] However, the fish that their cattle ate were not fresh from the sea.

> The *Muscatters* dig a large Hole in the Ground wherein they put it, 'till it remains so long that it rotts and comes to a kind of Earth. After this it is taken up, and boil'd with Water in great Earthen Pots, which makes a kind of thick Broth; and standing 'till it is cool, it is then given the Cattle, by which they grow extreme Fat, and yet their Flesh is very savory, not with either an ill Taste or Smell.[42]

The Dutch mentioned the marketing of Muscat loafsugar in Bandar Abbas in 1651.[43] In 1676 Batavia had become much worried about "the continued cultivation and culture of sugar on the coast of Arabia caused more and more oversupply in Persia and will be damaging for our trade."[44]

> Sugar, which apart from dates is the country's only produce, is cultivated to some considerable extent around the surrounding places or towns, viz. Semmed (Samad), Menneh (Manah), Behlah (Bahlah), Sahrel, Gabbie

39 Kaempfer, *Die Reisetagebücher*, p. 149 (with prices). For Omani products see also Anonymous, *Livro das Plantas*, p. 12, which included vegetables, grapes, onions and some wheat.

40 Floor 1985, "A description," p. 35.

41 Hamilton, *A New Account*, vol. 1, pp. 45-46.

42 Ovington, *A Voyage*, p. 426.

43 NA, KA 1077, Sarcerius to Batavia (25/03/1651), f. 580; Bocarro, *Livro das plantas*, p. 52 and Anonymous, *Livro das Plantas*, p. 12 had already mentioned this product in 1633 or thereabouts.

44 Coolhaas, *Generale Missieven*, vol. 4, p. 92 (07/02/1676). "Their horses they mostly get from Garick (Khark) and Persia. They buy them young, feed and train them here and then sell them as Arab horses." Floor, "A description," p. 31.

(Ghabbi) and in particular near Nizwa where sugar, also from the other places, is pressed and manufactured. The Imam or some merchants also purchase sugar cane in the areas where it is cultivated and has it brought to Nizwa, for it is only here that loaf-sugar is manufactured. There the Imam owns the two biggest manufactories jointly with a merchant who has a quarter share. The sugar manufactured by others is of little importance. The drier the air, the better and whiter the sugar is. The sugar-cane is sown in the soil between March and April and cut in December. The sugar having been manufactured, it is put into bags of 25 *man*-e Muscat [one *man* = 8 lbs.] and consists of three qualities: cabessa (*cabeça* or head), bariga (*barriga* or belly), and pe (*pé* or foot), or in Arabic, 'saugatje' (*saughat* or easy to swallow), 'amboneh' (*anbuh?*), and 'challal' (*halal* or permissible). The price of sugar fluctuates in proportion to the level of imports of that sweet produced by the Hon. Company in Persia. The ordinary price of the first quality is in Muscat 100 to 105, of the second quality 90 to 95, and of the third quality 80 to 85 laris. It is not very well possible to learn how much is manufactured and exported of it each year, because it is taken from Nizwa to the various sea-ports by camels and from there it is dispatched by ship to various countries. Moreover, the cultivation of sugar-cane is increased depending whether the previous good profits have been made on its yield. We were told that this country produces more than 5,000 to 6,000 chests of 22 Muscat *man*, of which Persia takes more than two-thirds; the remainder is taken to Bahrijn (Bahrain), al-Hasa, Bassura (Basra) and Mokha.[45]

In April 1706, van de Putt reported that 15 *trankis* arrived at Basra with so-called Omani bread sugar, textiles, pepper and other goods.[46] Padbrugge noted that the Omanis outside Muscat

> excel in agriculture and in the raising of cattle, mainly rams, goats, and camels, who are of two kinds and quality. With regard to their kind the difference is whether they have one or two humps on their back, like the dromedary. With regard to their quality the biggest difference amounts to the following: whether they can travel in one day from the court of Nizwa to Muscat, which normally is considered to take four days. Such animals they mostly keep as riding camels. They assert that they are as easy to handle as horses, but we believe to have experienced the opposite, for our ribs were creaking. That they are fast is true, this we saw when the Imam with his camel men passed us. … They also breed mules, but these are smaller than the Persian ones and hardly to distinguish from these.[47]

---

45 Floor, "A description," p. 31.

46 NA, VOC 1732, van der Putt/Basra to Wichelman (03/04/1706), f. 409-10; Ibid., idem to idem (05/10/1706), f. 411-13; VOC 1747, Basra to Casteleyn (?/11/1706), f. 543-45. There still was sugar cane production in the 1780s and in the 1850s, see Abdul Qadir, *Waqai*, p. 29 and Germain, "Quelques Mots," p. 342.

47 Floor, "A description," p. 27; see also Ovington, *A Voyage*, p. 423, 425-28; Bocarro, *Livro das plantas*, p. 52.

In general both rich and poor lived very frugal, their food mostly consisted of dried whey that was dried in the sun, which was then beaten tender between two stones. They ate it with some dates or some rice and salted or fresh fish. Sometimes, they also ate a little meat.[48]

Figure 8, Map of the Bay of Muscat, Dirk van der Velden, 1696, University of Leiden

---

48   Floor, "A description," p. 35 (It is odd that Wilmson did not mention rice, because that was of the main commodities imported from India); Ovington, *A Voyage*, p. 423.

TRADES AND CRAFTS

There were, of course, a large number of people engaged in trades and crafts to serve the population of Muscat as well as its maritime and commercial activities. However, it would seem that in particular the Omani artisan sector was not well developed.

> Trade and handicrafts are mostly carried out by the Sindis and Banyans in which pattern the prisoners from Diu can easily fit. Nevertheless one finds here many Arab gunsmiths and sword cutlers, anchor and bullet smiths, but they do not have the knowledge to smelt and cast iron. The coppersmiths make things that are used everyday quite well and properly. The hammers (*hamelslagen*) have not been well designed like ours, about which Dutch coppersmiths are very surprised. These consist of a very tiny grip which they bend a little; the hammering is done with red oxide which sticks very well to the copper. It also makes it suppler and only fills the hammer dents (*duppen*) and leaves the bosses elevated, which therefore are only hit by the hammer and evened out. We have made a large order for this red oxide in Persia so that our own coppersmiths may investigate it. How tar and paint are rubbed in to interchange between dark and red and new light red and how suitable it is for painting, the better it dries is perfectly known to Your Honour. There are several beautiful pieces of cannon (*clockspijs*) idle and totally unused due to the lack of good master craftsmen who might repair the widely burnt open fuse holes. The tinning with Sal ammoniac is also very common here as in Persia, because all their pots, vessels, and plates are all also made of copper. They also know how to turn materials rather nicely and small, because the beads of their rosaries, which the Catholics call *pater noster*, all have to be turned, in which they also have some dexterity. The potters are very good in glazing, but they are unfortunate in either having no good clay or not knowing well how to prepare it. They do not prepare the lead-ash for the glazing [process] as we do it by constantly stirring the melted lead with an iron claw. They just drop the molten lead in water, then take it out of the water again; they smelt it once more and pour it again in the water, and so on. This has to be a very slow process. But to return to the sifting, the ashes become cleaner, because only the thinnest and lightest particles mix with the water. To this one adds crushed up and sifted charcoal and in this way the glue for the glazing is ready. This produces a red color or black when it is a bit more heated or when some black [color] has been added. One gets a yellow or yellow-green color if one adds copper ashes in greater or smaller quantities to it.[49]

Therefore, it does not come as a great surprise that Padbrugge reported that, for example, carpenters, in particular ship's carpenters, were in short supply and generally less competent than their European counterparts. Padbrugge reported that "With regard to other crafts [such as carpentry, brick-laying, silver and gold-smithing, etc. they are not very good (*geen overvliegers*), which crafts] therefore are mostly taken up by the Sindis and Banyans."[50] During the discussion with Padbrugge in 1672 his Omani interlocutors

---

49 Floor, "A description," pp. 29-30. The word *clokspijse* actually means the metal of which cannons are cast, but that does not make sense here.

50 Floor, "A description," p. 30.

only once asked whether the Dutch East-Indies Company (VOC) could supply them with carpenters. "However, when they heard how much these people earned they did not raise this matter again. This probably led to a better welcome of the two Englishmen who were staying in Muscat and who had been well received by Sheikh Abdollah. On his departure, Padbrugge found that one of them, a carpenter, was instructing Omani carpenters how to repair damaged ships."[51] However, there was some capacity in Muscat to repair ships, because Kaempfer reported that in 1684 an Armenian merchant had come there to repair his damaged ship and his lost masts.[52]

System of Government

The Imam appointed a governor or *wali* to each town or district, who governed that jurisdiction on his behalf. This was also the case in Muscat. It was the governor's task "to administer justice on behalf of the Imam, to collect the country's revenues, to pay the militia out of that and to remit the remainder (for they keep tight strings on their purse) in the bait el mael (*bayt al-mal*) or the State treasury, of which only the Imam is in charge. He administrates it very honestly in such a way, that apart from a certain amount which he may use for himself, it is solely used for the country's welfare and he (if one may believe it) does not use even one penny for his own upkeep. This amount is so little that we do not dare to mention it in order to avoid that it would appear to be untruthful."[53]

There was further a *shahbandar* in charge of the customs administration as well as the weigh-house, which was next to the Dutch factory "and we believe that previously it was a water-gate, for during the Portuguese period it has been fit for that purpose, but not now. The year of construction is stated in Roman letters on top of the gate and to the best of our memory [it was] 1624."[54] It was the *shahbandar* who in 1674 came to the Dutch factory to count and weigh the VOC merchandise and who calculated the amount of customs due. Through these officials, the Imam controlled the finances, weigh-bridge and the defense of Muscat and he used only people of his own lineage and that of Sheikh Abdollah to run the administration. Sheikh Abdollah was the governor as of late 1671, one of his brothers was master of the weigh-bridge and the customs, and another brother was tax collector and in charge of the treasury in Nizwah. All other functionaries in Muscat such as comptrollers of the weighbridge and tax officials were all of the same lineage.[55]

Sometimes a qadi was also appointed next to the governor, whose task it was "to see to that that all court cases are scrupulously dealt with in accordance with their laws irrespective of persons and without connivance." There were no court houses, for justice was performed in public, in the open air, usually "in front of the governor's house or of that of the Imam's court, when he is in Muscat." The majority of cases were those between disputing merchants. "These cases, whatever their nature is, are immediately judged by

---

51 Floor, "A description," pp. 11-12.

52 Kaempfer, *Die Reisetagebücher*, p. 147.

53 Floor, "A description," pp. 31, 34. On the term *bayt al-mal* see the relevant article in the *Encyclopedia of Islam*.

54 Floor, "A description," p. 25.

55 Floor, "A description," pp. 18, 56; NA, VOC 1288, Report Padbrugge, f. 444vs.

the governor who also gives his verdict at once." This situation underlined the safety that existed in Muscat, day and night. After the drum was beaten in the evening nobody was "allowed to have a light or lamp burning."[56]

To defend his country against invasion, "According to Galiel (Khalil), the Imam had 15,000 men in arms from Jolphaar (Julfar) until the main hook of Rasal Gatte (Ra's al-Hadd), both along the beach doing guard duty as well as in the fortresses."[57] However, according to Wilmson's observations, "The sea-towns which have fortresses and in which the Imam keeps soldiers are Coriaat (Quryat), Muscat, Sohar, and Julfar or Cier,[58] which is situated on the inner side of Cape Musandam. Other small places with only redoubts were also to be found. Quite a few were situated on the coast with a force of five, six, eight to ten men of which places Muscat was the most important and "the key of Arabia."[59]

> The city [of Muscat] itself, situated in a plain between the two fortresses, has been enclosed in front and behind by a wall, while at the east side there are inaccessible mountains. Thus nature has made this place almost so strong that it only needs a small garrison [to ward off] enemies who come from outside. The Imam ordinarily only keeps here little more than 100 to 150 soldiers in his service, If he expects an enemy the Wali sends for 300 to 400 peasants from the surrounding villages, who then at this order come to serve the Imam with their gun, pikes, swords and shields, and that only for simple and frugal fare. The castles in the town are equipped with a few cannons only, similarly with ammunition; in all their fortresses are water-passageways; going along the bay it will amount to more than fifty pieces, amongst which even eighteen and twenty-four pounders of metal; the remainder are iron cannons, which they take and return from and to the ships according to their need.[60]

According to the Dutch merchant Padbrugge, "Most of the Imam's soldiers were from the Sindi coast, but recently he had dismissed most of them, because he had to pay for them. Now he uses his own people, who as soon as they are discharged return to their homes and work. Even important merchants allow themselves to be used in military operations out of love for their country they assert, but they also draw their pay and rations. The Imam at present has not more than 250 soldiers."[61] This maybe explains what Kaempfer wrote: "The soldiers looked as if they were pious, long-bearded respected village priests and clerics rather than martial warriors."[62] Wilmson reported that neither the Imam

---

56 Floor, "A description," p. 34. For some of the their legal rules and the safety and security of property, see Idem., pp. 34-35 (no punishment was allowed by the master of the servant or slave or by the head of household to a member of his family; any transgression had to be submitted in public to a magistrate for dispassionate and unprejudiced judgment. In case of murder, which seldom occurred, no hand was raised against the murderer; he was immured, however); see also Ovington, *A Voyage*, pp. 429-32.

57 Floor, "A description," p. 27.

58 Sir, often identified as Abu Dhabi (e.g. by Badger) and discussed by Slot, `*Arab al-Khalij*, pp. 40-41 as a place located somewhere between Sharjah and Mosandam (Niebuhr said it took its name from the residence of the Qawasem sheikh so it should certainly be between Sharjah and Ras al-Khaimah).

59 Floor, "A description," p. 32.

60 Floor, "A description," p. 32. For a description of the arms and equipment of the soldiers, which they had to buy themselves, see Idem, p. 27.

61 NA, VOC 1288, f. 445; Floor, "A description," p. 63, n. 130.

62 Kaempfer, *Die Reisetagebücher*, p. 150.

nor the Portuguese used the Baluchis (or Sindis) as soldiers, but only as sailors. When the Omani fleet sailed on January 23, 1673 Wilmson explicitly watched out for Baluchis and observed that among the crews many Baluchis were to be found. The Baluchis had come in great number with their families in barks from Kij-Makran in 1672 during the Iranian invasion of their territory (see above). Wilmson also stated that the Baluchis were known of old as good soldiers and as good shots. Merchants used them as soldiers on voyages to Mokha, Sind, and India and paid them good wages, namely 18 to 20 *laris* per month exclusive of the right to ship some goods free of charge. Wilmson did not investigate whether Baluchis would be willing to sign on with the VOC for voyages of two to three years' length, because he had not been ordered to do so. He also did not want to prevent that the Omanis would think that the VOC needed soldiers.[63] Wilmson further noted:

> that every time the Portuguese fleet sailed into the Gulf, the Omanis had to take cannons and crews and navigators from the merchandise fleet to man and arm their war fleet. This was an important handicap in mounting operations against the Portuguese, which had been put off several times. For several times the war drum had been beaten and not enough men had presented themselves. ... Their crews were inexperienced men such as porters, fishermen, boatmen etc. amongst whom many Baluchis. If prospects for booty looked bright there were sufficient recruits, but when the enemy fleet was expected to be at sea it was hardly possible to find anyone. Soldiers were recruited from the outlying villages at 9 to 12 laris per month. Their tactics were of the hit and run kind rather than of protracted resistance, for the Omani ships soon disengaged when the opposition was fierce. There was no discipline among the fleet, and if a crew did not want to fight it just did not partake in the battle. They also lacked a proper commander of the fleet or *saran* as they called him, while they do not know to handle cannons either. Their gunners were Canarese slaves who had run away from the Portuguese, and six Moors, who knew as little of cannons as the lowest ranking Dutch sailor. If something went wrong with their cannons therefore they had to divest the Muscat defenses of them.[64]

By 1700, the fortifications of Muscat were so out of repair that whenever they fired a gun part of the walls was shaken down.[65] There is no mention in other sources of the subterranean tunnel from the fort to the harbor, which in 1672 Struys allegedly saw.[66]

---

63 Floor, "A description," p. 58, n. 55; NA, VOC 1304, Report Wilmson, f. 482 vs.

64 Floor, "A description," p. 17. *Saran* probably is *sarhang*, a Persian word meaning 'general, commander, captain, chief.' The Cannarese slaves might have served as sailors or even as auxiliary soldiers aboard Portuguese ships taken in the Indian Ocean.

65 Lockyer, *An Account*, p. 208.

66 Straussens, *Reisen*, p. 200.

INTERNATIONAL TRADE IN MUSCAT.

The competitors of the Portuguese were not only happy with their ouster from Muscat, they also wanted to explore whether they might not do some profitable business there.[67] The VOC sent the flute *Concordia* on October 23, 1651 to the coast of Arabia to assess market opportunities.[68] Chief merchant Elias Boudaens reported, amongst other things, that after the capture of Muscat, the Imam had not yet levied any customs. The Imam told him that the port was open to anybody who wanted to trade there. He also offered the Dutch a house as a present. Boudaens considered the market of Muscat not interesting enough, however. Its main imports, according to leading Banyan merchants, consisted of rice, pepper, black sugar, and coarse textiles with an annual turnover of only Dfl. 20,000-25,000. This was too small an operation to even cover the operating cost of a Dutch factory, hence Boudaens advised against commencing an operation at Muscat. The population was also poor, who only owned the coarse fabrics in which they were dressed, while trade was mostly in barter.[69] When an English ship called on Muscat that year the Imam also invited the English East India Company (EIC) to come and trade there.[70] After the fall of Muscat in the early days of 1650, no Muscat ships went to Basra,[71] because they had no trade goods to sell.

Although the Dutch were not interested in the Muscat trade Asian merchants were. Boudaens observed Moslem and other Asian merchants who came to trade there in decrepit vessels.[72] This division between Asian and European merchants with regard the attractiveness of the port persisted throughout the Safavid period. Muscat had only a few export goods, which in the first two decades of the eighteenth century consisted of: horses, dates, fine brimstone, some coffee but not as fine as that from Mokha, some madder, and some pearls. Again, there was some manufacturing of coarse cotton linen and camelins.[73] The horse trade could be substantial, although it varied from year-to-year. For example, in 1680, some 400 horses had been ordered from Muscat for Cannanore, but these were not available.[74] Often vessels coming from India, but bound for Bandar Abbas, would first call on Muscat for two reasons. First, to avoid paying customs duties twice (first at Bandar Abbas and then at Muscat) by disembarking those goods destined for Muscat, and secondly, to order horses to be kept ready for their return journey.[75] It is of interest to note that Hamilton no longer listed sugar as an export product.

In 1659, trade was still at a rather low ebb in Muscat. Therefore, the English tried to take advantage of this by trying to obtain the right to establish a factory in Muscat,

67 Coolhaas, *Generale Missieven*, vol. 2, p. 417 (10/12/1650).
68 NA, KA 1072 bis, Instructie ende ordre voor den oppercoopman Elias Boudaen (06/03/1651), f. 839-42; NA., KA 1086, Sarcerius to Batavia (27/11/1651), f. 778.
69 NA, VOC 1188, Boudaens "Schriftelick relaes," f. 546r-vs; NA, KA 1072 bis, Boudaens to XVII (05/10/1651), f. 824vs. On the poor hinterland see Floor, "A description," pp. 30-32; Idem, *Dutch-Omani*, pp. 175-84, 234-52; Della Valle, *Voyages*, vol. 4, p. 412 (the bay of Kalbuh was settled by Arab fishermen and some Baluchis); Bocarro, *Livro das plantas*, p. 66. The land route allegedly offered to the Dutch in 1651 (Miles, *The Countries*, pp. 211) is a nice story, but is not based in historical fact.
70 Foster, *English Factories* 1651-1654, p. 73.
71 NA, KA 1072 bis, Boudaens to XVII (05/10/1651), f. 824vs.
72 NA, VOC 1188, Boudaens, "Schriftelijck relaes," (Surat 29/11/1651), f. 546vs.
73 Hamilton, *A New Account*, vol. 1, p. 47.
74 Coolhaas, *Generale Missieven*, vol. 4, p. 457 (29/04/1681).
75 Godinho, *Relação*, p. 75.

claiming that the presence of the English in Muscat would draw much trade to the city. To a certain extent this was a gratuitous claim, because at that time trade was on the increase. Apart from the initially customs-free trade policy at Muscat, later changed to a 2.5% customs duty, there also was the pleasant welcome that was accorded to merchants, which stood in contrast to the harassment and higher customs rates at Bandar Abbas. As a result there was a diversion of trade from Bandar Abbas to Muscat.[76] By the early 1660s, Muscat had become a major port-of-call for ships coming from India. In 1662, some 70-80 frigates arrived unhindered at Muscat with pepper, ginger, curcuma, coconuts and *dongrys* (coarse and inferior cotton cloth) from Malabar. They sold these goods at prices that were sufficiently competitive with VOC prices, so that van Wijck observed that his colleagues at Malabar had to be more attentive.[77] In 1664, some 125 to 150 ships did business at Muscat. Ships paid 2.5% *ad valorem* compared to 10-12% in Bandar Abbas and 9% in Bandar-e Kong.[78] Especially the trade from Konkan and Malabar came to Muscat.[79] In 1665 the Dutch observed that

> Mascate has drawn the entire Malabar and part of the Vingurla trade towards it. Congo has the entire trade with Sind as well as ships going from Basra to Surat. In Mascate customs are 2.5%, also for exports; while in Congo the merchants from Sind receive civil treatment and are charged customs of only 9%. From there, mostly Banyan merchants transported these goods upcountry. The goods that can be sold immediately (because one wants to have quickly return goods for Surat) and are for internal consumption all come to Gamron. Here [Bandar Abbas] it is still best [market], because the big merchants are here. In Congo it will be impossible for us to sell our goods, also because we have to pay customs.[80]

In 1666, the Dutch reported that the Imam of Muscat had increased the customs to 10%. Therefore, they expected that the merchants would return to Bandar Abbas, because they would have to pay tolls at the small ports of the Persian littoral as well. The Dutch expected that Bandar Abbas would flourish as a result, the more so if the war in Basra would continue.[81]

In 1672, the Dutch were asked to establish a factory in Muscat, to which they responded positively by establishing an agent there. However, military considerations more than trade played a role in both the Omani request and the Dutch reaction, which led to the withdrawal of the Dutch agent in 1675. At that time, Muscat carried on a sometimes lively trade with Sind, W. India, East Africa, and Yemen and with ports in the Persian Gulf itself. Both the volume and direction of trade was, of course, subject to fluctuations, both a function of international/regional developments as well as internal ones. Muscat was not the only port that traders called on the Omani coast. Jolfar also was a good harbor, "where many Indian barks carrying money, come to buy Dates, and pearls which are

76   NA, VOC 1242, Gamron to XVII (20/06/1664), f. 1091.
77   NA, VOC 1240, van Wijck to Batavia (13/05/1662), f. 690.
78   NA, VOC 1252, van Wijck to Batavia (19/01/1665), f. 716-17.
79   Floor, "A description," pp. 42-44.
80   However, the sales in Kong were to the *shahbandar* and the deputy governor who sold these goods to local merchants who would pay in Isfahan after having sold the goods there with small profits. Also, Kong was frequented by merchants from Bahrain, al-Hasa and the eastern part of the Gulf. However, there were no return goods for the VOC at Kong. NA, VOC 1252 (19/01/1665), f. 716-18.
81   NA, VOC 1259 (12/3/1666), f. 3311-12.

Fished all along that Coast from mascat to bahrem; there is a good Castle at Julfar."[82] Muscat trade was mostly with Sind, Kutch, Patan, Konkan, i.e. Rajapur and other ports held by the Shivaji, Surat (Gujarat), Karwar (south of Goa), the Cannarese and Malabar Coast, Mokha, Aden, Melinde (East Africa) and the Maldives. The imports were mostly textiles, rice and coffee, in addition to some minor products as well as 150-200 slaves. These slaves were were needed for the sugar 'plantations' and mills. Therefore, after 1650, the Omanis started sailing to the East Africa and targeted Portuguese held Mombassa to obtain slaves, as the more southern markets, namely Mozambique, was too far for them. Muscat's own exports were limited to dates, loaf-sugar, horses, and cash. Muscat also exported some Persian and Indian goods to its trading partners, but the range of products and its volume was limited. It was not the final market for most of the imports (with the exception of rice), but a point of transshipment. The majority of products were forwarded to the smaller Persian ports as well as to Basra, Bahrain, Qatar and Hasa.[83]

Muscat was "built on the Bottom of a small Bay, that almost has the Shape of an Horse Shoe."[84] Its harbor was closed by an iron chain and each arriving vessel was met by a guard-vessel, which ascertained whether the new arrival was friend or foe and the nature of its business. If friend and mercantile the ship was allowed into the inner bay, but it had to take in its sails. When the ship had come to anchor a guard was put on board, who stayed there until the ship departed. Nobody was allowed to leave the ship or come aboard after sunset. Likewise, no ship was allowed to depart before having shown a pass to the guards at the western water passage-way. Some ships only came to get water and firewood, but many came to trade. According to Lockyer, water was brought in pipes to the town for which people paid a fixed rate to the government. His ship had to pay 3 *mahmudi* or 3 shilling for every barrel, "but when the Dutch come here they pay nothing." Ships unloaded their cargo with lighters, which was then taken to the weigh-house where the goods were weighed, counted and sealed (in case of textiles). All goods had to be unloaded, unless an arrangement had been agreed upon prior to entering the inner-harbor.[85]

> Weighable goods are mainly packed according to a standard weight and are taken to the merchants' houses after having been counted and registered. If part of it is sold, the goods have to be taken to the weigh-house to be weighed; here the buyer's and seller's names, the date and the price of the transaction are also recorded in order to calculate the amount of tolls to be paid after the end of the monsoon or on departure of each ship. If the year has expired and some goods are still unsold, no toll is demanded however until they are sold or transported elsewhere.

---

82 Thevenot, *Travels*, vol. 2, p. 182.

83 For a detailed description of what was imported and exported from Muscat and to/from and the cost of transportation in 1673 as well as the sailing season, see Annex II; Barendse, *Arabian Seas*, vol. 1, pp. 319 (Muscat relied on grain imports from Sind), 410 (in the 1730s, more than half of the vessels calling on Muscat came from Konkan, mostly with cottons).

84 Hamilton, *A New Account*, vol. 1, p. 43.

85 Floor, "A description," p. 49; Kaempfer, *Die Reisetagebücher*, p. 148; Ovington, *A Voyage*, p. 429; Lockyer, *An Account*, p. 211.

Textiles (cleeden) are taken to the weigh-house, where they are registered and on each pack a seal is affixed, so that they cannot be changed. Nobody is allowed to open any pack in his house without the presence of an official. The settling of the account of toll to be paid is done in the same way as with the weighable goods.[86]

The weights used at Muscat in the 1670s were as follows:

Table 3: Weights used in Muscat (1673)

Name	Subdivision (in *man* of 8 lbs.)	Weight equivalent (in lbs.)
Great *bahar*	200	1,600
Small *bahar*	80	640
Candi	60	480
Feraseleh (*farsaleh*)	10	80
Mandilij (*man* of Delhi)	3	24
Man of Muscat	1	8
20 *parren*	Equals one *candi* of rice, wheat, etc. *	

Source: Floor, A description," pp. 49-50.

★ 1 For an explanation of the various weight terms see Hinz, Walther. *Islamische Masse und Gewichte* (Leiden, 1970); Floor, "Weights"; and *Hobson-Jobson*.

By 1700, gross goods were weighed at the customs house with a weight of 8.25 lbs., which refers to the *man* of Muscat in table 3, while in the city sometimes the *farasilah* and *bahar* were used, although, according to Lockyer, this was uncommon.[87]

After having being taken to the customs-house (*bangsar*) and the weigh-house, the goods were allowed to be taken to the merchant's house or lodgings. Around 1670 the brokerage for all trade and Muscat's weigh-house had been farmed to a Banyan, called Thewil for an amount of 30,000 *laris*. In addition he farmed 30-40 houses.[88]

He appoints a broker for each ship to whom they are obliged to pay 1½ per cent of all that which is sold. One per cent is for the main-broker (i.e. Thewil) and ½ per cent for his deputy broker; yes, even for the freight-goods which a ship takes from here on its return voyage.

Similarly, this broker allots to each ship or its crew one of the said houses for which he gets 5, 6 to 8 abbasis [per day?] depending on their size or location, until the day they leave. Someone who stays here until the end of the

---

86 Floor, "A description," p. 41. For the rates paid in the weigh-house, which varied per product, see Idem, p. 47.

87 Lockyer, *An Account*, p. 211.

88 Floor, "A description," p. 47. In 1682, a Moslem merchant, Hajji Mohammad, farmed the administration of the customs-house in Muscat. NA, VOC 1379, Casembroot report (25/11/1682), f. 2721.

monsoon makes a contract with him for the second journey from the last of
May or till the last of September or October for that whole period.

This did not include the brokerage for the horse trade, which was farmed separately
and was held in 1673 by a man called Khalil, who had paid 1,600 *mahmudis*. He recuper-
ated his invested by charging 29 *laris* per horse, of which buyer and seller each paid half.
The farmer also charged rent for the area where the horses were corralled; a fee of two
mahmudis per head per month. He also received 10 *mahmudis* for he transportation of
each horse, of which the merchant and the ship's captain (*nakhoda*) each paid half.[89] The
fact that so many key economic and commercial activities were farmed may indicate a
lack of a indigenous urban commercial community with sufficient capacity and funds
to sustain Muscat's trade. Moreover, farming provided the Sultan with a steady annual
income, free from the market fluctuations.

Initially the right of entrepot for all traders existed in Muscat, irrespective of the
religion or origin. This meant that merchants did not have to pay customs duties, even
when their merchandise had been taken ashore, or when the goods were forwarded to
other ports or markets. This was changed in 1672, probably due the oligopolistic position
taken by the new governor Sheikh Abdollah, about which later. Under the new rules,
"both Moors and Banyans have to pay the legal toll on all goods, which are taken ashore.
However, if a ship continues its journey, only toll is levied from that which was taken
ashore or that which was transshipped; in case of Moors sometimes allowances are made."
There was no export duty, because an import duty had already been paid, while all local
produce (loaf-sugar, dates, etc.) did not have to pay any export duties.[90]

After the conquest of Muscat, the Ya`arabi Imam initially levied no customs duties,
either from Moslems or non-Moslems. In fact, according to Wilmson when he arrived
in Muscat it was the very first time that Banyans had to pay customs duties. "Those who
possessed a house (*landshuis*) in the country had to pay 5 and others 10 per cent. Therefore
everybody was forced to take a house in the country, even though it was only a shop."
Moslems had to pay 2½ per cent (the *zakat* rate). On return from a voyage no duties were
levied if they had a document showing that they had paid their taxes. "However, they have
to make so many voyages with their merchandise that they have to pay tolls every time and
to show documentary proof thereof at the place of their residence."[91] The rates were raised
to 5% in 1671/72 and even to 7.5%.[92] The introduction of higher rates coincided with
the temporary closure of the port to foreign vessels, internal political troubles in Oman
and the overture to peace with the Portuguese as discussed below.[93] Klein has suggested
that rather than a quadrupling of rates, new rates were introduced reflecting Ibadi law,
i.e. low rates for Moslems (*zakat* rate), a higher one for *dhimmis* (adherent to an officially
tolerated non-Moslem religion) and the highest for those living in the *dar al-harb*, i.e. lands
outside of Moslem rule as well as unbelievers. In actual practice this rule was not strictly

---

89 Floor, "A description," pp. 47-48.

90 Floor, "A description," p. 47.

91 Floor, "A description," pp. 46-47.

92 NA, VOC 1279, de Haze to Batavia (16/05/1672), f. 955 suggests that there was a flat rate for all
    merchants, however.

93 NA, VOC 1259, van Wijck to Batavia (12/03/1666), f. 3311 (customs duties raised to 10%); Coolhaas,
    Generale Missieven, vol. 3, p. 598 (05/10/1667).

adhered to, however.[94] In 1673, Moslem merchants paid 2.5%; Banyans who had been exempt, then had to pay 5%, if they could prove that they were homeowners, in which case they were charged with a heavy real estate tax, otherwise the rate was 10%. A high rate of 8% was charged to Moslems and Banyans coming from pagan-held lands, such as Kuch as well as from Shivaji-held lands.[95] Around 1700, the customs rate was 2.5% for Moslems and 5% for non-Moslems. Lockyer's ship did not have to pay any duties at the Imam's instructions. He further reported that no duties were levied on exports.[96]

Table 4: Customs duties charged at Muscat in 1673

Country	Moslems or Moslem-owned goods in %	Banyans in %	Remarks
Sind	2.5	5	
Kutch	8	8	Higher rate as its ruler was an infidel
Patan	2.5	8	
Surat	2.5	5	
Rajapur	8	8	Because it is in the realm of the Shivaji
Vengurla	8	8	[Idem]
Karwar	2.5	-	
Basrur, Mangalore, Bhatkal	17.5	17.5	Because Omanis had to pay this rate [these ports were under the rule of the Hindu Ikkeri kings, but nominally belonged to the sultanate of Bijapur. They were Oman's main supplier of rice in India, as it had been for Hormuz.]
Basra	2.5	5	
Persia	2.5	5	
Mokha	2.5	5	

Source: Floor, "A description," p. 46.

One of the main problems in the 1670s was that trade arrangements as well the customs rates that were lowered or increased were based on political expediency and economic self-interest. The Imam's *wakil* or agent controlled the customs-house and trade itself, because he insisted on his right of first purchase. Nobody was allowed to sell or buy anything without Sheikh Abdollah's permission. The Malabar trade (coconuts, pepper, spices, coir, timber) was almost exclusively reserved for him. Sheikh Abdollah in general was not only interested in so-called weighable products (rice, pepper, spices), but also in textiles. He kept most of these goods until the end of the trading season to drive

94 NA, VOC 1259, Gamron to Batavia (12/03/1666), f. 3311.
95 Floor, "A description," p. 46. As most Indian traders were subjects of Islamic states, where they considered unbelievers, but in Muscat they paid the same tax as Moslems, because they came from Moslem states such as the Mughal Empire or from Sultanates in the Deccan.
96 Lockyer, *An Account*, pp. 208-09.

Figure 9, Muscat, 1670, Rijksmuseum, Amsterdam (1. Fish market; 2. Beach with much merchandize; 3. Two Dutch ships)

up prices, for he only sold when profits were high. These goods were then distributed over the ports of the Persian Gulf. Only the Imam was allowed to buy military goods such as coir ropes, planks, masts, cannon, and iron, i.e. all goods needed to outfit the navy. What he did not need was resold in the market.[97] To tilt the market to his advantage Sheikh Abdollah changed the rules when it suited him. Sometimes he bought an entire ship's cargo sometimes a part thereof. The ship's *nakhoda* had to present himself to Sheikh Abdollah's house with the bill of lading and a sample of his merchandise. Although many Banyan merchants were also present only Sheikh Abdollah was allowed to make a bid for the goods. He invariably bid lower than the going market rate, but the *nakhoda* had to accept else he was thrown into prison, which made Muscat a liability for ship owners and traders alike. The goods bought by Sheikh Abdollah were then taken ashore to the weigh-house and from there to the Imam's warehouse. The *nakhoda*'s remaining goods he took to his own lodgings, but he was allowed to sell them only after permission from Sheikh Abdollah. To be exempt from these impositions some merchants made a separate settlement with Sheikh Abdollah, i.e. they paid him a lump sum. In exchange for this payment merchants were allowed to sell their goods to the highest bidder. Even then he

97   Floor, "A description," p. 45.

might interfere, for it could happen that after a transaction had taken place and the goods were being weighed that Sheikh Abdollah liked the price (or rather the expected profit) and he then forced the buyer to accept him as a partner for half of the purchased goods. It even happened that when rice in bulk yielded a higher price than bagged rice that he forced the sellers of bagged rice (who already had paid customs duties to be allowed to sell their goods freely) to sell their rice in bulk.[98]

As to export products the Imam also was a major player in the market. He was a major producer of loaf-sugar, as discussed above, and thus also dominated this market segment. The other important export product, – horses was also under the Imam's (or rather his agent's) control. Not all horses sold in Muscat came from Oman, for each year the Imam sent an agent to Persia to buy 20 to 30 horses. In addition, 200 to 300 other horses were sold to Indian merchants, who exported them mostly to Konkan. Many, if not most of them, also came from Persia for Persian horse traders kept a large number of horses in stables in Muscat. However, the purchase of horses was conditional upon having bought one or more horses from the Imam's agent. Sometimes, the merchants had to buy all the Imam's horses, before he allowed others to be sold. To make high prices the Imam's agent usually waited with the sale till the end of the monsoon.[99]

Despite the dominant and oligopolistic role of the Imam's agent, Sheikh Abdollah, trade flourished. This was partly due to the fact that both Sayf b. Sultan (1680-1692) and Sultan b. Sayf I (1692 - 15 Oct 1711) promoted trade and expanded the wealth that they had inherited.[100] The Imam owned ships, which were mainly involved in trade with the Red Sea and East Africa.[101] It was further partly due to the fact that the trade of Muscat was entirely controlled by a group of Indian merchants associated with the Imam's agent, the admirals of the Muscat war fleet and tribal notables. This made it easier for W. Indian merchants to call on Muscat, for they were bound by ethnic, religious and in many cases also by family relations. The mercantile community of Muscat was small; most came from Sind, Gujarat and Kerala.[102] There were two important Arab wholesale merchants, Esma`il al-Basri and Esma`il Bandari, who as their names suggest had links with Muscat's two main markets, i.e. Basra and Bandar Abbas.[103] There were some Armenian traders who called on Muscat.[104] The Sindis played a special role with regard to textiles.

> From the textiles which are brought here from there Muscat consumes
> of the 800 packs little more than one quarter; the remainder is taken to
> Bahrain, Katijf (al-Qatif), Qatar, Basra, and Persia in the following manner.
> Those of Sind have their representatives here to whom they send their goods
> each year. These keep all that is consumed in Muscat and send the rest to the
> said places to other representatives who mostly reside there on their behalf to

98   Floor, "A description," pp. 43-46.

99   Floor, "A description," pp. 30, 48.

100 Ross, *Annals*, p. 56.

101 Floor, "A description," p. 40.

102 *ANTT*, DRI LIX, f. 86r-vs; Floor, "A description," p. 45; Allen, "The Indian Merchant," pp. 39-53; Foster, *English Factories*, vol. 5, pp. 126-27; Barendse, *The Arabian Seas*, p. 344.

103 Floor, "A Description," p. 61, n. 94.

104 Meier-Lemgo, K. *Die Briefe E. Kaempfers* (Mainz, 1965), pp. 267-314, no. 25; Baladouni and Makepeace, *Armenian Merchants*, pp. 39, 246.

sell these goods. They send the proceeds mostly via Congo (Bandar-e Kong) back to Sind.[105]

Muscat also gained wealth from Mecca pilgrims who came from India, and "it was much frequented by Merchants over the Deserts, and no less by those of Mocha in the Red Sea, and by the way of Grand Cairo; it vends all Drugs and Arab steeds, and pays Gold for Indian Commodities: Here they keep safe those Ships they steal or purchase, for Wood, nor Timber growing here."[106]

Because like other markets in the Persian Gulf Muscat also had a negative trade balance with India the lack of exportable goods was compensated for by the export of specie. It would appear that Muscat itself did not coin its own money. In 1673 the following coins were in use:

> The money which is current are abbasis, five shahis, and mahmudis. The small coins are [made of] spiaulter (zinc), and were introduced by the Portuguese and are still used. Their rate is 31 to 32 to one mahmudi depending whether many of them are brought from the other side of the Gulf, where they used to be coined in former times. Silver coins are full, half, quart and eight laris, which are exported by the Indians, who import others consisting of half copper, a reason why this trade had finally been forbidden altogether.[107]

Around 1700, the currency used was mainly *budgerooks*[108] and *mamoodas*. The former were of mixed metal, rather as iron, with a cross on one side and were coined by the Portuguese. Thirty *budgerooks* = 1 *mahmudi* = 8 pence. Surat rupee = 3.5 *mahmudis*; Spanish dollars = 7.5 *mahmudis*. Further, Venetians, *Ibrahimis* and other coins were in use.[109]

The main exports at that time included various drugs, coffee, and ivory. These were not real exports, because none of these products were of Omani origin, which emphasizes Muscat's role of a transhipment port. Although Muscat controlled the pearl fishing, pearls there were almost as expensive as in Europe. According to Lockyer, horses were exported to the Malabar coast (more probably the Cannarese coast), on which more than 1,000% could be made with the right selection of animals. There was so much fish at Muscat that there was a lively export trade. Lockyer saw that in Bandar Abbas several trankis arrived with dried fish and onions, on which the sellers made at least 100% profit. As to imports, Lockyer listed: China commodities, all Indian products; from Europe fir-masts, lead,

---

105   Floor, "A Description," p. 41 (also for a breakdown of the kind and quantity of fabrics consumed in Muscat in 1672).

106   Fryer, *A New Account*, vol. 2, p. 156.

107   Floor, "A Description," pp. 31-32. The zinc coins most likely were struck in Goa, Diu, Daman and Chaul and the alloy used was composed of copper (40.4%), zinc (25.4%), nickel (31.6%), and iron (2.6%). Teixeira de Aragão, *Descrição geral e histórica das moedas cunhadas em nome dos reis, regentes e governadores de Portugal*, 3 vols (Lisbon, 1874-80), vol. 3; Vaz, J. Ferraro and Sousa, M. Correia de. *Dinheiro luso-indiano (Indo-Portuguese Money)* (Braga, 1980).

108   From the Portuguese *bazarucco*, a coin of low denomination and of varying value and metal. It was current in Goa and elsewhere on the W. Indian coast. For its possible etymology and further details, see Hobson-Johnson c.v. Budgrook.

109   Lockyer, *An Account*, p. 211.

steel and iron in bars, guns, anchors, nails, etc. He was very surprised that the governor of Muscat refused his present saying he could accept nothing from strangers without displeasing the Imam or anything that might be perceived as bribes.[110]

The Demise of the Ya'ariba Dynasty

In 1719, Imam Sultan b. Sayf died and with his death the suppressed sentiments of those who had opposed him came to the fore. His contested successor Imam Muhanna' b. Sultan (1719-20) only lasted one year, before he was killed. He was remembered for his good administration and the promotion of trade to which end he even abolished customs duties at Muscat.[111] The result of this succession conflict was an intense struggle between two major factions that resulted in a civil war that would last till 1728 and ultimately led to the demise of the Ya'ariba dynasty.[112] Due to dynastic problems at the end of 1722, Oman also was unable to maintain its influence in the Persian Gulf.[113]

In 1736, the Ya'ariba Imam of Oman, Sayf b. Sultan II had been unable to suppress a rebellion and appealed to Nader Shah for help; a coincidence that suited the latter's plans very well. The joint forces were very successful at Muscat, but then the Imam and Latif Khan quarreled with one another, the latter was forced to withdraw his troops to Jolfar.[114] In 1739, Sayf b. Sultan II again welcomed the arrival of the Persian troops, for events had taken a bad turn. The combined forces defeated the rebel troops, seized several towns, and finally captured Muscat itself. When the Imam realized that the Persians wanted to occupy his land rather than just help him regain it, he switched sides and joined the rebels. The Persians were defeated and had to fall back to Jolfar.[115] The war in Oman, meanwhile, did not go well for the Persians. The garrison at Jolfar was under constant pressure and in great difficulty. In July 1739, the deputy-governor of Bandar Abbas literally begged the Dutch to send supplies to Jolfar.[116] Meanwhile, the Persian authorities commandeered all local vessels in Bandar Abbas to send supplies to Jolfar, for it was a matter of life and

110   Lockyer, *An Account*, pp. 208, 210, 212.

111   Ross, *Annals*, p. 57.

112   Coolhaas, *Generale Missieven*, vol. 7, p. 573 (30/11/1721). For an account of the civil war see Ross, *Annals*, pp. 56-74.

113   Hamilton, *A New Account*, vol. 1, p. 50; Lorimer, *Gazetteer*, p. 79.

114   NA, VOC 2417, Resolutions Gamron (23/03/1737), f. 3822-24 and (30/03/1737), f. 3860-61; NA, VOC 2448, Resolution Gamron (30/04/1737), f. 319-32; Lockhart, "Navy," p. 10.

115   NA, VOC 2449, Resolution Gamron (06/05/1739), f. 2090-91; NA, VOC 2416, Gamron to Batavia (25/02/1739), f. 87-91; Idem, Resolutions Gamron (08/08/1738), f. 183-83; (12/08/1739), f. 190-91; (29/09/1739), f. 244-46; (03/10/1739), f. 255-56. On 17 July 1738/31 Rabi' al-Avval, Mohammad Taqi Khan had written to Koenad that the latter's lack of enthusiasm to lend him a ship was quite evident. However, he did not need his ships anymore, because he was almost finished there (Muscat). "If the Imam of Muscat, Sayf, wants to oppose me, I have 7 to 8 ships on the roadstead of Jolfar, one English Company ship, and about 100 small vessels of Arab and other subjects of the Shah. Sayf has only two rotten, decrepit ships and the royal fleet can handle those." NA, VOC 2476, Mohammad Taqi Khan to Koenad (Kong, received 14/09/1738), f. 260-61; Idem, Bushire to Gamron (17/08/1739), f. 1066; Ibid., idem to idem (16/09/1738), f. 1077; Ibid., idem to idem (12/11/1738), f. 1097; Ibid., idem to idem (12/01/1739), f. 1106; Ibid., Hoogeboom c.s. to Koenad (Qeshm, 23/07/1738), f. 1130; see also Ibid., f. 1140, 1146.

116   NA, VOC 2510, resolutions Gamron (16/07/1739), f. 1370-73, (29/07/1793(, f. 252; Ibid., Mohammad Taqi Khan to Koenad, f. 1248-53.

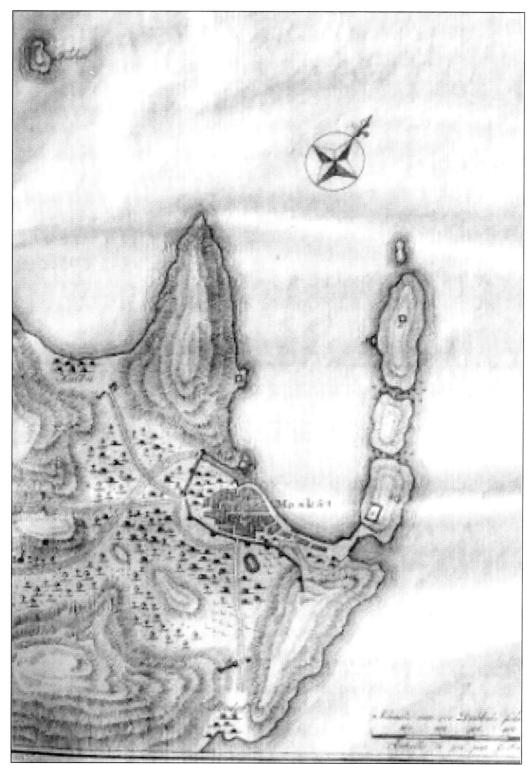

Figure 10, Plan of Muscat according to Niebuhr

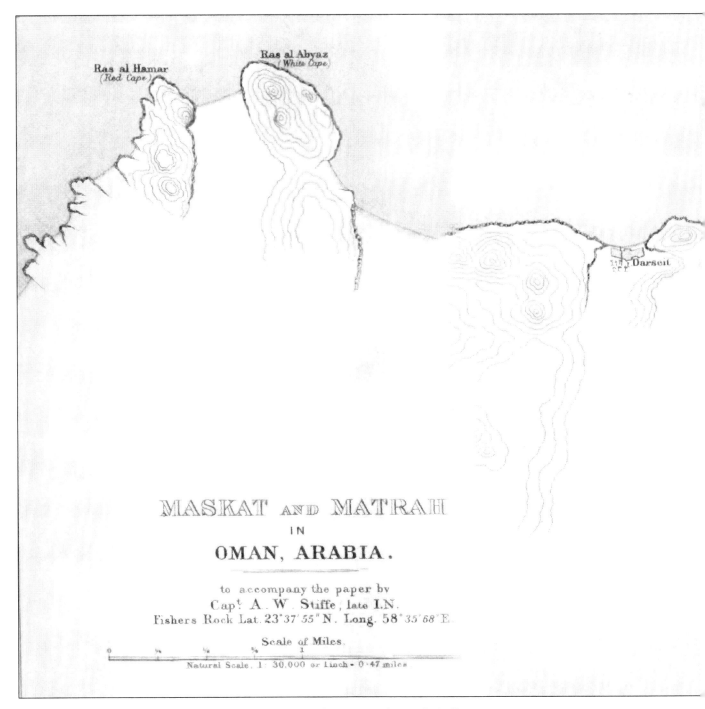

Figure 11, Map of Muscat and Matrah, Stiffe

death for the Persian troops there.[117] Around the same time, peace talks began between the Imam and the Persians, which finally led to the end of hostilities. The Persians probably took the initiative with these talks since Nader Shah needed his fleet for operations in Sind. In September 1739 Mohammad Taqi Khan was already making preparations for this

_____

117   NA, VOC 2510, Resolution Gamron (29/08/1739), f. 278-79; Idem, Gamron to Batavia (25/11/1739), f. 110-111.

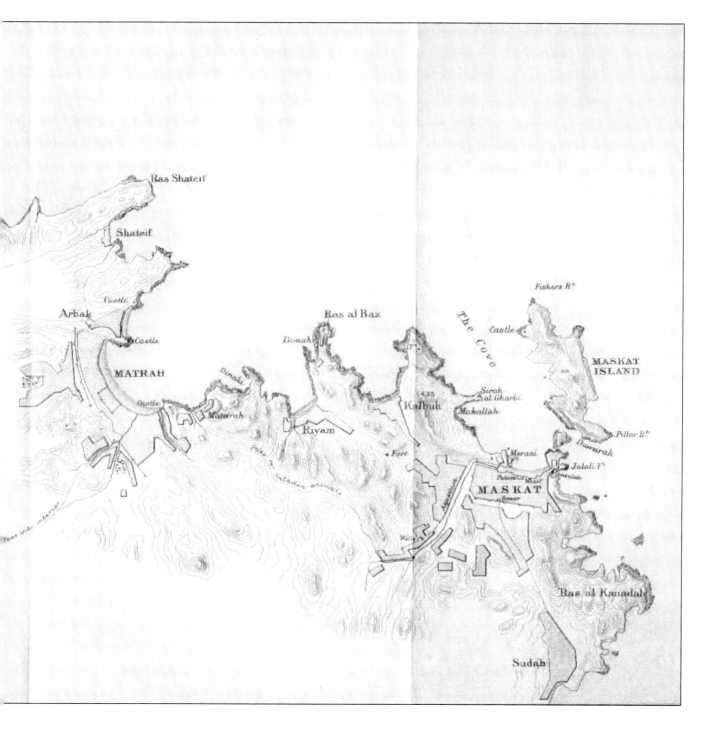

campaign. When he arrived in Bandar Abbas on 4 November 1739 he asked the Dutch
to transport troops and supplies to Divil.[118]

118   NA, VOC 2510, Resolution Gamron (10/11/1739), f. 411-16; Idem, Gamron to Batavia (25/11/1739), f.
      119-20; Lockhart, "Navy," p. 11. For a discussion of the location of the port of Divil see Monique Kervran,
      "Le port multiple des bouches de l'Indus: Barbarké, Dēb, Daybul, Lahori Bandar, Diul Sinde," in Rika
      Gyselen ed. *Sites et monuments disparus d'après les témoignages de voyageurs.* Res Orientales VIII (1996),
      pp. 45-92.

In 1742 the Imam of Oman again appealed to Nader Shah for help. The shah willingly complied with this request. After defeating the rebellious Hulas at Khasab, Kalb 'Ali Khan, the new *sardar*, accompanied by Mohammad Taqi Khan Shirazi and the Imam, arrived in Bandar Abbas on 2 June 1742. On 18 June they sailed to Oman with about 8,000 cavalry. This campaign initially was very successful for the Persians, for they were able to seize most towns and, by ruse, even the forts of Muscat. The Imam found out too late that he had been deceived by his allies. By July 1743 Mohammad Taqi Khan Shirazi held the greater part of coastal Oman.[119]

As a result of a revolt led by Ahmad b. Sa'id Al Bu Sa'id, the governor of Sohar and the renewed war with the Ottoman Empire, the Persians were unable to maintain their positions in Oman and were driven back to Jolfar (now called Ras al-Khaimah). As rebellions were breaking out all over the country the Persian troops in Oman also rebelled in March 1747. On 13 April 1747 some 40 *trankis* with about 4,000 men arrived in Bandar Abbas coming from Oman. These troops had rebelled and were commanded by Mir Mehr Ali. Qalij Khan (Galieds Chan), the commander of all these troops, followed with 3,000 men on 27 April 1747. After the sack of Bandar Abbas, Khalij Khjan left Bandar Abbas and marched to Bandar-e Kong.[120] This was the end of the Persian occupation of Oman and the beginning of a new ruling dynasty over Muscat and other parts of Oman, that of the Al Bu Sa'id.

Figure 12, View of Muscat from anchorage, Stiffe

119 NA, VOC 2593, f. 1797, 1803, 1806, 1808vs.; Lockhart, *Nadir Shah*, pp. 215-16.

120 Floor, *Nader Shah*, pp. 176-77; Slot, *'Arab al-Khalij*, p. 311, referring to the Gombroon Diary entries between 30/03/1747 and 25/05/1747.

4

Muscat under al-Bu Sa`id Rule 1749–

MUSCAT

As in previous times, during the eighteenth and nineteenth century, sailing into or out of the Persian Gulf, Muscat was the first or last port of call for ships. In both cases this was to take in fresh water, fruits, vegetables, meat and other provisions. Arriving in the Persian Gulf, the stores of water and food aboard ships needed to be renewed, while crews were often ill and weak and needed restoration. Departing ships wanted to be sure that they had ample stores of fresh water and provisions before embarking on the dangerous crossing of the Indian Ocean. Of course, trade was another reason why ships called on Muscat as well as the fact that between Aden and the Persian Gulf, the harbor of Muscat was the only one where ships of any size could find safe anchorage. Also, since the 1860s, Muscat was the port of call for Gulf mail steamers.[1] In 1834, Roberts, the US envoy to Muscat opined that "Muscat being the key to the Persian Gulf is a place of great resort in winter months, for vessels from the Persian Gulf and the western parts of India."[2]

When arriving at the port the first thing that struck the ship's crews was Muscat's forbidding aspect, because nothing green was to be seen from the roadstead. The French botanist Aucher-Eloy even wrote that compared with the barren hills around Muscat, those of the Sinai were a garden.[3] The view from the sea was 100-130 m high barren, rugged, multi-colored volcanic rocks and the almost inaccessible hills that enclose the town, dominated by *Jabal Bardah* (جبل بردہ) or Saddle Hill. Behind the white town, whose color nicely contrasted with the green color of the water of the harbor, stretched the serrated and arid Green Mountains (*Jabal al-Ahdar*– جبل احضر), so-called because it shows

---

1 Stiffe, "Ancient"; Bent, "Muscat," p. 169; von Oppenheim, *Vom Mittelmeer* , vol. 2, p. 323; Allemann, "Mascate," p. 90; Fraser, *Narrative*, p. 5.

2 Roberts, *Embassy*, p. 361.

3 Potter, "The Eastern Coast, p. 163; Francklin, *Observations*, p. 36; Aucher-Eloy, *Relations* , vol. 2, p. 667; Fraser, *Narrative*, p. 5; Roberts, *Embassy*, p. 353; Ruschenberger, *A Voyage*, vol. 1, p. 67; Taylor, *A Voyage*, p. 164; Pfeiffer, *A Woman's Journey*, p. 236; Binning, *A Journal*, vol. 1, p. 123; Curzon, *Persia*, vol. 2, p. 439; Stiffe, "Ancient"; Maurizi, *History*, p. 21 ("except a few stunted bushes; yet foxes, called taleb by the Arabs, are found on the island which forms its entrance."); Maindron, "Mascate," p. 464 (around Muscat there were only six bushes and two trees).

some vegetation.⁴ The conical peaks surrounding the city were crowned everywhere with small watch towers, which guarded the passes that were barred with walls and gates.⁵

On opposite ends of Muscat Bay, enclosing the sandy beach, there are the two large forts on rocky promontory, Jalali (جلالي) and Mirani (ميراني), which command the harbor and city; one of them served to defend a small bay or bight, formed by the rocks that form Muscat harbor. Forts to the right were called Jurra-i Kalani (جره كالاني) and the other closer to town Jalali. The forts on the left side were called Jurra-i Khurd (جره خورد) and Kaptani.⁶

At high water, the passage between the rocks was not more than one fathom. "A vessel that cannot navigate the rocks as is sometimes difficult in the north-westers, may run into the bight without fear of danger and find good anchoring ground there, though close in."⁷

Muscat harbor, usually referred to as cove and shaped like a horse-shoe, was not as spacious as that of Matrah, but according to Parson, hundreds of vessels could drop anchor there. It was only 1,200 m deep and 800 m wide. The small island situated at the harbor's entrance, lying off the northern end of the Muscat island, was called Fisher's Rock. On the western side of the bay a 200 meter outcropping spur forms a sheltered cove called Makallah. One side of Muscat Island was covered by names of ships in white oaint that recorded their first arrival. According to Curzon, this custom started because the crews of British naval ships were not allowed to go ashore, "for fear of the possible consequences of their hilarity." Thus, the only playground was this barren rock that looked like an empty slate asking to be filled with a paint-pot.⁸

The Muscat harbor sheltered vessels from the winds, but not the northerly, when outer cove became a dangerous anchorage and in winter gales crashed heavy seas into it.⁹ Otherwise:

> The harbor of Muscat is exceedingly pretty, with its reddish volcanic promontories, and its deep blue sea studded with tiny craft; canoes painted red, green, and white, steered by paddles, swarm around the steamer, fisherman paddling themselves about a plank or two tied together, hawk their wares from boat to

4 Stiffe, "Ancient"; Bent, "Muscat," p. 169; Lorimer, *Gazetteer*, vol. 2, p. 1180; Dieulafoye, *A Suse*, pp. 198-99 (drawing of Muscat).

5 Ruschenberger, *A Voyage*, vol. 1, p. 67; Stiffe, "Ancient," p. 609; Allemann, "Mascate," p. 85; Curzon, *Persia*, vol. 2, pp. 440-41; Sadid al-Saltaneh, *Tarikh*, p. 43.

6 Abdul Qadir, *Waqai*, p. 27. The Portuguese called Jalali, São Jão and Mirani, Capitan. Miles, *The Countries*, p. 463. On the state of the forts, armament and garrison in 1830, see Stocqueler, *Fifteen Months*, vol. 1, p. 254. According to Lorimer, *Gazetteer*, vol. 2, p. 1181, the subsidiary maritime defenses were called Sirat al-Sharqiyah (صيرة الشرقيه) and Sirat al-Gharbiyah (صيرة الغربيه). For pictures, see Peterson, *Historical*, photos 89-91.

7 Potter, "The Eastern Coast, p. 163; Fraser, *Narrative*, p. 6; Lorimer, *Gazetteer*, vol. 2, p. 1180; Dieulafoye, *A Suse*, p. 193 (drawing of the forts); Buckingham, *Travels*, pp. 505-06 (with a detailed description how to navigate into the cove); Sadid al-Saltaneh, *Tarikh*, pp. 43-44.

8 Lorimer, *Gazetteer*, vol. 2, p. 1180; Parsons, *Travels*, p. 210; von Oppenheim, *Vom Mittelmeer*, vol. 2, p. 324; Curzon, *Persia*, vol. 2, p. 439 (with the names of British ships); Allemann, "Mascate," p. 77 (with the names of a few of those ships); Roberts, *Embassy*, p. 352; Maindron, "Mascate," pp. 328-29 (with names of ships). Costa Graziosi G., "The ships' names of Muscat Bay," *Journal of Oman Studies*, 7 (1985), pp. 105-120. For a picture of the painted names, see Peterson, Historical, photo 91 and below fig. 27. For a map of Muscat harbor, see Stiffe, "Ancient Trading Centers". For a drawing of the harbor of Muscat, see de Rivoyre,*Obock*, p. 60.

9 Owen, *Narrative*, vol. 1, p. 337; Roberts, *Embassy*, p. 352; Parsons, *Travels*, p. 210; Miles, *The Countries*, p. 462.

boat; the oars of the larger boats generally made with a flat circular piece of wood fastened onto a long pole, and are really more like paddles than oars; then in the northern corner lie huddled together large dhows. Most of these belong to Banyan merchants and are manned by Indian sailors.[10]

No vessels were allowed to enter the harbor after sunset nor might a boat go from one ship to another to prevent circumvention of payment of customs duties. The Serang [sic; *sarhang* or commander] of the Sultan had to help each arriving ship, for which he may collect a certain sum, "which they are never backward in demanding, whether they attend or not." When an arriving vessel signaled it needed a pilot some one would come, otherwise nobody would pay attention. "It is best to make them attend till the vessel is secured, as they have excellent boats for carrying out warp anchors." However, by 1816 there was no longer a Serang, who moored the ships. Nevertheless, if a ship needed help and it signaled help was given. Also, the old rule that ships were not allowed to enter into port, bring goods ashore or do business ashore after sunset, was no longer enforced. "though shore-boats are not permitted to come off the ships in the harbour after dark, yet ships'-boats are allowed to remain on shore, and to go off at pleasure."[11]

Muscat was still a walled town, except for "the part fronting the harbour," while it was flanked by two forts, Jalali and Mirani, which were dilapidated and displayed the Arab blood-red flag. The apothecary of the British Agency, de Rozario called them "the Gulali, the Capitainie, and two Seeras." Around the thin five meters high city walls, which had eight round towers and square bulwarks and battlements, was a deep moat that in 1816 Buckingham described as "originally a dry ditch, but it is now nearly filled up." Thereafter things improved for in 1890 Curzon described it as "a fosse in fair repair." The moat was about seven meters wide and four meters deep and nicely covered with stones.[12] In 1816, the forts were guarded by a few captains with a few hundred gunners, while around 1900, both forts were held by 100 badly armed men, mostly Baluchis and Arabs, one-quarter of which were the Sultan's private retainers.[13] In 1851, Binning got the impression that the role of the guards in the forts "was to exercise their lungs for the purpose of keeping themselves, and every one else, awake, because the stillness of the night was interrupted by the shouting and the howling of the watchmen on the fortifications. The echo in this cove is certainly very great."[14]

---

10 Bent, "Muscat," p. 171; Allemann, "Mascate," p. 85 (a raft of 2-3 trees tied together); Palgrave, *Narrative*, vol. 2, p. 364; Shepherd, *From Bombay*, p. 43.

11 Niebuhr, *Reisebeschreibung*, vol. 2, p. 498; Milburn, *Oriental Commerce*, vol. 1, p. 114; Buckingham, *Travels*, p. 525

12 Roberts, *Embassy*, p. 353; Potter, "The Eastern Coast, p. 163; de Rozario, "An Account," vol. 4, p. 235; Lumsden, *A Journey*, p. 27 ("an inferior wall, with gateways and towers at intervals"); Buckingham, *Travels*, p. 507; Blakeney, *Journal*, p. 200; Maurizi, *History*, p. 22; Binning, *A Journal*, vol. 1, p. 123; Germain, "Quelques mots," p. 345, 354; Allemann, "Mascate," p. 85; Zwemer, *Arabia*, p. 81; Curzon, *Persia*, vol. 2, p. 440; Palgrave, *Narrative*, vol. 2, p. 364; Peterson, *Historical*, p. 20 (*al-Sirah al-Gharbiya* and *al-Sharqiyah*); Maindron, "Mascate," pp. 464-65; Niebuhr, *Reisebeschreibung*, vol. 2, p. 499; Sadid al-Saltaneh, *Tarikh*, pp. 44, 60.

13 Lorimer, *Gazetteer*, vol. 2, p. 1181; Curzon, *Persia*, vol. 2, p. 440; Buckingham, *Travels*, p. 507; Weeks, *From the Black Sea*, p. 141 (the guards "wearing wide, loose turbans of some striped material, lounge on the benches. Their ponderous matchlocks are hung on the wall behind them."); Lumsden, *A Journey*, p. 27 ("the guards had their bows slung upon the walls, while they were all employed making baskets.")

14 Binning, *A Journal*, vol. 1, p. 122; Buckingham, *Travels*, p. 519 ("sentinels who repeat their cries from tower to tower."); Sadid al-Saltaneh, *Tarikh*, pp. 60-61.

Figure 13, Bab al-Kabir of Muscat, Allemann

The city's suburbs, which were two to three times larger than the city itself, were protected by the hills that hemmed in the city, across which a wall had been built. This wall, according to Niebuhr in 1764, was weak and had only 8 towers, although more bulwarks had guns.[15] Some 50 years later, around 1810, the wall was described as "built of large stones laid one upon the other, is from 8 to 10 feet in height, and extends from Matra to Sedab, a distance of 20 miles."[16] The passes through those hills were protected by folding gates with wooden doors and towers, guarded by armed Baluchis or Bedouins. The main guard towers were Borj Sa`ali (برج سعالي), south-east of the town, Bostu (بستو) behind the middle of the city, Borj al-Morabba` (المربّع) up the Wadi al-Kabir, Borj Damodar (دمودر) west of the town, and Borj Madaimin (مديمن) towards Riyam and Borj Makallah west of the harbor.[17]

The walled city was 800 meters long from east to west and 400 meters wide. It covered one-third of the front part of the plain between the sea and the surrounding

---

15   Niebuhr, *Reisebeschreibung*, vol. 2, p. 499; Geary, *Through Asiatic Turkey*, vol. 1, p. 12.

16   Maurizi, *History*, pp. 25-26.

17   Lorimer, *Gazetteer*, vol. 2, p. 1181; de Rozario, "An Account," vol. 4, p. 234; Shepherd, *From Bombay*, p. 59; Curzon, *Persia*, vol. 2, p. 440; Maindron, "Mascate," p. 465 (the Bordj-el-Naubé was also known as the 'castle of the three salvos,' because every night one of its guns fired three times to announce that the gates were closed and that curfew had started. It probably is the same as the Borj Sa`ali, because both were in the east).

Figure 14, A walled and gated mountain pass, Allemann

hills.[18] Its north bordered on the bay and the east on the hills; a gap called Moghab separated it from the Jalali hill. In 1786, Muscat had four gates; two faced the sea and the north. Between these two gates was "a depot for buying and selling and the customs house (*firdah*)." The two other gates faced the south at the foot of these hills. There were three more gates called Sidab, Riyam and Kalbuh, respectively facing the south, west, and south-west.[19] The south and west sides of the city were walled, which walls, by 1900, were in reasonable condition with towers at intervals. In the middle of the south-side wall there was the Little Gate (*Bab al-Saghir*), outside of which there was a good market of 40 shops, mainly for the sale of provisions. According to de Rozario, by the 1860s this was the "principal seat of the market." This gate led to the Miyabin suburb. To the south-west side was the Big Gate (*Bab al-Kabir*) through which traffic to Matrah and the Tuyan suburb flowed. These gates were guarded day and night by sleepy guards. They were closed a few hours after sunset. Another gate on the north-west corner near Ft. Mirani was called *Bab al-Mithaʿib* (drains) constituting a row of four small iron-grated posterns,

---

18   de Rozario, "An Account," vol. 4, p. 234.
19   Abdul Qadir, *Waqai*, p. 27.

through which Wadi al-Kabir (and its run-off water) continued to the beach.[20] The path from the Little Gate led to Sidab, situated in a small cove via a pass that was protected by a tower and gate. From the Big Gate led at least four routes, viz. to Kalbuh, Riyam, and one to Matrah via a very deep and rugged path. The middle road led to Riyam, and to go there was a four hours journey; the path to the left led to Sidab. At Riyam, the roads from the interior united. The fourth route led to Tuyan or "The Wells" to the Wadi al-Kabir. From there was a road that led to a pass, protected by a tower and gate that led to Sayh al-Harmal (Sehal Harmel) and the village of Ruwi. Here there was the wall and gate that surrounded Muscat in an arch (see above).[21]

The city was divided into seven quarters (*mahallat*): Moghab (British consulate; houses of its staff; hospital), Banyan (Indian *suq* and residents), Al Bu Sa`id (Sultan's palace and residences of his relatives); Waljat (mainly Arab residents), al-Suq (main market; mixed population), al-Baharinah (Shi`as and their *ma'tam*s and other residents) and Wadi al-`Awr (mainly Baluchis).[22] In the beginning of the nineteenth century, only Arabs and Banyans were allowed to live in the walled city. It was only after 1828 that Persians were also given this right.[23]

In 1764, Niebuhr reported that outside the walled city was a large plain, but he did not mention the presence of any dwellings there. However, elsewhere he mentions that there was a quarter with huts outside the city.[24] Twenty-two years later, there were between the town and hills some orchards and dwellings of common people-washer men, water carriers and Afghans.[25] Thereafter, outside the city walls, all available land in the valley was covered by dwellings, which formed a number of suburbs, which occupied about two-thirds of the remaining area of the plain.[26] As Stiffe rightly pointed out, each cove had a town or village at its head, at the water's edge, which might all be considered suburbs of Muscat.[27] In fact, the villages of Sidab and Kalbuh and the hamlets of Riyam, Matairah, Falaj and Arbak and the village of Darsait were separated from Muscat and Matrah by small hills, but were so close to them that "in a practical point of view they may be looked upon more as suburbs than independent centres of habitation."[28]

As soon as you left either of the two main gates, just outside the walls, there was the fish and provision market, reeking with horrible smells and alive with noise.[29] The markets formed an integral part of the vast suburbs of so-called *barasti* huts made of "date stick reed, split bamboos, and mats, gable roofed and rarely exceeding twelve feet in height,"

20 Lorimer, *Gazetteer*, vol. 2, p. 1182; Binning, *A Journal*, vol. 1, p. 123; Germain, "Quelques mots," pp. 345, 354; Stack, *Six Months*, vol. 1, p. 16; de Rivoyre, *Obock*, p. 84; Allemann, "Mascate," pp. 77, 85; de Rozario, "An Account," vol. 4, p. 234; Zwemer, *Arabia*, p. 81; Buckingham, *Travels*, p. 507 ("the walled town is certainly less than a mile in circuit."); Peterson, *Historical*, p. 20; Maindron, "Mascate," pp. 465, 606 (for a description of the guards taking their ease and comfort), For a detailed description of the lay-out of the town, see Sadid al-Saltaneh, *Tarikh*, pp. 44-46. For pictures of the gates, see Peterson, *Historical*, photos 95-96, 99-101.

21 Maurizi, *History*, pp. 25-26 ("About 3 miles from Muscat, the road divides into three"); Miles, *The Countries*, p. 467; for a description of the route to the village of Besheyr, see Palgrave, *Narrative*, vol. 2, pp. 373-77.

22 Lorimer, *Gazetteer*, vol. 2, p. 1182-83.

23 Milburn, *Oriental Commerce*, vol. 1, p. 114; Potter, "The Eastern Coast, p. 163.

24 Niebuhr, *Reisebeschreibung*, vol. 2, pp. 498-99.

25 Abdul Qadir, *Waqai*, p. 27.

26 de Rozario, "An Account," vol. 4, p. 234.

27 Stiffe, "Ancient," p. 609.

28 Administration Report 1899-1900, p. 24.

29 Bent, "Muscat," p. 174.

which were inhabited by a mixture of humanity. Between the huts there were palm trees, almond trees, tamarind and the ubiquitous camel thorn.[30] According to Binning in 1851, the houses in the quarter where the Indians lived were "cleaner and better than the ordinary run of Muscat dwellings. I observed that the exterior walls of these domiciles were decorated with rude fresco paintings of elephants, tigers, and other Indian objects."[31]

Muscat had several suburbs, each of which had one or more quarters just like the city itself. Immediately adjacent to the city were the large suburbs of Takiyah and Tuyan, which were mainly inhabited by Baluchis from the Mekran and Africans from Zanzibar.[32] De Rozario called the two main suburbs "Tooyan and Meeabeen (Miyabin)," which were divided by a hill. The former "bears west and consists of a river-bed, in the centre of a flat piece of rich dark soil land, called the Zabadia-the fat land. The Meeabeen bears east and was rocky, with some cultivation only at two places." It was used as the burial place of Muscat and was the residence of lower class Arabs and Baluchis.[33] Ida Pfeiffer did not call them suburbs, but two villages, of which the first one, which was larger than Muscat, contained several burial-places. The cemetery for the Al Bu Saʿid family was south of the Rawiyeh tower.[34] These were "the two natural divisions of the suburban area," the other smaller ones were usually subsumed under their name.[35] These quarters were as follows:

---

30 Miles, *The Countries*, p. 467; Potter, "The Eastern Coast, p. 163; Buckingham, *Travels*, p. 507; Roberts, *Embassy*, p. 354; Ruschenberger, *A Voyage*, vol. 1, p. 74; Geary, *Through Asiatic Turkey*, p. 12; Stiffe, "Ancient," p. 609 ("Of the date tree, and largely of a dwarf palm called *pish*, brought from Makran"); Bent, "Muscat," p. 174; Curzon, *Persia*, vol. 2, p. 441 (Baluchis); Allemann, "Mascate," p. 86; Maindron, "Mascate," p. 609.

31 Binning, *A Journal*, vol. 1, p. 125; Buckingham, *Travels*, p. 518 ("there is a strange mixture of Indian architecture in the Banian's shops and warehouses, gilded and decorated in their own fantastic way, which contrasts with the sombre melancholy of the Arab houses and alleys by which they are surrounded.")

32 Administration Report 1899-1900, p. 25.

33 de Rozario, "An Account," vol. 4, p. 234; Sadid al-Saltaneh, *Tarikh*, pp. 45, 57.

34 Pfeiffer, *A Woman's Journey*, p. 236; Sadid al-Saltaneh, *Tarikh*, p. 56.

35 Administration Report 1899-1900, p. 25; Zwemer, *Arabia*, p. 82; Shepherd, *From Bombay*, p. 58 (this area was also used for exercising horses, sometimes at a break-neck pace, at least this was the case in 1856).

Table 5: The quarters and suburbs of Muscat and their number of houses ca. 1900

Name quarter	Limits and number of houses	Remarks
1. Moghab	From Ft. Jalali to the customs house; 8 houses	British Consulate and houses of its staff; Agency hospital
2. Mahallat Banyan	Surrounds the customs house; 30 houses	Most of the Indian bazaar and most of the Indian residences
3. Mahallat Al Bu Sa'id	From the customs house to Ft. Mirani; 10 houses	Sultan's palace and residences of his relatives
4. Waljat	From east end of town to US vice-consulate; 70 houses	Arabs of various tribes
5. Mahallat al-Suq	From US to French vice-consulate; 100 houses and 300 shops	Main bazaar; mixed population
6. Mahallat al-Barahina	From French vice-consulate to Bab al-Kabir; 70 houses	13 houses occupied by Shiites as *ma'tam* or places of lamentation.
7. Wadi al-'Awr	From Mirani to Bab al-Matha'ib; 40 houses	West of 3, which cuts if off from the sea; mainly Baluchis
	SUBURBS	
8. Safafir (copper-smiths)	Adjoins town on the side towards Sidab; 50 houses	Mainly Bahrainis
9. 'Ajam	Between 9 and 7; 40 houses	Mainly Persians
10. Takiyah	On the road to Sidab; the furthest suburb from town in this direction; 100 huts	Largest suburb; mainly Baluchis; has a blockhouse on a mound.
11. Hinna (henna sellers)	On the west side of road to Sidab, nearer to town than 9; 80 huts	Africans, Persians, Arabs
12. Baharinah (بحارنه)	Adjoins 10, in between town and Bosto hill; 50 houses	Mostly Persians
13. Nisasil (weaver)	Between 11 and 13; 50 houses	Persians from Qeshm Island etc; they are weavers.
14. Khutmah	Outside Bab al-Kabir; 50 huts	Arabs and Baluchis
15. Bab al-Matha'ib	Outside the gate of the same name; 40 huts	Baluchis, some Africans and Arabs
16. Dabghah (tannery)	West of Wadi al-Kabir towards Kalbuh; 100 huts	Mostly Baluchis
17. Jafainah	Reaches towards the pass to Riyam; 50 houses	Baluchis
18. Dalalin (brokers)	West of Wadi al-Kabir; 60 houses; US Presbyterian mission	Bayasirah and freed slaves
19. Halalu	Around Ft. Rawiyah west of Wadi al-Kabir; 50 houses	Africans; Arabs; a fruit and flower garden belonging to the Sultan
20. Tuyan	Extends up to Wadi al-Kabir above Rawiyah;	Baluchis; divided into 3 parts: Lughan (40 houses of Baluchis); Hammaliyah (15 houses of Africans); Sheikh (50 houses of Baluchis).

Name quarter	Limits and number of houses	Remarks
21. Zabadiyah	East of Wadi al-Kabir opposite Rawiya; 45 houses	Arabs
22. Zijal	Below and south of Bosto hill; 45 houses	Jadgals; they are shopkeepers
23. Miyabin	Separated from 21 by a rocky pass; 40 houses	Arabs (mainly Bani Wahaib) and Africans.

Source: Lorimer, *Gazetteer*, vol. 2, pp. 1182-85. For a map of the location of these quarters, see Peterson, *Historical*, photo 8.

Other quarters that were under Muscat were: (i) the village of Sidab, which is southeast of Muscat and separated from it by a small hilly pass. It was inhabited mostly by fishermen and lower class Arabs; (ii) the village of Kalbuh situated to the west and separated by a small pass from the city. It had 15 stone houses and 20-30 huts inhabited by Baluchis, slaves, and some Arabs; (iii) Makallah, a small cove in the harbor, in which the Coal Depot of the British government was situated, which had a capacity of 1,700 tons. At certain times of the year people of Socotra lived there, who periodically came to Muscat to fish and to dive for jetsam. Percy Cox described how these fisherman caught mullet with large rectangular fishing-baskets, which they anchored to the bottom with stones.[36]

MATRAH

The bay of Matrah was more spacious than that of Muscat; it was 1,400 m wide and 1,200 m deep. It was generally considered less safe as a harbor, because it was only protected from the north-west wind, but it was, according to Lorimer, "more easily entered, and is preferred as a harbour by ordinary native craft." However, Buckingham disagreed. He wrote that Matrah's harbor was as good as that of Muscat and in fact, offered "a better shelter from northerly and north-west winds." Like Muscat, Matrah was enclosed by rugged mountains, which were guarded by block-houses, but unlike Muscat it had an easy road leading to Oman's interior. As such it was a caravan-terminus and explains why it was the commercial center, where most of the rich merchants lived. Nevertheless, according to de Rivoyre, its people seemed to be poorer than those in Muscat. Matrah was almost as big as Muscat, although by 1900 it was the largest city of Oman (1,200 m wide and 250 m long). It had a wider harbor and its aspect was greener than Muscat, for around the city were some gardens. It was a walled town with four bastions and a number of towers and three guarded gates, the most important known as Bab al-Kabir, which was a stone gate; the other gates were called Bab Juri (in the north-west of the town and after Tuyan) and Bab al-Mitha`ib. According to Bartle Frere, the gates "were kept by a picturesque rabble of Arabs and Beloochees." The town was defended by a small Portuguese fort, north of which was the customs-house, called *furdah* (فرضه). South of the customs-house was the

---

36 Administration Report 1899-1900, pp. 24-25, 27, 32; Bent, "Muscat," p. 174; Allemann, "Mascate," pp. 77, 94; Lorimer, *Gazetteer*, vol. 2, pp. 1185, 1193; Curzon, *Persia*, vol. 2, p. 441; Ward, *Travels*, p. 55; Sadid al-Saltaneh, *Tarikh*, p. 58. For a picture of the location of this station, see Peterson, *Historical*, photos 12 and 70.

suq. East of the Tuyan gate and the Khojah fort was another customs-house, this one for the imports from the interior of Oman. North of which was a public square known as *arsah* (عرصه), where the Omani imports were offered for sale. The government collected 5 paisas per every 100 paisas of sale. However, imported firewood paid 10 paisas per camel load and 6 paisas per mule load. People from the interior also came to Matrah to buy provisions such as coffee, herbs, cottons, and sugar. Matrah was cooler than Muscat, whose inhabitants retired there during the hot season. It was the favorite retreat of Sultan Turki, where he had a villa.[37] In 1873, the Khojahs proudly showed Bartle Frere the two towers they had been allowed to build as landward defenses a long time ago. However, these defenses did not always provide the necessary protection, for in January 1874 Matrah was plundered for five days by rebels led by Sheikh Saleh b. Ali al-Harithi.[38]

In 1816, Buckingham opined that there were more well-built houses in Matrah than in Muscat. But these apparently did not last, for in 1835, Wellsted described Matrah as a very large collection of huts, situated at the extremity of a cove. He wrote this, because there was hardly any house made of stone; *barasti* huts dominated.[39] However, in 1891 there were a few well-constructed buildings, such as the US consul's, i.e. Mr. Mackirdy's mercantile house, but generally the houses were mean. Only one out of seven was what in India was called a pukka building. Further, there were 10-12 mosques.[40] Its *suq* was an extremely miserable place, according to Fraser. It was "scarcely protected from the rays of the sun by a wretched covering of date leaves; all narrow, dirty and offensive, and a very peculiar and disagreeable odour saluted our senses, as we traversed the place."[41] In 1905, there were 434 shops in Matrah, of which 11 belonged to Banyans. Of these 434 shops three were butcher shops and 11 *halwa*-sellers shops.[42] As in Muscat there was not one, but several suburbs and quarters, each with their own distinctive names. In general, they were called Jabru (or Jibru) and Tuyan, the former being the northern and the latter the southern suburb. These two suburbs were separated by a natural barrier, a high projecting hill. People lived there in densely populated huts, in which there was barely ventilation, near a graveyard and mounds of rubbish and filth and human and other excreta in various stages of decomposition, in particular in Jabru and Tuyan and in the `Iryaneh quarter of the town.[43] In Jabru the two poorest classes lived, the Mekrani Baluchis and Persian

---

37 Lorimer, *Gazetteer*, vol. 2, p. 1197; Sadid al-Saltaneh, *Tarikh*, pp. 72-74 (instead of al-Mitha'ib he renders the name as Misa'ib/مصاعیب); Buckingham, *Travels*, p. 523 ("Muttrah is less a place of business than Muscat"); Martineau, *The Life*, vol. 2, p. 105; Zwemer, *Arabia*, p. 82; von Oppenheimer *Vom Mittelmeer*, vol. 2, p. 330; Bent, "Muscat," p.172; de Rivoyre, *Obock*, pp. 65, 74; Aucher-Eloy, *Rélations* , vol. 2, p. 553; Bombay Records, p. 629; Potter, "The Eastern Coast, pp. 163-64; Johnson, A Journey, p. 11; Lumsden, *A Journey*, p. 27; Fraser, *Narrative*, p. 22 (the nearby garden were irrigated by *aflaj*); Binning, *A Journal*, vol. 1, p. 132; Dieulafoye, *A Suse*, p. 205; Miles, *The Countries*, p. 461; Sadid al-Saltaneh, *Tarikh*, p. 72 (*arsah* means vacant lot, courtyard). For the gardens around Matrah, see Keppel, *A Personal Narrative*, vol. 1, pp. 28-29, whose description of crops being raised in numerous pits dug for irrigation, suggests that this refers to *gav-chah tarkari* wells, as they are called in Persian.

38 Martineau, *The Life*, vol. 2, p. 106; Administration Report 1873-74, p. 76; Goswami, *The Call*, pp. 112-13.

39 Buckingham, *Travels*, p. 523; Wellsted, *Travels*, vol. 1, p. 32; Fraser, *Narrative*, p. 22; de Rivoyre, *Obock*, p. 74; Birks, *The life*, vol. 2, p. 369. The huts were all burnt down by the Wahabis in 1813. Maurizi, *History*, p. 85.

40 Birks, *The life*, vol. 2, p. 369. Pukka refers to a building constructed with durable materials such as stone, bricks and clay tiles. Sometimes mortar is used as a binder; the purpose is to have a lasting building without too much maintenance.

41 Fraser, *Narrative*, p. 22.

42 Sadid al-Saltaneh, *Tarikh*, p. 73.

43 Administration Report 1899-1900, pp. 25, 27.

Figure 16, Makallah Bay, anchorage for small boats, Stiffe

beggars. Nazia Moya (sic; Nazimawjah) and Takiyah were two quarters of Matrah that were mostly occupied by Africans, who also were living in unsanitary conditions.[44]

Table 6: The quarters and suburbs of Matrah and their number of houses ca. 1900

Name	Position	Number of houses and remarks
1. Sur al-Lawatiyah (سور اللواتيه)	Center of town; facing sea	300 houses; Khojah fort
2. Takiyah (تكيه)	South of nr. 1	150 houses of slaves and servants of the Khojahs; also Baluchis and Jadgals
3. Harat al-Siyagh (jeweler/حارة الصياغ)	On the sea; immediately n.w. of nr. 1	50 houses of Hindu silversmiths, Baluchis, Bayasirah
4. Sarmalla (سرملا)	On the sea; immediately north of nr. 3	25 houses of Baluchis and Bayasirah
5. Harat al-Shamal (حارة الشمال)	At extreme n.w. end of town; between 4 and Arbaq village	125 houses of Manadharah; Baluchis; Africans and Hindus

44   Administration Report 1899-1900, p. 28. For a detailed description of the lay-out of the town, see Sadid al-Saltaneh, *Tarikh*, pp. 72-73. Nazimawjah comes from the Swahili word for 'garden of banana trees,' see Peterson, *Historical*, p. 102.

Name	Position	Number of houses and remarks
6. Harat al-Suq (حارة السوق)	On sea front from nr. 1 to customs-house	500 houses of Baluchis, Jadgals, Arab, Hindus, Khojahs; here is the main bazaar
7. al-Wadi (الوادي)	On both sides of Khor Bambah	80 houses (Khojah Sablahs, Baluchis, Africans, 4 shops)
8. Nazimawjah (نازموجه)	Between Takiyah and 7; 6 to its north	30 houses of slaves and servants of the Khojahs; also Baluchis, Jadgals and a few Hindus
9. 'Iryanah (عريانه)	Bounded by 6 to the north and 7 to the west; on the island side	300 houses of Baluchis, Arab brokers and Bayasirah.
10. Dalalil (brokers/دلا ليل)	South of Portuguese fort	60 houses of Arabs and Bayasirah
11. Dikkah (دكّه)	South of 10 and east of 9	120 houses of Baluchis and Bayasirah
12. Jabru (جبرو)	Inland, west of 5	60 houses of Persians and Baluchis; with a Shiite *ma'tam*
13. al-Khazzazin (الخزّافين)	Inland, west of 3 and 5	100 houses of mixed tribes
14. 'Ajam (عجم)	Inland, west of 12	250 houses of Persians and Baluchis; a new and growing quarter
15. Harat al-Balush (حارة البلوش) a.k.a Gharaifah (غريفه)	Adjoins 2 and 8 on s.w. side	300 houses of Baluchis, Jadgals, Bani Hadram, Bayasirah and 30 houses of Bani Jabir
16. Tuyan (طويان)	Outside Bab al-Kabir	180 houses of tribes as in 14
17. Zabadiyah (زبادية)	South of 15; east of the road	50 houses of slaves and servants of Kholahs and others

Source: Lorimer, *Gazetteer*, vol. 2, pp. 1198-99.

In addition, Dr. Jayakar, the British Agency physician, mentioned Matrah Harbor, Dikkah (100 houses of Baluchis), Bazaar and Kitleh (nr. 6 of Table 6) as Matrah city quarters or suburbs.[45] In the 1830s, the Hindi quarter or Hallat al-Hunud is mentioned (either nr. 3 or 6 of Table 6), in which Hindus lived, as the name implies. Also, in the 1830s, there was a 'walled' Baluchi quarter (nr. 14; *Harat al-Balush*) or town inside Matrah with sentries at the only gate that opened up to the beach. The quarter occupied an arid plain of about half a square mile filled with palm huts, not higher than ten feet; some were round, others had conical roofs. The huts had small court yards fenced by palm leaves. There was a small white mosque with a graveyard in part of the town, filed with white tombs; the ones of the poor sprinkled with coral fragments.[46] In this quarter lived not only Baluchis, but also Jadgals.[47]

Most curious was the so-called forbidden fort or the Hallat Sur al-Lawatiyah, which was adjacent to the Indian quarter. Here the Khojahs or Lawatiyahs (sing. Lawati or

---

45   Administration Report 1899-1900, pp. 28, 33; Dikkah is also mentioned by Peterson, *Historical*, p. 62.

46   Roberts, *Embassy*, p. 358; Ruschenberger, *A Voyage*, vol. 1, p. 77.

47   Administration Report 1899-1900, p. 26; Lorimer, *Gazetteer*, vol. 2, p. 1193.

Lutyani) lived, who did not allow any foreigner, Arab or otherwise, to enter their walled city; allegedly inside their women went about unveiled.[48] The Khojah fort had a population of about 1,000 people. The southern side of the fort was 210 paces, the northern side, facing the sea, was 200 paces, the western side was 240 paces, while its eastern side was diagonal, each side of which was 87 paces long. The fort had two gates; the one to the south was called the *Bab al-Amwat* (gate of the dead), because the deceased were carried out through that gate to the cemetery.[49]

In addition, the hamlets of Matairah, Riyam, Shataifi, Falaj (with the only entrance to Matrah) and the villages of Arbaq and Darsait were part of Matrah.[50]

POPULATION

It is difficult to form a reliable idea about the population of Muscat and Matrah, because both had a fluctuating population, while the estimates of its size likewise fluctuate. According to Brucks, "at times it amounts to near thirty thousand souls; at other times there is not more than ten or twelve thousand." Because in summer, i.e. from May until October, most permanent residents left Muscat moving to Sama'il, Nizwah, Jabal al-Ahdar and other places. Of the floating population, Bedouin Arabs and pilgrims from India, Persia, Afghanistan and C. Asia formed the main two groups.[51]

Table 7: Estimated population of Muscat and Matrah

Muscat	Suburb	Year	Source
10,000	3,000	1816	Buckingham, *Travels*, p. 507
30,000	-	1817	Heude, *A Voyage*, p. 31
10,000	-	1820	Mignan, *A Winter Journey*, vol. 2, p. 243
10-12,000	-	1821	Fraser, *Narrative*, p. 6
2,000	-	1824	Keppel, *Personal Narrative*, vol. 1, p. 18
60,000	-	1828	Germain, "Quelques mots," p. 346
12-30,000	-	1830	Bombay Records, p. 631
60,000	-	1838	Fontanier, *Voyage*, vol. 1/2, p. 28
12,000	5,000	1834	Roberts, *Embassy*, p. 354
<20,000	-	1834	Ruschenberger, *A Voyage*, vol. 1, p. 70
55,000	43,000	1846	Osgood, *Notes*, p. 93
12,000	-	1850	Binning, *A Journal*, vol. 1, p. 124
4,000	6,000	1852	Pfeifer, *A Woman's Journey*, p. 236

---

48 Ruschenberger, *A Voyage*, vol. 1, p. 78; Miles, *The Countries*, p. 461; Sadid al-Saltaneh, *Tarikh*, pp. 72-73.

49 Administration Report 1899-1900, p. 26; Lorimer, *Gazetteer*, vol. 2, p. 1200; Sadid al-Saltaneh, *Tarikh*, pp. 72-73.

50 Administration Report 1899-1900, p. 34.

51 Bombay Records, p. 631; Lorimer, *Gazetteer*, vol. 2, p. 1185; Administration Report 1876-77, p. 104; Palgrave, *Narrative*, vol. 2, pp. 367-68; Fraser, *Narrative*, p. 11 (wealthy Muscatis went to Sidab, the Sultan to Barkah); Germain, "Quelques mots," p. 345; Wellsted, *Travels*, vol. 1, p. 15 ("Few Afghans settle permanently here," they only came for the hajj); Zwemer, *Arabia*, p. 79.

Muscat	Suburb	Year	Source
60,000	-	1856	Benjamin 1859, p. 178
40,000	>40,000	1863	Palgrave, *Narrative*, vol. 2, p. 369
30,000	4,000	186	Germain, "Quelques mots," 346-47; de Rozario, An Account," vol. 4, p. 236
60,000	-	1874	Fogg , *The Land*, p. 161
40,000	-	1876	Administration Report 1876-77, p. 101
40,000	-	1878	Geary, *Through Asiatic Turkey*, vol. 1, p. 13
65,000	-	1886	Dieulafoye, *A Suse*, p. 208
5,000	-	1890	Curzon, *Persia*, vol. 2, p. 441
10,000	5,000; 2,000 visitors	1900	Administration Report 1899-1900, p. 24-25; Lorimer, *Gazetteer*, vol. 2, 1185
10,000		1905	Sadid al-Saltaneh, *Tarikh*, p. 46
3,000	35,000	1910	Miles, *The Countries*, p. 467
Matrah			
10,000	-	1817	Heude, *A Voyage*, p. 27
19,000	-	1834	Ruschenberger. *A Voyage*, vol. 1, p. 70
8,000	-	1834	Roberts, *Embassy*, p. 352
8,000	-	1846	Osgood, *Notes*, p. 93
>12,000	-	1850	Binning, *A Journal*, vol. 1, p. 132
25,000	-	1863	Palgrave, *Narrative*
20,000	-	1886	Dieulafoye, *A Suse*, p. 208
15,000	-	1899	Administration Report 1899-1900, p. 25
14,000	5,000	1906	Lorimer, *Gazetteer*, vol. 2, p. 1185

From the above Table, with the various estimates of the population of the two cities, it is clear that the figures for Muscat often seem to be much too high, while those of Matrah appear to be more realistic. A figure of around 10,000 inhabitants for Muscat plus some 2,000 to 3,000 in the suburbs seems to be one that reflect reality for the early part of the nineteenth century. Wellsted gave a figure of 60,000 for Muscat and Matrah together. Ten years later, Fontanier also mentions this figure, but comments that to him this figure appeared much too exaggerated, even for Muscat and Matrah together.[52] The data further suggest that there was a rise in population after the 1850s, but, if true, the reason for this is not known. It may be connected to the political turmoil in the interior of Oman. Neither do we know for certain why towards the end of the nineteenth century the population of Muscat seems to decrease, in fact, more so than that of Matrah, which overtook Muscat in the number of inhabitants. A likely reason for this decrease is political, i.e. the plunder and destruction of Muscat in the second half of the nineteenth century. The more so, because, in 1898, Bent remarked that at that time "most of Muscat is now in ruins; fifty years ago the population must have been nearly three times greater than it is now."[53] On the other hand, a similar observation made by Germain in the 1860s suggests that Muscat's decline, both in population and of the city's buildings, had begun 30 years earlier. This decline in population coincided with the steady emigration of people from

52 Wellsted, *Travels*, vol. 1, p. 22; Fontanier, *Voyage*, vol. 1/2, p. 28.
53 Bent, "Muscat," p. 172. Muscat was also plundered in 1877, see Administration Report 1877-78, p. 128.

Oman to Zanzibar in the 1870s and Muscat's economic decline due its loss of its entrepot function after 1850.[54] This suggests that the population of Muscat remained rather stable, apart from seasonal fluctuations, for most of the nineteenth century, a phenomenon that is also seen in other Persian Gulf ports such as Lengeh, Bandar Abbas and Bushehr.[55]

Another item of interest reported on the composition of the population is that allegedly women outnumbered men by ten to one in Kalbuh, while for the whole of Oman Germain estimated that this ratio was four to one, which seems quite unlikely.[56] His likely source, the British Agency apothecary de Rozario, reported that Arab men did not like to marry Arab women, because they were not very docile and agreeable. Therefore, they preferred an Abyssinian or African concubine. As a result, marriages were few and the number of 'pure' Arab offspring was on the decline. He added: "strange as it may seem, the proportion of males to females is 1 to 20, and, stranger still, the rate of male to female births bears almost the same proportion."[57] Other contributing factors for the low birth rate among 'pure' Arabs may have been the fact that men rarely married before the age of 20 and women before eighteen.[58] Moreover, according to the British Agency physician, Arabs in Muscat suffered from impotence due to homosexual habits which were normal during youth.[59]

It is also difficult to form an idea about the development and change of the ethnic composition of the population. This is because the population of both Muscat and Matrah was a mixture, while the travelers are not always very precise in the use of their ethnic labels. Moreover, this was made more difficult by the process of miscegenation. There was, for example, frequent intermarriage with Africans, although not with the higher class Arabs and or with Indians.[60] Consequently, most of the inhabitants of the two cities were of a mixed race, descendants of Arabs, Persians, Indians, Syrians, Kurds, Afghans, Baluchis, Africans, Abyssinians, etc.[61] Given the variety of ethnic groups living in both cities it is interesting to see whether it is possible to establish who they were and how their numbers and status changed over time.

AFRICANS

Africans had come as slaves to Muscat in the seventeenth century as a result of the Omani raids of Portuguese strongholds along the East African coast, such as Melinde, Mombassa, and Mozambique. Their influx increased after Oman had extended its rule over Zanzibar

---

54   Germain, "Quelques mots," p. 346; Administration Report 1877-78, p. 129; Landen, *Oman*, pp.124, 126.

55   Floor, *Lengeh*; Idem, *Bandar Abbas*; Idem, *Dutch-Omani*.

56   Germain, "Quelques mots," p. 347.

57   de Rozario, "An Account," p. 326.

58   Binning, *A Journal*, vol. 1, p. 125.

59   Administration Report 1876-77, pp. 102-03; Administration Report 1899-1900, p. 26. However, in 1791, Captain Matthew Jenous, *The Route to India*, quoted by Ward, *Travels*, p. 9, opined that the Muscatis were "perfectly free from any *mauvaise honte*."

60   Wellsted, *Travels*, vol. 1, p. 17; de Gobineau, *Trois Ans*, vol. 1, p. 113. According to Johnson, *A Journey*, p. 11, "The inhabitants of Muttra seemed to be altogether cleaner and fairer than those of Muscat, and to have less affinity with the Abyssinian race."; see also Dieulafoye, *A Suse*, p. 206.

61   Wellsted, *Travels*, vol. 1, p. 14-15; Roberts, *Embassy* , p. 354; Fontanier, *Voyage*, vol. 1/2, p. 41; Geary, *Through Asiatic Turkey*, p. 13; Lorimer, *Gazetteer*, vol. 2, pp. 1185, 1200.

Figure 17, Walled city of Muscat and suburbs, Allemann

in 1698 and became a major player in the slave trade.[62] Consequently, many slaves, who were called Zanzibaris, settled in Muscat and Matrah as elsewhere in Oman and mixed with the local population. In 1862, Palgrave estimated that they and mulattos formed one-fifth of population of Muscat.[63] In 1877, according to the British political agent in Muscat, of the fixed population the largest group was formed by negroes, estimated at 10,000. Pure Abyssinians were comparatively few, probably because they were gradually absorbed by the Arabs, because they were usually female and thus their children were considered to be Arab. A few Nubians were also part of the population. The Sedee [Sidi] or negroes were usually employed as laborers and workers and were healthy up to 40 years of age. Thereafter they suffered much from chronic muscular and articular rheumatism and gonorrhea. Women, occupied with domestic chores, were less subject to disease. The Abyssinians were less hardy than the Sidis. The mulattos were a considerable class, but were not considered to be different from the Arabs and were estimated at 15,000.[64] Therefore, the African population, both slaves and freed ones, were mainly from East Africa. By 1900, there still were very few Abyssinians (*Habush*) and Nubians (*Nuban*).[65]

---

62 Niebuhr, *Beschreibung*, p. 306; Risso, *Oman & Muscat*, p. 82.

63 Palgrave, *Narrative*, vol. 2, p. 366. All sources attest to their good treatment; for an exception of a cruel master, see Shepherd, *From Bombay*, p. 65

64 Administration Report 1876-77, pp. 101-02. Early in the nineteenth century they also served as the Sultan's household troops as well as of important Sheikhs. Maurizi, *History*, p. 104; Bombay Records 1856, p. 197.

65 Lorimer, *Gazetteer*, vol. 2, p. 1185.

BALUCHIS.

This imprecise term in fact denoted two ethnic groups that came from the Mekran and Sindi coast. Baluchis had already been employed by the Portuguese and the Ya`ariba rulers of Oman in the seventeenth century, but their presence in Oman began even earlier.[66] The establishment of Omani rule over Gwadar around 1794, of course, facilitated migration of groups from that area to the other side of the Persian Gulf. It would seem that the term Baluchis used by European travelers actually referred to two different ethnic groups. The first group was the Baluchis from the Mekran coast or Baluchistan proper. The second group were the so-called Jatgals, Jadgals or Zadjal, who "though racially distinct from them, are socially and in their domestic habits much like" Baluchis.[67] The Jadgals probably came from Sind and spoke a language different from Baluchi.[68]

   In 1876, the Baluchis living in Muscat and Matrah numbered about 5,000, while about 1900 they made up half of the population of Matrah.[69] They married young, were prolific, and concubinage was rare among them.[70] Though thrifty, they were generally very poor. Whereas Omani Arabs and Persians seldom intermarried, Arabs gave

---

66   See above Ya`ariba section; Barendse, *Arabian Seas*, vol. 1, p. 68.

67   Administration Report 1899-1900, p. 26. In 1816, Buckingham, *Travels*, p. 517 described these two groups as "Sindians and Belooches from the coast of Mekran."

68   Administration Report Year 1876-77, p. 104; Maurizi, *History*, pp. 7 ("Belluchees, or Bellucci, Jedegals, or Gedegals; the former are natives of Mekran; the latter from Sindy, or Sindi"), 167; Saldanha, *The Persian Gulf Précis*, vol. 7/III, pp. 2, 24 (Jadgal chief in Gwadar, originally from Sind; retained their language). On the Jadgals or Jadzals, see Peterson, "Oman's diverse society," p. 37.

69   Administration Report 1876-77, p. 103; Lorimer, *Gazetteer*, vol. 2, p. 1200.

70   de Rozario, "An Account," vol. 4, p. 236.

Figure 18, Masked woman, Allemann

wives to the Baluch, who often settled permanently in Oman. In fact, Baluchis intermarried with all groups.[71] This was because the Arabs ranked them one rung higher than the Banyans, whom they despised.[72] Many Baluchis, of whom there were some 2,000 in Muscat in 1898, were employed as household troops of the Sultan, worked as porters, servants, craftsmen, petty traders and a few as mariners.[73] Sadid al-Saltaneh estimated the Baluch at 4,000 persons in 1905, or about 40% of the city's estimated population.[74]

INDIANS.

The term Indian is somewhat of a misnomer and, in fact, travelers usually employed more distinctive terms to denote the various Indian groups. There were five groups of Indians: (i) Banyans; (ii) Khojahs, (iii) other Moslem Indians, (iv) Portuguese-Indians, and (v) a few Parsis and Sikhs. Moreover, there was economic rivalry between

these various groups.[75] The size of the Indian community fluctuated depending on their welcome. Prior to 1800, this community was quite sizeable, but with the imposition of Wahabi influence and intolerance in the early years of the nineteenth century most of them left. However, under the tolerant rule of Sultan Sa`id II (r. 1806–1856), who attracted Indians traders with special immunities, the size of the Indian grew significantly. However, under the rule of his son Thuwayni (r. 1856-66), due to the latter's negligence

---

71 Wellsted, *Travels*, vol. 1, p. 15-16; Osgood, *Notes*, p. 94.

72 Ruschenberger, *A Voyage*, vol. 1, p. 77; Germain, "Quelques mots," p. 348; Landen, *Oman*, p. 143.

73 Maurizi, *History*, pp. 7, 9, 15, 30 (2,000 Baluch soldiers); Bombay Records, p. 633 (1,500 Baluch soldiers); Wellsted, *Travels*, vol. 1, p. 15-16; Ruschenberger, *A Voyage*, vol. 1, p. 77; Osgood, *Notes*, p. 94; Palgrave, *Narrative*, vol. 2, p. 332; Administration Report 1876-77, p. 103; de Rivoyre, *Obock*, p. 93; von Oppenheim, *Vom Mittelmeer*, vol. 2, p. 328; Lorimer, *Gazetteer*, vol. 2, p. 1185; Geary, *Through Asiatic Turkey*, vol. 1, p. 17.

74 Sadid al-Saltaneh, *Tarikh*, p. 46.

75 Landen, *Oman*, p.141.

Figure 19, Baluchi guards, Fogg

or "the unchecked injustice of some subordinate harpy" their number decreased, to increase again under Sultan Turki (r. 1871-88) and fall thereafter due to Muscat's decline.[76] Although most of the Indians were British subjects it was only as of 1873 that they enjoyed full extra-territorial protection and thus, were outside Omani jurisdiction.[77]

BANYANS

The term Banyan is derived from *vaniya* (pl. *vaniye*) a Gujarati word meaning 'trader.' The Portuguese used this word, in the form of Banyan or Banian or some other similar form, to refer to any Indian trader, and this appellation was later adopted by other Europeans, because during the Portuguese control over Muscat and other Omani ports, Banyans were also living and working there, as they continued to do after the Portuguese ouster from Oman in 1650. Estimates of the number of Banyans in Muscat differ widely. In the eighteenth century they constituted one of the largest Indian communities in the Persian Gulf. After 1785, the Thatta Bhatias were slowly being replaced by Bhatias from Kutch and Khojahs from Hyderabad called Lawatiyas.[78]

Apart from the Bhatias there were "the Banians proper, or Lohannas, who are comparatively few in number." Both groups formed the Hindu part of the Indian population.[79] De Rozario reported that there were Bhatias from Kutch, called Kutchis and Lavanees (Lavanis) from Multan, called Multanis. The name Lohani comes from Lohanpur, the capital of the medieval Lohani kingdom in Multan. Whether the Lohannas are the same

76 Palgrave, *Narrative*, vol. 2, pp. 369-70.

77 Lorimer, *Gazetteer*, vol. 1, p. 629; Landen, *Oman*, p. 143.

78 Allen, "The Indian Merchant," pp. 41-43 (with a discussion of why this happened); Markovits, *The Global World*, p. 11; Martineau, *The Life*, vol. 2, p. 105.

79 Saldanha, *The Persian Gulf Précis*, vol. 3, p. 8 (Précis of the slave trade)

as the Lughan, after whom a quarter is named in the Tuyan suburb is unclear.[80] Despite the existence of these two distinct groups, European sources almost without exception refer to both as Banyan, as I also do in what follows, because the other sources only refer to Banyans.

The Banyans came from various places. The following locations are mentioned: N.W. Province, Sind, Kutch, Bombay, Gujarat, and even Konkan, which is possible, because Muscat had a centuries old trade relations with the Malabar Coast.[81] In 1765, Niebuhr estimated the Banyan community of Muscat at some 1,200 persons.[82] According to Maurizi, around 1810, there were 4,000 of them, while in 1835, Rabbi David Beth Hillel and Wellsted, estimated their number at respectively 1,000 and 1,500. They were, according to Wellsted, "a body of principal merchants."[83] In 1840, they were estimated at some 2,000, while in the 1860s, de Rozario gave a number of 200 Banyan males.[84] This sudden drop in the number of Banyans was due to the unwelcome, if not hostile, atmosphere that existed under Sultan Thuwayni's rule (r. 1861-66), under the uncertain rule of Sultan Salim (r. 1866-68) as well as under that of the usurper Azzan b. Qays (r. 1868-71). After the establishment of the more welcoming government of Sultan Turki, instead of the older generation of Banyans (in particular Kutchi Bhatias), a new group of younger traders came to Muscat.[85]

Banyans usually remained for 15-20 years, but they never brought their wives or families with them. They only occasionally "intrigue with Arab females," while those who were married were rare.[86] The Banyans remained religiously and socially apart from the rest of the population. They were pure vegetarians and mainly worked as shopkeepers and merchants. In 1875, they numbered about 500, reflecting Muscat's decline as a trade

---

80 de Rozario, "An Account," vol. 4, p. 236; there also were Lohannas or Lavanis in Mandavie (i.e. Mandvi), the most important port of Kutch, see Hamilton, *The East Indian Gazetteer*, vol. 2, p. 204. The Lohannas were originally from Sind. The name Luvanas or Lavanis is due to the fact that they claim descent from Lava, the son of Rama. For more details concerning Bhatias and Lohannas, see Gosvami, *The Call*, pp. 29-32. For the Lughan, see Peterson, "Oman's diverse society," p. 49; Idem, *Historical*, pp. 55-56. Bartle Frere also mentioned two groups: the Bhatias and the Karachi Banyans, presumably meaning the Lohannas. Martineau, *The Life*, vol. 2, p. 105.

81 Wellsted, *Travels*, vol. 1, pp. 18-19 (NW Province); Fraser, *Narrative*, p. 6 (Sind, Kutch and Gujarat); Buckingham, *Travels*, p. 507, 517 (Guzerat and Bombay); Germain, "Quelques mots," p. 347 (Kutch and Gujarat); Palgrave, *Narrative*, vol. 2, p. 369 (Kutch, Gujarat and Konkan); Miles, *The Countries*, p. 468 (Kutch); Helfer, *Travels*, vol. 2, p. 5 (Sind, Kutch, Gujarat); Martineau, *The Life*, vol. 2, p. 105 (Karachi).

82 Niebuhr, *Beschreibung*, p. 305 estimated the Banyan community of Muscat at some 1,200 persons in 1765. According to Sadid al-Saltaneh, *Tarikh*, p. 88 the Banyans from Kutch and Mandvi came during the reign of Sultan Sayyed Hamad b. Sa'id (r. 1786-1792).

83 Maurizi, *History*, p. 23; Fraser, *Narrative*, p. 6 (1,000 Indians); Buckingham, *Travels*, p. 507 (1,000 Banyan and other Hindus); Beth Hillel, *The Travels*, p. 113; Wellsted, *Travels*, vol. 1, p. 18; Aucher-Eloy, *Relations*, vol. 2, p. 546 (many) Brucks 1856, p. 631.

84 Markovits, *The Global World*, p. 17; de Rozario, "An Account," vol. 4, p. 236.

85 In 1866, many Banyans left Muscat temporarily at the insistence of Col. Pelly, the Persian Gulf Resident, see Goswami, *The Call*, pp. 103-04. For the reasons of the departure of the older generation and the arrival of younger traders, see Allen, "The Indian Merchant," p. 46.

86 Wellsted, *Travels*, vol. 1, p. 18-19; Germain, "Quelques mots," p. 348; de Rivoyre, *Obock*, p. 67 (they married young and for short periods they returned home); Dieulafoye, A Suse, p. 206; Helfer, *Travels*, vol. 2, p. 6. They did not intermarry, neither a Banyan woman would marry with a non-Banyan "nor do the men every marry Arabian women." Maurizi, *History*, pp. 129-30.

emporium.[87] By 1900, this number had dwindled to about 200 men, 50 women and some children. There were relative few of them in Matrah; in 1900 there were 30 men, of which 7 or 8 had their families with them. The presence of Banyan women and children was a recent innovation.[88] The sharp drop in the size of Indian community in Muscat meant that it was even smaller than that of the native 'pure' Arabs. In fact, the number of Banyans continued to fall, so that in 1905 there were only 53 Banyans left in Muscat.[89]

In the late nineteenth century the Banyans in Muscat were led by four families of Dowlatgirji Manrupgirji, a Gosain Brahman from Kutch nicknamed the 'Ace,', who resided near Mandvi and delegated the management of his business to a local manager; Ratansi Purshottam, nicknamed the 'king'; Virji Ratansi, a banker nicknamed the 'queen,' and Damodar Dharamsi, nicknamed 'the jack' who occasionally farmed the customs. Other Hindus named themselves after this quarter.[90]

The Banyans dominated the trade of Muscat and Matrah; they had a quasi-monopoly of the pearl trade as well as of the cloth, piece-goods and coffee trade; they also were the owners of the large ships registered in Muscat/Matrah.[91] "The wealthy and influential Hindoo merchants, who carry on, or control the principal commercial operations, reside in Muscat."[92] There was also an insurance company run by Banyans to provide maritime insurance for ship and cargo.[93] They were "brokers to most Arab merchants and agents to any European ship that trades to this place."[94]

Allegedly, from time immemorial, the rulers of Muscat annually sold the right to collect customs duties at Muscat and Matrah to one of the Banyan traders. This person practically became the banker of the government towards the end of the nineteenth century.[95] In 1874, according to the British political agent, the customs were still in the hands of the same Hindu firm that had held it for the last 200 years. The Sultan received

87 Administration Report 1876-77, pp. 103-04; Germain, "Quelques mots," p. 348; Maurizi, *History*, p. 129; Osgood, *Notes*, pp. 98; 99-100 (Banyan diet); de Rivoyre, *Obock*, p. 67. In 1881, there were 700 Hindus in Muscat, according to Stack, *Six Months*, vol. 1, p. 17.

88 Lorimer, *Gazetteer*, vol. 2, pp. 1185, 1200.

89 Administration Report 1899-1900, p. 26.

90 Allen 1981, p. 48, n. 65; Ward, *Travels*, p. 73. For a discussion of the role of the Bhimani family and its control over the customs house, see Goswami, *The Call*, pp. 95-101, 119-21; for Purshottam, see Landen, *Oman*, p. 139. For a list of Indian merchants and their trade, see Sadid al-Saltaneh, *Tarikh*, pp. 64-65.

91 Wellsted, *Travels*, vol. 1, p. 21, 24; Maurizi, *History*, p. 23; Stack, *Six Months*, vol. 1, p. 17; Lorimer, *Gazetteer*, vol. 2, pp. 1181, 1185, 1187-88; Osgood, *Notes*, p. 96 (with negative remarks about their business methods; also a description of the finger language used in negotiations - for a discussion of this method of calculation or dactylonomy and its diffusion, see Jean-Gabriel Lemoine, "Les anciens procédés de calcul sur les doigts en Orient et en Occident," *Revue des Etudes Islamiques* 6/1 (1932), pp. 1-58); Miles, *The Countries*, p. 468. For some of these business methods, see Bhacker, *Trade and Empire*, pp. 70, 99, 159, 177; Allen, "The Indian Merchant," pp. 45, 47-48.

92 Administration Report 1873-74, p. 78; Maurizi, *History*, p. 129; de Gobineau, *Trois Ans*, vol. 1, p. 113; Landen, *Oman*, pp. 131-44. For merchants other than Indians, see Sadid al-Saltaneh, *Tarikh*, pp. 65-66.

93 Ruschenberger, *A Voyage*, vol. 1, p. 136.

94 Brucks 1856, p. 631.

95 Administration Report 1900-1901, p. 16; Maurizi, *History*, p. 29; de Rivoyre, *Obock*, pp. 64 (Rustanjee), 91; Risso, *Oman & Muscat*, p.192 (Mowji). The earliest mention of a Banyan farming the Muscat customs is in 1801, when one Mowjee, a Banyan from Kutch. He probably was Gopal Mowjee Bhimani, a member of the family who held onto this post. Bhacker, *Trade and Empire*, pp.171-72. In 1827 another Banyan is mention as customs farmer. Bombay Records, p. 632 (180,000 dollars). Before that time, at least in the 1780s, the customs master was Ruzayq b. Bakhit. Bhacker, *Trade and Empire*, pp. 24-25. Under Azzan b. Qays the customs were farmed by an Arab administrator, which was not a very efficient arrangement. Goswami, *The Call*, pp. 90-100.

120,000 Maria Theresia dollars for the customs farm, which included customs duties, transit dues on produce from the interior, petty monopolies, etc.[96] The financial administration was efficiently handled by the Sultan's "Hindustani officials," but, so the British political agent opined, could be much improved if managed by a professional. Therefore, in 1900, the Sultan decided to manage the customs himself and he made more money than before after paying 20,000 dollars in expenses.[97]

KHOJAHS

This term, derived from the Persian honorific *khvajeh*, meaning 'lord, master,' referred to those converted to Nizari Ismaili Islam in the Indian sub-continent from about the thirteenth century onward. More particularly, it included certain groups, predominantly from Gujarat and Kutch, who, despite being Moslem, retained strong Indian ethnic roots and caste customs. They probably arrived in Oman at least from the mid-eighteenth century, if not earlier.[98]

Their origin as well as their date of arrival in Muscat is unclear, but it is quite likely that they came from Hyderabad in Sind. This tradition among the Lawatiyahs or Hyderabadis about their place of origin is rejected by some scholars, such as Calvin Allen and Philip Ward, who mistakenly believe that Hyderabad was only founded in 1768 and, therefore, given their alleged length of residence in Muscat the Lawatiyahs could not have hailed from there.[99] However, 1768 was only the year when the Kalhora king moved his capital there. The city of Hyderabad already existed well prior to 1720. This fits Ibn Ruzayq's statement that the Lawatiyahs were among the notables who welcomed the first Al Bu Sa`id Sultan in Matrah in the late 1740s, indicating that they were long-time residents of that city.[100] They suffered under the conservative religious rule of Azzan b. Qays (1868-71), but after the return of tolerant Al Bu Sa`id rule in 1871 a second wave of Khojahs came to Matrah. They spoke Khwajki (a dialect mixture of Sindi and Kutchi) among themselves and Arabic to outsiders.[101]

The Khojahs and petty dealers mainly lived in Matrah; in 1900 there were only 10 of them in Muscat, where they had 41 shops, while they had 67 shops in Matrah. However,

---

96   Administration Report 1873-74, p. 78; Administration Report 1875-76, p. 78 (The Customs farm has changed hands three times this year. It is now held for 1,10,000 dollars). Sett Khatao Bhimjee farmed the customs for $95,000 and one year later for 1,25,000 dollars. Administration Report 1880-81, p. 207; Administration Report 1881-82, p. 137; Maurizi, *History*, p. 29 (180,000 dollars annually around 1810); Owen, *Narrative*, vol. 1, p. 343 (farmed to a Banyan); Fontanier, *Voyage*, vol. 1/2, p. 42 (farmed to a Banyan); Sadid al-Saltaneh, *Tarikh*, p. 46.

97   Administration Report 1900-1901, pp. 16-17.

98   Allen, "The Indian Merchant," p. 49; Badger, *History*, vol. 2, p. 163. Peterson, "Oman's diverse society," p. 41.

99   Allen, "The Indian Merchant," p. 50; Ward, *Travels*, p. 73, both of whom, apart from the Hyderabad date of 1768, give other theories about their origin.

100   Allen, "The Indian Merchant," p. 49; Badger, *History*, vol. 1, p. 163; Lorimer, *Gazetteer*, vol. 1, p. 535 mentions that during a dispute in 1889 the Khojahs claimed that their rights went back one century. For the existence of Hyderabad prior to 1720, see Floor, *Afghan Occupation*, p. 330 (with a list of names of the Bangesalies from Hyderabad in Bandar Abbas in 1728) and Idem, *Nader Shah*, p. 229, where, in 1739, mention is made of the presence of Banyan merchants (Bangesalies and Derwellies) in Bandar Abbas from Hyderabad, called Hyderabadis like the Lawatiyas; see also Barendse, *Arabian Seas*, vol. 2, pp. 784-85; vol. 3, p. 948.

101   Ward, *Travels*, p. 73.

most Khojahs went daily to Muscat, "some in smart boats of their own, others in omnibus boats or canoes."[102] The Khojahs, who were also known locally as Lawatiyah (sing. Lawati or Lutyani), formed an important part of the commercial community of Muscat and Matrah; they numbered in total about 1,000. They lived in Matrah "in a small fortified place of their own, which is remarkable for its absolute want of any sanitation. They are thus socially distinct and separated from the rest of the Mahomedans." According to some, the fort perhaps is a former Portuguese fort. In the 1620s, Rui Freire, indeed, had built a fort there to house Portuguese factors who came from the mountains and could not reach Muscat, because of the lack of roads, but it may also be a fort built in the 1640s by the first Ya`aribah Sultan.[103] According to the head of the Khojahs in 1873, Soleyman Khojah,

> They had in old times managed to get all their houses together-windows and doors inside, dead walls outside-and little by little connected the houses by substantial walls, a tower or two, and a gateway. Over the door leading into the interior was a date two hundred and forty years ago; now they shut the gates at dark and keep all inside subject to their Sumat or assembly of elders.[104]

If the number 240 is correct then this means that the fort's gate was built in 1633, which favors the identification of the original fort as Portuguese, because the Omani fort was built later.[105]

The Khojahs were mainly shopkeepers and merchants. They controlled the trade in dried fish (which the vegetarian Banyans, of course, refused to deal in) and dealt in the other daily needs of people, such as trading in grains, dates, and textiles. Some of them also worked as artisans such as in carpentry and boat building.[106] In 1905, there were a number of houses uninhabited inside the fort, while there were 330 shops. They were the only Indians to bring their families with them. Their women led a sedentary life; their houses suffered from a lack of ventilation, were overcrowded and lacked sanitation, according to the British Agency physician. To the untrained eye of Bartle Frere, however, the quarter was "thriving and clean but crowded."[107] They married young, were prolific, but child mortality must have been high, because the males never seemed to be able to exceed beyond the 500 limit, according to de Rozario. He further, noted that after 1859, their social and economic condition worsened, because, in that year, the British-Indian

---

102 Administration Report 1873-74, p. 78; Lorimer, *Gazetteer*, vol. 2, pp. 1185; Martineau, The *Life*, vol. 2, p. 105. In 1905, there were 13 Khojahs in Muscat. Sadid al-Saltaneh, *Tarikh*, pp. 46, 73.

103 Anonymous, *Relãçao das plantas*, p. 11; Bocarro, *Livro das plantas*, p. 54, which also has a drawing of the fort (fig. vi). For the fort built by the first Ya`ariba Sultan, see Lorimer, *Gazetteer*, vol. 1, p. 401 or above. According to Sadid al-Saltaneh, *Tarikh*, pp. 73, 78, the Lawatiyah fort was built by Sultan Sayyed Hamad b. Sa`id (r. 1786-1792).

104 Martineau, *The Life*, vol. 2, p. 106 (the fort's gate at the beach had a large guardhouse, where guests were received. Given that the guards were Baluchis and that households had African slaves suggests that some trusted outsiders had also access to the otherwise closed Khojah community).

105 Ward, *Travels*, p. 73 reports that a Khojah told him that the date on the gate indicated construction in the sixteenth century. If that is correct, it is more likely that the Khojah fort was an old Omani fortress.

106 Landen, *Oman*, p. 140; Administration Report 1876-77, p. 81; de Rozario, "An Account," vol. 4, p. 238; Administration Report 1899-1900, p. 26.

107 Administration Report 1876-77, p. 103; von Oppenheim, *Vom Mittelmeer*, vol. 2, p. 329; Lorimer, *Gazetteer*, vol. 2, pp. 1185, 1200; Martineau, *The Life*, vol. 2, p. 106.

government decided on technical grounds that they were not British but Omani subjects. As a result, they enjoyed less protection and were more imposed upon by the Omani government and constrained in their business affairs.[108] In 1905, one third of the Khojahs were Omani subjects, while the remainder were British subjects.[109]

OTHER INDIAN MOSLEMS

In addition to the Khojahs there were other Indians, who had converted to Sunni or Shiite Islam, viz. Bohras and Memons.[110] These Indian Moslems, who were mostly traders, goldsmiths and carpenters lived inside the city, but in better sanitary surroundings than in Baluchi and Arab quarters.[111]

INDIAN CHRISTIANS

Towards the end of the nineteenth century, this very small group consisted of some 20 Indo-Portuguese, who worked as shopkeepers, sellers of alcohol, clerks and servants.[112]

PARSIS AND SIKHS

At the end of the eighteenth century two Parsi merchants, Bhimji Hirji and Mowji Rowji from Gujarat, resided in Muscat. It is not known how many Parsis lived in the twin cities, but there were Parsi merchants in Matrah and Muscat; in 1886 their dress was peculiar enough to catch Jane Dieulafoye's eyes in Muscat. Palgrave mentioned the presence of Sikhs in Muscat. These may have been the guard detail of the British agency. At the end of the 1890s they numbered some twenty-five.[113]

ARABS

In Muscat the original Arab inhabitants were the Bani Wuhayb and in Matrah the Bani Hasan. Although Muscat and Matrah were the biggest cities of Oman, among those who lived in these two cities, Arabs formed the smallest minority already in the 1830s.[114] This allegedly was different from the situation in 1816, when Buckingham reported that nine-tenths of the inhabitants of the walled city were 'pure' Arabs, a term that neither

---

108   de Rozario, "An Account," vol. 4, p. 236; Sadid al-Saltaneh, *Tarikh*, p. 143.

109   Sadid al-Saltaneh, *Tarikh*, p. 73.

110   Allen, "The Indian Merchant," p. 49; Goswami, *The Call*, pp. 34-37 (who submits that there were no Memons in Muscat).

111   Administration Report 1899-1900, p. 26.

112   Lorimer, *Gazetteer*, vol. 2, 1185; Administration Report 1899-1900, p. 26; Birks, *The life*, vol. 2, p. 366; Sadid al-Saltaneh, *Tarikh*, p. 65.

113   Buckingham, *Travels*, p. 517; Fraser, *Narrative*, p. 27; Keppel, *A Personal Narrative*, vol. 1, p. 27; Palgrave, *Narrative*, vol. 2, p. 367; Dieulafoye, *A Suse*, p. 206; Nadri, *Eighteenth-Century Gujarat*, p. 63; Maindron, "Mascate," p. 625.

114   Owen, *Narrative*, vol. 1, p. 338. Peterson, *Historical*, p. 22; Lorimer, *Gazetteer*, vol. 2, pp. 1200 (in Matrah the "predominant Arab tribes are Bani Hasan, Siyabiyin, Rahbiyin and Bani Jabir).

he nor any other traveler defined.[115] By 1900, 'pure' Arabs remained a small group and rarely exceeded 500 in Muscat as gradually they were absorbed by the mixed group due to concubinage.[116] Arabs of mixed marriages were known as Mawalid and usually were black.[117] Therefore, some authors report that the Arabs (i.e. 'pure' and mixed) formed the larger part of the population of Muscat. Osgood and von Oppenheimer explicitly state that Arabs formed the largest group among Muscat's population; however this is not supported by most other sources.[118] Also, there was an unknown number of Arabs from other parts of the Middle East (Bahrain, Iraq, Arabia), most of whom were transients.[119]

BAYSARIYAH

This low-status group (Bayasirah; sing. Baysari) is already referred in the tenth century in India to denote Moslems born locally of an Arab father and an Indian woman. The term probably was derived from the Gujarati word *adh-besra*, meaning 'mixed blood.' In tribal Oman, the term Bayasirah referred to low-status people, who may represent remnants of the pre-Arab local population, migrants from Sind, and/or were offspring of Omani Arab fathers and slave mothers; in short, their origin is unknown.[120]

ZATUT

This was another low-status group, who, although Moslems, were looked down upon by all other Moslems and thus were socially isolated.[121] According to the British consul, "The Jutts, or Zatoots, as the Arabs call them, form a class by themselves, and are the descendants of the Jutts who emigrated a thousand years ago from India." They were divided into Arab Zatoots and Baluch Zatoots (Zatut; sing. Zutti) and in 1876 their number was about 200. They were peddlers and were sometimes incorrectly referred to as Gypsies. They should not be mistaken either for Jats, a group of low-caste agriculturalist and herders from Sind, many of whom converted to Islam.[122]

115 Buckingham, *Travels*, p. 507. Palgrave, *Narrative*, vol. 2, p. 163, also submits that Muscat was still a place where 'pure' Arabs lived.
116 Administration Report 1876-77, pp. 102-03; Administration Report 1899-1900, p. 26.
117 Lorimer, *Gazetteer*, vol. 2, p. 1185.
118 Osgood, *Notes*, p. 94; Aucher-Eloy, *Rélations*, vol. 2, p. 546; von Oppenheimer, *Vom Mittelmeer*, vol. 2, p. 527.
119 Palgrave, *Narrative*, vol. 2, pp. 265-66, 364.
120 Government of India, *Gazetteer*, vol. 1, part 1, appendix V, p. 516. In tribal Oman, the term referred to low-status people, who probably hailed originally from Sind. Wilkinson, "Bayasirah," pp. 75-85; Lorimer, *Gazetteer*, vol. 1, p. 298; Peterson, "Oman's diverse society," p. 48.
121 Administration Report Year 1876-77, p. 104; von Oppenheim, *Vom Mittelmeer*, vol. 2, p. 329.
122 Administration Report Year 1876-77, p. 104; von Oppenheim, *Vom Mittelmeer*, vol. 2, p. 329 (150-200 Zatoots). On the Zatut, see Peterson, "Oman's diverse society," p. 48. It is perhaps interesting to note that in Dashti (a district s.e. of Bushehr) there was a group of camelmen of unknown origin known as Jatut. Lotimer, *Gazetteer*, vol. 2, p. 369.

PERSIANS

The Persian speaking or Ajam community in Oman has ancient roots in Oman, dating from before the Islamic conquest. Moreover, there were commercial and other contacts between the populations on both sides of the Persian Gulf throughout the centuries. In fact, during the kingdom of Hormuz both Arab and Persian coastal areas were part of that same kingdom from the thirteenth century until 1622. Some Persians may also have stayed behind after the Persian invasion of Oman between 1739–47. Others, in particular from the Lar, Bandar Abbas and Minab area, came across after 1800, because until 1868, the Sultans of Oman held the governorship of Bandar Abbas and Minab on behalf of the Persian Shah.[123] In 1816, many Persians were living in Muscat's suburbs.[124] Nevertheless, because of the Persian invasion (1737-47), Persians were mistrusted and were not allowed to live in the walled city of Muscat. According to Lt. Potter, none but Arabs and Banyans, or Christians, were permitted to live within the walls of Muscat; "the fugitive Persians and Blochees, &c. of which there is a great number, live without the gate in mat-houses."[125] Only a small number of Persians was allowed into town. After the marriage of Sultan Sa`id II with a Persian princess in 1828 that order and several other restrictions were lifted. In the early part of the nineteenth century, Persians were mostly merchants; those from Bandar Abbas, Lar and Minab made swords and matchlocks.[126] They were described in the 1830s as being mostly merchants dealing in Indian piece-goods, coffee, hookahs, and rosewater.[127] Despite their long time presence, Persians were looked upon as strangers, and were even unpopular.[128] According to a report by a Persian official in 1860, half of the population hailed from Persian ports, while he also mentioned that there was a group of Bahrainis. This figure clearly is inflated as the writer (the Persian agent at Bombay) wanted to make the case for the importance of his function and the need to increase his salary.[129] In 1876, some 100 Persians lived permanently in Muscat, some of whom were in the Sultan's employ as gunners; others worked as fishermen and small traders, while there were also a few Persian merchants.[130] Mohammad Ali Kebabi was a very influential Persian merchant from Bandar Abbas, while his son Ahmad Kebabi, likewise a very influential merchant, who even became Sultan Thuwayni's and Sultan Salim's vizier.[131] Around 1900, according to von Oppenheim, there were not more than 200 Persians in Muscat, who worked as sword smiths, tradesmen, craftsmen, and weavers making silken fabrics that were exported to other Gulf ports, cities in S. Arabia and Zanzibar. However, at that time, Lorimer states that the Persian community was considerable, being employed as shopkeepers, fishmonger, weavers, and makers of beds and quilts.[132] In fact, in 1905, Sadid al-Saltaneh estimated the Persian population of Muscat at 800 men and 800 women and

123 Floor, *Bandar Abbas*.
124 Buckingham, *Travels*, p. 507, 517 (from Bushehr).
125 Potter, "The Eastern Coast, p. 163.
126 Wellsted, *Travels*, vol. 1, p. 16-17; Potter, "The Eastern Coast, p. 163; Ruschenberger, *A Voyage*, vol. 1, p. 70; Osgood, *Notes*, p. 94 (who mistakenly gives the year 1848).
127 Wellsted, *Travels*, vol. 1, p. 17.
128 Palgrave, *Narrative*, vol. 2, pp. 365-66.
129 Habibi and Vothuqi, *Barrasi-ye tarikhi*, p. 216, doc. 59 (November 1860).
130 Administration Report 1876-77, p. 104; Geary, *Through Asiatic Turkey*, p. 13.
131 Sadid al-Saltaneh, *Tarikh*, pp. 47, 142, 149, 152, 159-60; Floor, *Bandar Abbas*, pp. 75, 88.
132 von Oppenheim, *Vom Mittelmeer*, vol. 2, pp. 328-29; Lorimer, *Gazetteer*, vol. 2, pp. 1183, 1185.

children. Twelve of them were artillerists in government service, the remainder worked in humble occupations.[133] The Ajams dominated the baking of flat bread until modern times. The flat bread was prepared and baked in the *suq*. The dough was made on the spot, in a wooden dish, then divided into small pieces that were flattened into large thin flakes, "which are smeared over with salt water, and stuck into the inner side of a round tube. These tubes are made of clay, are about eighteen inches in diameter and twenty-two in length; they are sunk one half in the ground, and furnished with an air-draft below. Wood-charcoal is burnt inside the tube at the bottom." Ida Pfeiffer had a few loaves made in this oven, she tasted and liked them very much.[134] In Matrah, Persians also belonged to very poor and mostly eked out a living as beggars (see above).

JEWS

In 1764, Niebuhr mentions that Jews were not subject to special dress rules as elsewhere in the Moslem world. Maurizi and Buckingham mention that in the early nineteenth century there were a few Jews in Muscat, who were said to have come from Basra.[135] A larger group came in 1835 from Baghdad, fleeing from oppression from the local governor. Thereafter, the size of the group fluctuated widely, usually being in the single digits.[136] In 1898, there was still a small group of Jews living and working in Matrah and six in Muscat.[137] Many Jews were employed as making silver ornaments, money-changers or *sarraf*s; a few also made a living in the liquor retail trade.[138]

LANGUAGES GALORE

Given this medley of ethnic groups, it is not a big surprise that it was reported that at the beginning of the twentieth century 14 languages were spoken regularly in the *suq*s of Muscat and Matrah.[139] This was because most of the above groups continued to speak their own language, which more than anything else, was the ethnic distinction or even identity that marked them off from other groups.[140] Although these various ethnic groups interacted on a daily basis, each kept very much to their own group and "home intimacy" was rare.[141] Despite the multitude of languages spoken, usually one language was the lingua franca for all groups, which, in Matrah, seems to have been Hindi. The lower classes spoke bastardized Arabic, but also knew Hindi and almost always understood Persian as well, according to Dieulafoye. The Omani elite and wealthy, in addition to Arabic, sometimes

---

133　Sadid al-Saltaneh, *Tarikh*, p. 56; Allemann, "Mascate," p. 74.

134　Bhacker, *Trade and empire*, p. 135; Pfeiffer, *A Woman's Journey*, p. 237.

135　Maurizi, *History*, p. 23; Buckingham, *Travels*, p. 506 (three or four), 517 (from Basra).

136　Wellstead 1838, vol. 1, pp. 21-22; Fontanier, *Voyage*, vol. 1/2, pp. 43-45; Beth Hillel, *Travels*, p. 112 (four families); de Gobineau, *Trois Ans*, vol. 1, p. 113 (a few); Lorimer, *Gazetteer*, vol. 1, pp. 400, 472; vol. 2, p. 1185; Peterson, *Historical*, p. 83.

137　von Oppenheim, *Vom Mittelmeer*, vol. 2, p. 329; Lorimer, *Gazetteer*, vol. 2, p. 1185.

138　Wellsted, *Travels*, vol. 1, p. 22; de Gobineau, *Trois Ans*, vol. 1, p. 115.

139　W.G. Grey, "Trades and Races of Oman," *Quarterly Journal of the Mythic Society*, vol. 2, no. 2 (January 1911), p. 4.

140　See Peterson, "Oman's diverse society," on this subject.

141　Palgrave, *Narrative*, vol. 2, pp. 365-66.

Figure 20, Local school, Allemann

knew Turkish and Persian. They sent their sons for education to Bombay, Calcutta or sometimes to Persia, in the latter case especially to study medicine. For those less wealthy the only available education, be it not affordable for most, was the rudimentary curriculum of a *maktab* to learn the Koran. "When a boy can read the Koran his education is considered to be complete. Those who intend to become Nakhodas are taught a little arithmetic, and navigation, at Bombay or at Calcutta."[142] In 1831, according to Stocqueler, there were 15 small *maktab*s, and one larger school, "supported by the government where the education is of a higher order, and whence the cazees for the interior districts are selected."[143] In 1891, Bishop French noted that there were a few school for boys and girls in Muscat and Matrah, where they learned to read the Koran until they were nine or ten

---

142 Ruschenberger, *A Voyage*, vol. 1, p. 87; Heude, *A Voyage*, p. 24; Fraser, *Narrative*, p. 26; Keppel, *A Personal Narrative*, vol. 1, p. 13; Hamerton 1985, p. 242; Maurizi, *History*, pp. 104, 122; Binning, *A Journal*, vol. 1, p. 130; de Rivoyre, *Obock*, p. 75; Dieulafoye, *A Suse*, p. 208; de Rozario, "An Account," vol. 4, p. 238; Birks, *The life*, vol. 2, p. 370 (Arabic is the colloquial in Muscat). Most crafts, of course, were learned through on-the-job training, passing on know-how from one generation to the other. de Rozario, "An Account," vol. 4, p. 238.

143 Stocqueler, *Fifteen Months*, vol. 1, p. 257.

years old. In 1905, American missionaries established a school just outside Bab al-Kabir, where Arabic and English was taught.[144] There were some highly educated people in Muscat, of course, one of the them was Mahmud b. Khamis, the Sultan's interpreter, a Zanzibari, who had been educated at Highgate in Great Britain. The walls of his sitting-room were "hung with coloured prints of ballet-dancers, race-horses, and engravings of Shakespeare's plays. His library consisted of French and English standard works on history, biography, science, and novels of various hands."[145] Another educated Muscati was Hamid b. Mohammad b. Ruzayq, the author of the *History of Imams and Seyyids of Oman* and a member of the Bombay Commission reporting on the secession of Zanzibar.[146]

STREETS

Many visitors of Muscat report that its streets were straight.[147] However, they were no thoroughfares, but rather mere lanes.[148] In fact, according to the American envoy Roberts, "the lanes, or rather slits, between the buildings, are very irregular, encumbered with filth and rubbish."[149] Houses were built so close together that when you stretched both arms sideways you could touch the walls on either side of every street. As a result, no horse, donkey or camel was seen, nor a cart as it would be almost impossible for them to pass through the narrow streets. Also, as Stocqueler found out when he rode on a horse through the maze of streets, that was only possible by "bobbing my head every twenty yards rather than kiss the projecting beams and roofs of houses." As a result, there was not much room for open squares or gardens. The Frenchman Maindron wrote that Muscat's "squares were large as a napkin, and the streets had the width of a hand."[150] Outside the walled city, in the suburbs built of sticks and mats, the streets were crooked and narrow. According to Maindron, they were less than one meter wide.[151] According to Buckingham, "In the town, every one, as far as I observed, even the Imaum himself, went on foot."[152] As a result, the streets and markets were very crowded, filled with "Arabs, Jews,

144 Birks, *The life*, vol. 2, pp. 370, 380, 382; Sadid al-Saltaneh, *Tarikh*, p. 57.

145 Shepherd, *From Bombay*, pp. 49, 61.

146 For the translation of this book, see Badger, *History*.

147 Fontanier, *Voyage*, vol. 1/2, p. 28; Aucher-Eloy, *Rélations*, vol. 2, p. 546; de Rivoyre, *Obock*, p. 67; Maindron, "Mascate," pp. 334, 463; Taylor, *A Voyage*, p. 174 (narrow and winding).

148 Martineau, *The Life*, vol. 2, p. 105 ("more like passages in a rambling house than thoroughfares"); Geary, *Through Asiatic Turkey*, vol. 1, p. 20.

149 Roberts, *Embassy*, p. 354; Abdul Qadir, *Waqai*, p. 27; Aucher-Eloy, *Rélations*, vol. 2, p. 546; Keppel, *A Personal Narrative*, vol. 1, p. 18; Lumsden, *A Journey*, p. 26; Pfeiffer, *A Woman's Journey*, p. 237; Binning, *A Journal*, vol. 1, p. 124; Buckingham, *Travels*, p. 507; Maindron, "Mascate," p. 323 (the width of a desk); Francklin, *Observations,*, p. 35; Stocqueler, *Fifteen Months*, vol. 1, p. 8 ("narrow alleys, nicknamed streets."), 254; Shepherd, *From Bombay*, p. 58 (people jumping out of the way and dogs barking at our heels).

150 Maindron, "Mascate," pp. 334, 462 (hardly 3 meters wide).

151 Keppel, *A Personal Narrative*, vol. 1, p. 18; Lumsden, *A Journey*, p. 26; Buckingham, *Travels*, pp. 507, 519; Pfeiffer, *A Woman's Journey*, p. 236; Geary, *Through Asiatic Turkey*, vol. 1, p. 12; Allemann, "Mascate," p. 80; Fraser, *Narrative*, p. 7; de Rozario, "An Account," vol. 4, p. 234; Helfer, *Travels*, vol. 2, p. 9 (the unveiled Mme Helfer and the veiled wife of the US consul went to the Sultan's palace on donkeys); Maindron, "Mascate," p. 608.

152 Buckingham, *Travels*, p. 519; Palgrave, *Narrative*, vol. 2, p. 371.

Figure 21, Canoes made of a few tree trunks, Allemann

Hindoos, Belooches, Turks, and Africans," although sometimes, as Maindron experienced, they were totally deserted.[153]

Many Bedouin visitors usually wore a dagger, a sword on the left shoulder, an immensely long single-barreled matchlock gun and a round shield on the back. The scabbards and gun often were silver-plated. They left their camels and horses at Matrah and from there came by canoe to Muscat. Despite the presence of such arms, the city was a safe place, day and night. Although people were shooting their guns each night it was only by accident if somebody would be hit. People going out at night had to carry

153   Heude, *A Voyage*, p. 22; Lumsden, *A Journey*, p. 26; Buckingham, *Travels*, p. 519; Taylor, *A Voyage*, p. 167; von Oppenheim, *Vom Mittelmeer*, vol. 2, p. 326; Maindron, "Mascate," pp. 334, 461.

Figure 22, Typical street, Allemann

a lighted lantern.[154] Nevertheless, the Sultan employed some mountain folks from the Hadramaut, who were armed with a matchlock, or a two-handed saber, a leather shield on their back, and pistols and daggers in their belt, who functioned as police. They were placed at several points in the markets and made rounds. By 1905, this task was executed by 12 Africans, who were called *natur* or guard (pl. *nawatir*). They received each three riyals per month. The government collected 7.5 riyal per month from the fish-seller shops to pay these guards. According to Lorimer, each month, on their account, the government collected a tax called *hirasah* from all shopkeepers.[155]

In the 1860s, the city was half-ruined; many streets were impassable because of the rubble, which was never cleared away.[156] Although the main streets were narrow, they were generally even and free from dirt, according to the British consul in 1877. Twenty years later, Bent disagreed as he found the lanes in the markets filthy and smelly. The streets in the bazaar opposite the Banyan quarter were covered with mats as protection against the sun and thus ventilation was not great in the bazaar; also, little light penetrated the by-lanes creating a gloomy atmosphere. Walking during the hot season, even for a short distance, was an unpleasant task. In Matrah, in particular in the Khojah quarter, the alleys were also very dirty and obnoxious smells were common.[157]

After the periodical heavy rains rapid streams formed in the mountains, "which carry with them into the sea, all kind of rubbish."[158] Worse, the mat covered streets were converted into "so many canals by the water running from the mountains and frequently demolished a considerable portion of the city."[159] In December 1823 the Muscat bazaar had to be traversed knee-deep in the mud; people had to wait until the sun had dried the mud before they could walk the streets without getting muddy.[160]

154 Niebuhr, *Reisebeschreibung*, vol. 2, p. 498; Maurizi, *History*, p. 24; Ruschenberger, *A Voyage*, vol. 1, p. 72 (Bedouins); Heude, *A Voyage*, p. 22 ("Unprotected strangers are often plundered by these miserable wretches [African slaves] on the outskirts of the city"); Buckingham, *Travels*, p. 519; Osgood, *Notes*, p. 94 (Baluch soldiers); Palgrave, *Narrative*, vol. 2, p. 368; de Gobineau, *Trois Ans*, vol. 1, p. 115 (Bedouins); Aucher-Eloy, *Rélations*, vol. 2, p. 555 (Baluch soldier); Curzon, *Persia*, vol. 2, p. 442; von Oppenheim, *Vom Mittelmeer*, vol. 2, p. 327 ("all men are armed"); Geary, *Through Asiatic Turkey*, vol. 1, pp. 15-16; Dieulafoye, *A Suse*, p. 205; Taylor, *A Voyage*, p.186; Skinner, *Adventures*, vol. 2, p. 287; Maindron, "Mascate," p. 332, 607.

155 Fontanier, *Voyage*, vol. 1/2, p. 41; Germain, "Quelques mots," p. 346; de Rivoyre, *Obock*, p. 93; Allemann, "Mascate," p. 81; Dieulafoye, *A Suse*, p. 205; Lorimer, *Gazetteer*, vol. 2, 1185, 1189; von Oppenheim, *Vom Mittelmeer*, vol. 2, p. 326 (with drawings of daggers and swords); Maindron, "Mascate," pp. 607-08; Sadid al-Saltaneh, *Tarikh*, pp. 47-48.

156 Germain, "Quelques mots," p. 345, 354.

157 Administration Report 1876-77, p. 105; MacGregor, *Narrative*, vol. 1, p. 6 ("the streets are narrow, but, for the East, are cool and clean"); Bent, "Muscat," p. 172; Allemann, "Mascate," p. 80; de Rozario, "An Account," vol. 4, p. 235.

158 Benjamin, *Eight Years*, p. 179.

159 Roberts, *Embassy*, p. 353.

160 Owen, *Narrative*, vol. 1, p. 336. For a picture of the making of a *barasti* hut, see Peterson, *Historical*, photo 209, see also photo 177 of the *barasti* suburb.

HOUSES

There were three different types of traditional houses in Oman. The usual term is *arish* for the *barasti* huts, but the term *kargin* was also used for this type of dwelling. These were made from local wood and filled in with palm fronds and covered with palm leaves. The other one is called round house, *bayt al-dawwar*. These were made of stones and the roof was made of local wood, palm leaves and grass. The last one is called *bayt al-qufl*. These were strong houses built of large stones, their walls were thick and their floors were closed with a lock (*qufl*).[161]

In 1764, Niebuhr found the houses in Muscat mean and poorly built.[162] In 1786, according to the visiting mission from Kerala, the houses of the Imam and the city's notables were all two-storied and were 45 in number. The mode of construction was simple and traditional. "Wooden planks are laid over the four walls and covered with lime and earth; the second storey is built in a similar way. The houses of the common people and the Indian merchants are roofed over with twigs and date-palm leaves laid close together, both lengthwise and breadth-wise, over beams, and then covered up with earth." The houses of the brokers and the Banyans numbered 97, on which they had to pay taxes. In addition, there were 1,500 to 1,700 houses that belonged to Arabs.[163] It is interesting to note that these dwellings were not built with sandstone in the eighteenth century as they were in the nineteenth century. Lt. Porter observed 'that though all the Rocks about this place are Lime Stone, and that the lime works out of the Rocks itself without the help of fire, there is very little made use of it, and the large houses in the Town are built with Mud instead of Cimman."[164] This description suggests that later new stone houses were built on top of the old ones.

According to Fontanier, in the 1830s, houses in Muscat were large and well constructed, but lugubrious from the outside. Stocqueler counted that there were 300 houses.[165] Of course, he meant the houses of the wealthy, because the majority of the population lived in so-called *barasti* huts, which, as the name indicates, were made of palm fronds. Apart from the Sultan's palace, the *Bayt al-'Alam*, which was a plain three-story building situated adjacent to the bazaar, in a narrow, dark mat-covered street, and "a few other decent looking houses, miserably built of stone, coated with chunam, the larger portion are small, dark, and filthy made of palm branches only, or at best covered with mats, or coated with mud."[166]

The Sultan's palace, a large, plain three-storied house facing the harbor, was the finest of the native houses, but very much inferior to the new residence (built in 1889-90) of the British political agent, situated at the southern extremity of the town, where it could

---

161 Floor, *Dutch-Omani*, p. 250, n. 55.

162 Niebuhr, *Reisebeschreibung*, vol. 2, p. 499.

163 Abdul Qadir, *Waqai*, p. 27.

164 Porter, "The Eastern Coast of Arabia", p. 164. Cimman or chunam is quick-lime or plaster. In the 1670s, there were stone houses in Muscat, see above.

165 Fontanier, *Voyage*, vol. 1/2, p. 28; Stocqueler, *Fifteen Months*, vol. 1, p. 254.

166 Roberts, *Embassy* , p. 353; Ruschenberger, *A Voyage*, vol. 1, p. 67; Stocqueler, *Fifteen Months*, vol. 1, p. 254; Aucher-Eloy, *Rélations* , vol. 2, p. 555; de Rivoyre, *Obock*, p. 62; Lumsden, *A Journey*, p. 26; Allemann, "Mascate," pp. 78, 80 (with a photo of the gate of the Sultan's palace). Maurizi, *History*, p. 22 writes that around 1810, "Seyed Said was busily erecting a handsome palace in the style of European architecture."

Figure 23, Baluchi huts, Allemann

catch all the breeze coming through the gap.[167] The houses of the Sultan's relatives and of wealthy merchants were in fine style and appeared comfortable. The interior, according to Pelgrave, was done according to Persian taste. Some, if not all, were equipped with thick crenellated walls and shooting slits, which were useful in case of an attack by the

167   Bent, "Muscat," pp. 171-72; Fraser, *Narrative*, p. 7; Buckingham, *Travels*, p. 506; Binning, *A Journal*, vol. 1, p. 124; Curzon, *Persia*, vol. 2, p. 441 (from the Sultan's residence flew the red flag); Zwemer, *Arabia*, p. 81 (the British Resident's and the American consul's house are the best); de Gobineau, *Trois Ans*, vol. 1, p. 103 (description); Lorimer, *Gazetteer*, vol. 1, p. 536 (the new British Agency building, constructed in the site of the old one, was re-occupied in July 1890); Taylor, *A Voyage*, p. 187 (for a description of the interior of a house of a notable); Maindron, "Mascate," pp. 475-77. For particulars about these houses, see also Ward, *Travels*, p. 60. For a picture of the *Bayt al-`Alam* and the British Residency, see Peterson, *Historical*, photo 68.

tribes from the interior.[168] This security aspect of the stone houses was also clear from other aspects, both exterior and interior. One entered the house stooping through a low doorway and entered a low, dark basement with mud-floor, without windows. From there via a rickety ladder in a dark corner, one climbed "over a shaky landing, up another short ladder, through a dimly-lighted narrow passage, into a long lofty room, lighted by two windows" facing the sea. This and similar experiences that Shepherd had in the houses that he visited in 1856 "gave the impression of mistrust on part of the owners. Low and small doorways, few, or no windows towards the land, confined approaches to the upper rooms, and ready means of escape, indicate the cautious provision, of persons living under a despotic rule, liable to incursions from surrounding Arabs."[169] These waterfront houses were usually 2 or 3-storied and coated with white cement.[170] Some of these mansions of the wealthy survived until some 50 years ago.[171] Binning remarked "that many of the wooden door-frames of these houses were beautifully carved in very tasteful arabesque pattern."[172]

Two Portuguese religious buildings (a church and a monastery) were still standing, "although much mowed down by time." One was used as the Sultan's palace/office and stables and the other as the customs-house. The former was known as *El Gresa* or *Graisa* or *Gharayzah*, a corruption of the the term *igrezia*, the Portuguese word for church. According to Wellsted, in 1835 one church was in ruins.[173] The customs-house was merely an open square of twenty feet with benches around it. It was open to the sea and was roofed. In particular after mid-day, it was constantly crowded with merchants, clerks, brokers, and pilots, because it was also the Commercial Exchange. Here also the customs officials weighed imported goods. The building proper, dating from 1624 according to an inscription on one of its gates, was used as a warehouse and was small as was the wharf and the customs office. Here all whole-sale transactions were concluded under the supervision of the customs farmer, "who is supposed to see that there may be no monopoly."[174] From the customs house you entered the city through a narrow gate and arrived into a narrower bazaar, where one had to move through a crowd of traders, buyers and passers-by. After some 40 meters one arrived at a stone archway, guarded by soldiers, which led to a cool corridor, "surrounding a square of orange and lime trees, in the centre of which, once

168 Wellsted, *Travels*, vol. 1, p. 13; Buckingham, *Travels*, p. 518; Owen, *Narrative*, vol. 1, p. 337; Pfeiffer, *A Woman's Journey*, p. 236; Osgood, *Notes*, p. 89; Allemann, "Mascate," p. 80; Palgrave, *Narrative*, vol. 2, p. 365; Fontanier, *Voyage*, vol. 1/2, p. 26 (description of the furniture in the Sultan's house). One of these houses was the "Bait Graiza originally built for Ghaliah bint Salim ibn Sultan, niece of Sultan Sa`id ibn Sultan, about 1835, and later on became the Mission Hospital, being converted to a consular residence when M. Paul Ottavi was made the first French Consul." Ward, Travels, p. 68.

169 Shepherd, *From Bombay*, pp. 45-46.

170 Stiffe, "Ancient," p. 609; Geary, *Through Asiatic Turkey*, vol. 1, p. 14; Shepherd, *From Bombay*, p. 43.

171 For a discussion of some of these houses, see Peterson, *Historical*, pp. 16-19.

172 Binning, *A Journal*, vol. 1, p. 124. For a picture, see Peterson, *Historical*, photos 21-22, 126.

173 Niebuhr, *Reisebeschreibung*, vol. 2, p. 499 (one is the residence of the *wali*, the other a warehouse); Maurizi, *History*, p. 22 ("serves as a judiciary"); Osgood, *Notes*, p. 81; de Rozario, "An Account," vol. 4, p. 234; Wellsted, *Travels*, vol. 1, p. 11 (the remaining church was used as the Sultan's palace); de Rivoyre, *Obock*, pp. 62, 66 (for a description of the custom-house), 68; Curzon, *Persia*, vol. 2, p. 440; Helfer, *Travels*, vol. 2, p. 4; von Oppenheim, *Vom Mittelmeer*, vol. 2, p. 325. These Portuguese buildings have now all disappeared, see Peterson, *Historical*, pp. 20-21 and photos 74 and 76.

174 Buckingham, *Travels*, p. 518; Maurizi, *History*, p. 111; de Rozario, "An Account," vol. 4, p. 234; Sadid al-Saltaneh, *Tarikh*, p. 45. For a description of the busy square, see Shepherd, *From Bombay*, p. 50.

Figure 24, Sultan's palace and disembarkation landing, Allemann

played a fountain, the basin being now filled up by the carriage of a brass nine-pounder."
Here one had arrived at the fore-court of the Sultan' palace.[175]

As indicated above, the new houses of the Sultan, his relatives and wealthy Muscatis
were mainly built of sandstone. It is known that the Sultan's house was built around
1810, because Maurizi writes that "when I left, Seyd Said was busily erecting a handsome
palace in the style of European architecture."[176] The wealthy lived in houses constructed
of mud and sandstone, which were covered with gypsum-stucco and had a small central
courtyard. According to de Rozario:

> the mud mixed with fragments of old mortar, gravel and other rubbish,
> makes up a pretty durable fabric; but those built with sandstone and mortar
> are the strongest. The interior is plastered with Gutch, a material that forms
> an exceedingly smooth surface, that improved by time, so as to require no
> washing over. Parts, subject to action of water, are plastered with Sarooj,

---

175 Shepherd, *From Bombay*, pp. 50-52; Sadid al-Saltaneh, *Tarikh*, p. 45.
176 Maurizi, *History*, p. 22.

a material absolutely proof against water. The Sarooj is a combination of
Peroxide of Iron with lime and other matter.[177]

The houses had a few small windows, often with iron bars, were square-shaped and
had no attached compounds. The rooms generally were square around the courtyard.
"The walls are thick and are not easily heated even when the dry hot wind is blowing.
Ventilation in most houses is good, windows and doors, though small, are sufficient in
number to ensure a constant current of air."[178] These houses all had two floors, although
no one lived on ground floor, but the servants or they were used as lumber store or
store-rooms.[179]

> The roofs are flat and surrounded by small walls and are convenient to sleep
> on in summer; they are plastered, thus providing protection against the rain
> and the heat of the sun. Small temporary sheds of date branches are generally
> built on the roofs during the hot weather as protection from dew, which is
> heavy at that time of the year.[180]

When the hot desert wind or *shomal* blew into Muscat, the people sleeping on the
roof were "during the night watered, like plants, with a watering-pot. This may account
for the fact that muscular rheumatism is by no means unknown in Muscat."[181]

Most other houses were mean and one-storied, like in the market, with a flat earthen
roof, which gave the city the appearance of a large burrow.[182] However, in 1821, Fraser
remarked on the dilapidated condition of almost all buildings, due to bad construction.
"The plaster was dropping off the wall of the forts; disclosing the masonry in an equally
bad state; and not a gun was fired without bringing down clouds of dust, and abundance
of the stones and mortar from the embrasures."[183] In 1898, Maindron found the entire
city covered with dust and many buildings in ruins.[184]

In 1786, between the city and its surrounding hills there were some orchards and
2,000 huts made of palm fronds, the dwellings of the common people - washer men,

---

177   de Rozario, "An Account," vol. 4, pp. 235, 238 ("Masons are good and excel in ornamental work"). For a description of the interior of the house of the British agent, see Shepherd, *From Bombay*, pp. 45-47. For *gach* (Persian: plaster) and *saruj* (Persian: mortar), see Floor, *Traditional Crafts*, p. 58.

178   Administration Report 1876-77, p. 104; Lorimer, *Gazetteer*, vol. 2, p. 1182; de Rivoyre, *Obock*, p. 68; Keppel, *A Personal Narrative*, vol. 1, pp. 17-18; Lumsden, *A Journey*, p. 27; Pfeiffer, *A Woman's Journey*, p. 237; Fraser, *Narrative*, 1984, p. 7; Binning, *A Journal*, vol. 1, p. 124; de Rozario, "An Account," vol. 4, p. 235; Geary, *Through Asiatic Turkey*, vol. 1, p. 14; Maindron, "Mascate," pp. 337, 339, 461-62.

179   Geary, *Through Asiatic Turkey*, vol. 1, p. 14; von Oppenheim, *Vom Mittelmeer*, vol. 2, p. 326; de Gobineau, *Trois Ans*, vol. 1, p. 101; de Rozario, "An Account," vol. 4, p. 235.

180   Administration Report 1876-77, p. 104; Geary, *Through Asiatic Turkey*, p. 14; von Oppenheim, *Vom Mittelmeer*, vol. 2, p. 325; Maindron, "Mascate," pp. 623-25 (Banyans slept on cots in the street near the British Agency to enjoy cooler air; the British consul asked the Sultan to have the street cleared. The latter saw no reason to do so).

181   Geary, *Through Asiatic Turkey*, vol. 1, p. 14.

182   Owen, *Narrative*, vol. 1, p. 336; Ruschenberger, *A Voyage*, vol. 1, p. 72; Lumsden, *A Journey*, p. 26; Lorimer, *Gazetteer*, vol. 2, p. 1182; Administration Report 1876-77, p. 114.

183   Fraser, *Narrative*, 1984, p. 7; Binning, *A Journal*, vol. 1, p. 124. The same held for the stone houses in the 1860s, see de Rozario, "An Account," vol. 4, p. 235.

184   Maindron, "Mascate," p. 334

water carriers and Afghans.[185] These suburbs were found in places such as near the pass to the interior by "the Sudoaf Road, and round a noxious muddy pool, numerous miserable mat-hovels are erected, by the native Arabs in this gap, as they are not allowed to build any thing more substantial, for fear they should cover the advance of an enemy."[186] This type of dwelling of so-called *barasti* huts built of palm fronds and matting was the norm for the poor; they were small and were nearly standing on top of each other. They had one advantage over the stone houses, viz. that ventilation was constant, but during hot weather the temperature inside was high and in winter, especially at night when the north-western wind blew it was very cold.[187] In 1824, according to Keppel, what he called mat tents, "are in the form of a Bengal routee, having an enclosure in front, in which the cattle are lodged at night."[188]

People did not have much household furniture and utensils. According to Maurizi:

> the poor repose upon the bare ground, those in better circumstances upon
> straw mats, or upon couches, woven with straw, and supported with four legs,
> like an European bed; the richest merchants and Sceks [sic; Sheikhs] alone
> possess these couches interwoven with cotton, and covered with a Persian
> carpet. They never sleep upon mattrasses or sheets, but lie down in the clothes
> they have used during the day, and which even the chiefs do not change more
> than once or twice a week.[189]

Apart from a mat as bed, the poor used their hands as pillow, while an earthen pot was their only cooking vessel; dried camel dung and date palm branches were their fuel.[190]

EMPLOYMENT

Muscat was a sea port and a trading city, in fact, it "forms an entire bazaar," according to Owen.[191] Indeed, most people were either directly involved with trade or in ancillary activities, while the remainder of the population mostly worked in the service industry (food, transport, construction, domestic). "At most seasons of the year, the poor are happy to engage their services, to anybody who is able to give them employment, but when the season for gathering dates arrives, it is very difficult to procure a servant."[192] Most everyday economic activity was concentrated in the small and confined *suq*. To provide

185   Abdul Qadir, *Waqai*, p. 27.
186   Owen, *Narrative*, vol. 1, pp. 334-35. This muddy pool probably was the nearby swamp mentioned by
       Capt. Taylor, Bombay Records, p. 10 and refers to the Tuyan suburb with its wells.
187   Administration Report 1876-77, p. 104; Geary, *Through Asiatic Turkey*, vol. 1, p. 14; Pfeiffer, *A Woman's
       Journey*, p. 237; Fraser, *Narrative*, 1984, p. 7; de Rozario, "An Account," vol. 4, p. 234.
188   Keppel, *A Personal Narrative*, vol. 1, p. 24.
189   Maurizi, *History*, p. 108.
190   Roberts, *Embassy*, p. 353.
191   Owen, *Narrative*, vol. 1, p. 336.
192   Maurizi, *History*, pp. 100-01.

protection against the ferocious sun's heat, poles were placed in between walls of the streets at a height of some 6-7 meters (18-20 feet), over which layers of mats were placed, which were plastered over with 7-10 cm (3-4 inches) of stiff mud. Every 20-30 meters there was an opening in the roofing to let in light. This created a gloomy or mostly dusky atmosphere, because the streets looked like subterraneous passages. The smell was often heavy, although there was ventilation.[193] Merchants were almost naked sitting in their shops fanning themselves.[194] In front of each house there was a small opening, where people displayed goods for sale.[195] In the narrow filthy lanes there were "stalls of earth raised above the common foot-way" filled with goods.[196] Every handicraft or product was displayed "on platforms, erected in front of the small stone shops, which are only about ten feet square."[197] Thus, many of the narrow lanes, formed an entire *suq*, "by every cast of Indian merchants, who dwell in narrow alleys, partly covered by open mats of palm-leaves, slightly interwoven, to keep out the sun," but not the rain.[198] The *suq* was a place lively with crowds and shops were filled with goods.[199] Palgrave is the only one who makes mention of "The great Keysareeyah, a remarkably well-built and vaulted construction, consisting of several arcades, and containing shops worthy of Bombay or Madras."[200] Normally, the word *Qaysariya* refers to the center of the market, where all the expensive goods were stored and sold. However, given that Palgrave is the only one mentioning this building, one may assume that he misunderstood the word, which most likely is a corruption of the word *gharayzah* (from *igrezia*, the former Portuguese church), which had been used as the customs-house for many years.[201]

The bazaar was very thriving and lively.[202] In 1834, according to Roberts, a few black-smiths, carpenters, coppersmiths, sandal makers, and rope makers were almost the only trades seen. They worked in the streets under open sheds. The blacksmiths used primitive bellows with two skins so arranged that one filled while they blew the other; they had dug two holes, one for fire and other for water, while a stone served as their anvil.[203] A crew member of the ship on which Roberts also sailed reported that the *barasti* huts

---

193 Geary, *Through Asiatic Turkey* (London, 1878), p. 14-15; Lumsden, *A Journey*, p. 26; Ruschenberger, *A Voyage*, vol. 1, p.72; de Rivoyre, *Obock*, p. 68; Allemann, "Mascate," pp. 80-81 (with a photo of a bazaar lane)

194 Griffiths, *Travels*, pp. 394-95.

195 Owen, *Narrative*, vol. 1, p. 337.

196 Ruschenberger, *A Voyage*, vol. 1, p. 72; Curzon, *Persia*, vol. 2, p. 442; Buckingham, *Travels*, p. 518. For a picture, see Peterson, *Historical*, photo 106.

197 Osgood, *Notes*, pp. 89-90.

198 Owen, *Narrative*, vol. 1, p. 336; Birks, *The life*, vol. 2, p. 370 (the bazaars "are almost like mole-burrows underground.") The market probably was known as Chorah Bazaar, which was plundered and set fire to by the departing rebels in March 1895. Administration Report 1894-95, p. 18.

199 Fontanier, *Voyage*, vol. 1/2, p. 40; de Rivoyre, *Obock*, pp. 68-69.

200 Palgrave, *Narrative*, vol. 2, p. 369.

201 Skinner, *Adventures*, vol. 2, p. 287 ("the bazars are good."); Helfer, *Travels*, vol. 2, p. 4 (every luxury was available).

202 Griffiths, *Travels*, p. 395 ("an infinite variety of dried grains, gums, medicines, &c."); Allemann, "Mascate," p. 81; de Rozario, "An Account," vol. 4, p. 238; Geary, *Through Asiatic Turkey*, vol. 1, p. 15. For a lively description, see Osgood, *Notes*, pp. 91-92; Shepherd, *From Bombay*, p. 62; Bombay Records 1856, p. 239. In 1891, Bishop French could not find a decent tailor to make clothes for him. Birks, *The life*, vol. 2, p. 374; Francklin, *Observations*,, p. 35.

203 Roberts, *Embassy*, p. 354; Osgood, *Notes*, pp. 90-91 (the fruit bazaar). The smiths were ordinary, while horse-shoeing was an unknown art. de Rozario, "An Account," vol. 4, p. 238.

were occupied by barbers, weavers, and bracelet-makers.[204] In 1831, Stocqueler reported that in Muscat and environs, the following items were produced: porous jugs and bowls, matting, cotton and silk piece-goods, *halwa*, clarified butter, woolen cloths, small carpets, swords, fire-arms, daggers, spears, and brass cannons.[205] Early in the nineteenth century there were no producers of fire-arms and sabers in Muscat; these were all imported. Likewise, although gunpowder was made locally it was of such bad quality that it only could be used for salutes; for all other purposes gunpowder was imported.[206] Between Sibi and Matrah a cannon foundry was established around 1810 managed by a Persian refugee; when he wanted to show off his newly cast mortars, one of them blew up.[207] In 1835, Wellsted remarked that Persians from Bandar Abbas, Lar, and Menon (sic; Minab), manufactured swords and matchlocks, for which there was a great demand in the interior.[208] In the meat market you could buy roasted meat alternated with onion skewered on a bamboo stick.[209] According to British consul, "The jewellery and gold and silver work of Muscat is mostly done by Cutchees and Sindians, and is very superior."[210] Around 1900, the *suq* in the walled city comprised some 300 shops, including 20 arms dealers; 80 money lenders, 100 sellers of piece-goods and 100 provision merchants.[211]

In addition to the sale of goods in shops, all kinds of goods, like slaves, were also hawked in the streets.[212] All perishable goods not sold by brokers in the morning were auctioned in the evening. "Everything is sold by the mahmudi."[213] Also, there were peripatetic craftsmen who plied their craft in the street, such as Hindu barbers who work in the streets. "After shaving the head, a part of the face, and over the *eyelids*, extracted the hairs from the nose and ears, trimmed the mustaches, and perfumed the beard with sweet-scented Arab oil, they conclude by cutting the finger and toe nails."[214]

The slave-market was near the landing place, where "every evening sales were made towards sunset."[215] Slaves were sold three times a week. They were clean and in as sleek condition,

---

204 Ward, *Travels*, p. 17.

205 Stocqueler, *Fifteen Months*, vol. 1, p. 257.

206 Maurizi, *History*, p. 102. Firing a salute was dangerous, because the recoil of the ancient Portuguese cannon, mounted on moulding wooden carriages, was so irregular that each single one might cost the gunner an arm or a leg . However, Sultan Turki said: "I rather loose all my gunners than my reputation as a gentleman." Dieulafoye, *A Suse*, p. 208; Curzon, *Persia*, vol. 2, p. 440 (ancient iron guns with rusty nozzles. "One of the iron guns had stamped upon it the word Hollandia and a bronze gun bore the blazonry of the royal arms of Portugal."); Geary, *Through Asiatic Turkey*, vol. 1, p. 27 (with more details on old guns found there).

207 Maurizi, *History*, p. 105; the Sultan had also bought some cannon and mortars from Bombay, which the same Persian had trouble operating. These artillery pieces were placed on Omani warships, which Persian bombardiers operated, Idem, pp. 82-83.

208 Wellsted, *Travels*, vol. 1, p. 17.

209 Osgood, *Notes*, p. 90.

210 Administration Report 1876-77, p. 81; de Rozario, "An Account," vol. 4, p. 238.

211 Lorimer, *Gazetteer*, vol. 2, p. 1182. In 1905, according to Sadid al-Saltaneh, *Tarikh*, p. 47, there were 450 shops in the *suq*, of which 15 *halwa* sellers; the *halwa* was sold one two riyals per Muscat *man*. The government took one-third of the rent of the shops from the owners.

212 Roberts, *Embassy* , p. 355; Stiffe, "Ancient," p. 609.

213 Fraser, *Narrative*.

214 Roberts, *Embassy*, p. 355; Osgood, *Notes*, p. 91; Ruschenberger, *A Voyage*, vol. 1, p. 72.

215 Roberts, *Embassy*, p. 354; Aucher-Eloy, *Relations* , vol. 2, p. 555; Lumsden, *A Journey*, p. 26 ("mart for slaves ... and sold by public sale three times a-week.")

Figure 25, A lane in the *suq*, Allemann

(with a cloth girdle round their middle, for their only covering) as their owners or purchasers could have wished. The latter, indeed, in walking between the ranks, seemed extremely particular in handling and feeling the bodies and skins of their intended purchases; extending their inspections to such minute particulars as astonished me. ... A tall lusty Arab was parading a boy of ten or twelve, and crying out his price; vociferating, with an impudence truly professional, his age and stature, his qualities and cast.[216]

This market, according to Roberts, was "a great resort for Arab dandies; decorated with fine sabres and silver-hilted crooked daggers, which are worn in the shawls that encircle their waists; their long beards well perfumed, and their turbans arranged according to the prevailing fashion, they examine females as well as males, with little regard to delicacy, or even to common decency."[217] The slaves themselves hardly paid attention to

---

216 Heude, *A Voyage*, p. 24; see also Johnson, *A Journey*, p. 12.
217 Roberts, *Embassy*, p. 354. On the slave trade, see Bhacker, *Trade and Empire*, pp.130-31.

Figure 26, A sword auctioneer, Fogg

the auction, unless they were taken around and examined. Keppel commented about the behavior of some 20-30 young African girls that "they sat giggling and chatting with the utmost nonchalance."[218] After the abolition of the slave trade in 1845, allegedly there was no longer a slave-market in Muscat. However, according to Palgrave, "the public negro mart has been courteously transferred from Mascat to Matrah."[219]

There was not only a *suq* in the walled city near the Sultan's palace, but outside the wall in the suburb was a *suq* which was very busy in the morning.[220] There was a constant auction going on; "men walk about calling out the last bid for some article they carry for sale, which seems to go on until some offer is made which they will accept."[221] Here certain crafts and trades were concentrated such as the production of *halwa*, which, if we were to believe Fontanier, was the only industry in Muscat. Indeed the production of *halwa* was so ubiquitous that all travelers were struck by the importance of this product. It was a compound of sugar, ghee and the gluten of sesame, according to Geary, while Stiffe opined that it was made chiefly of the gluten of maize; Fontanier wrote that is was made from gum Arabic mixed with sugar. Bent wanted his readers to know that *halwa*

218   Keppel, *A Personal Narrative*, vol. 1, p. 21; Johnson, *A Journey*, p. 12.

219   Binning, *A Journal*, vol. 1, p. 122; Palgrave, *Narrative*, vol. 2, p. 372.

220   Palgrave, *Narrative*, vol. 2, p. 372.

221   Stiffe, "Ancient."

was made by Africans stirring it with their feet. This did not prevent *halwa* from being a much sought after article that was sold in earthenware pots for export.[222]

In the suburbs and the village of Riyam there were weavers who dug a hole for their feet, with their seat a step higher, and used a primitive loom with a palm leaf shelter. The weavers were of Persian descent, and came "from the neighbourhood of Sohar, chiefly being the descendants of the old Persian conquerors and settlers." There they made "the fine check cloth, with red and yellow ends that are used as turbans in Oman." However, more popular was the "Brown cloth made of the brown cotton called here Khodranj, and greatly worn and prized in the country."[223] According to de Rozario, weavers were creditable. "Pugrees and loongees weaved, are peculiar and neat, and much prized by the Arabs of Oman and Zanzibar. ...Women are capable of coarse knitting and sewing, but owing to irregular application and inventive genius the art is stationary."[224] In 1855, Consul Hamerton reported that "the industrial resources are almost nothing: woolen cloths, useful to Arabs only, for tents and cloaks; some cottons of good quality, used only by Arabs; silks, also used by Arabs; leather, but of poor quality; iron, chiefly arms. Oman cannot be said to have an export trade in manufactures; most things now required are imported. Yet in Oman, formerly, there existed considerable manufactories of silks."[225] Other local products included "pottery jars called murtuban, turbans, abas, girdles, cotton, canvas, and gunpowder."[226]

One branch of the service industry was omnipresent, viz. that of beggars, who were everywhere. It was not uncommon to see groups of blind people on streets corners asking for alms.[227] However, in 1875, Geary saw no beggars, which was odd indeed, as other travelers do mention them.[228] However, in 1891, Bishop French noted beggars, among whom were lepers, sitting at all street corners of Muscat.[229]

Of course, given the wealth of fish in the cove and waters of Muscat, many people made a living supplying the fish-market with its produce. Fishermen used various methods to make a good catch. One was where they threw a five meter wide net, with a rope attached for retrieval that was weighed down with stones. Once the net had sunk to a depth of 3-4 meters two fishermen jumped over board and drove the fish into the net, the weights closed the bottom thus, catching the fish within the net's meshes,

---

222 Johnson, *A Journey*, p. 14; Fraser, *Narrative*, p. 8; Fontanier, *Voyage*, vol. 1/2, p. 40; Binning, *A Journal*, vol. 1, p. 128; de Rozario, "An Account," vol. 4, p. 237; Geary, *Through Asiatic Turkey*, vol. 1, p. 15; Stack, *Six Months*, vol. 1, p. 17 (a confection of wheat-starch, sugar and almonds); de Rivoyre, *Obock*, p. 82; Stiffe, "Ancient," p. 612; Bent, "Muscat," p. 172; Curzon, *Persia*, vol. 2, p. 442; Shepherd, *From Bombay*, pp. 62-63; Bhacker, *Trade and Empire*, p.137.

223 Roberts, *Embassy*, p. 354; Ruschenberger, *A Voyage*, vol. 1, p. 77; Administration Report 1876-77, p. 80; Allemann, "Mascate," p. 94; von Oppenheimer, *Vom Mittelmeer*, vol. 2, p. 329. Maurizi, *History*, p. 103, qualifies weaving output when he writes that "the spinning-wheel and the loom are little in use, as the extreme heat renders much clothing necessary, and that usually worn can be imported from India cheaper than it can be manufactured."

224 de Rozario, "An Account," vol. 4, p. 238; see also Bhacker, *Trade and Empire*, pp.133-35.

225 Bombay Records 1856, pp. 238-39, 289.

226 Fraser, *Narrative*, p. 18; Osgood, *Notes*, p. 90; Lorimer, *Gazetteer*, vol. 2, p. 1183 (weavers from Qeshm); Landen, *Oman*, pp. 144-46.

227 Johnson, *A Journey*, p. 11; Roberts, *Embassy*, p. 354; Ruschenberger, *A Voyage*, vol. 1, p. 72; Osgood, *Notes*, p. 93.

228 Geary, *Through Asiatic Turkey*, vol. 1, p. 15.

229 Birks, *The life*, vol. 2, p. 382 (there were some 50 families of lepers who occupied one part of the village of Mateirah).

Figure 27, Water taxi, Allemann

which was then hauled up. During the 1830-50s, the presence of fin-back whales kept sharks out of Muscat bay, so that fishing activity was heavy. At that time, fishermen in Muscat spat on their bait for good luck as was common in the USA. In the evening the fishermen returned.[230]

Although there was a boat yard at Muscat (below the Mirani fort), where vessels were built and repaired, building and repairing ships was Matrah's business. At least in the beginning of the nineteenth century the largest vessels were also caulked at Matrah.[231] It was also at Matrah where the sailors and shipwrights lived, who did all the repairs and caulking.[232] Working on vessels was not the only economic activity going on in Matrah. In fact, most people work in weaving cloth, or making the woolen cloaks so generally worn in Arabia. "Scarcely a hut but contained its spinning-wheel, with a female busily

230 Ruschenberger, *A Voyage*, vol. 1, pp. 68, 355-57; Wellsted, *Travels*, vol. 1, p. 14; Johnson, *A Journey*, p. 15; Fraser, *Narrative*, p. 8; Shepherd, *From Bombay*, p. 55 (the whale was called Muscat Tom). For other methods of fishing, see Osgood, *Notes*, p. 75. On fisheries in the Persian Gulf in general, see Administration Report 1876-77, p. 81 and Administration Report 1880-81, pp. 54-77.

231 Abdul Qadir, *Waqai*, p. 27; Roberts, *Embassy*, p. 358; Owen, Narrative, vol. 1, p. 337; Lorimer, *Gazetteer*, vol. 2, p. 1187; Millburn, *Oriental Commerce*, vol. 1, p. 115; Miles, *The Countries*, p. 412.

232 Fontanier, *Voyage*, vol. 1/2, p. 23. However, boat building suffered a steep decline after 1860. Landen, *Oman*, p. 120

employed before it."[233] Also, Banyans (these must have been Khojahs) baled small dried fish for export. As in Muscat *halwa* was prepared there in large copper pans stirred with sticks by sweating naked Arabs. Others activities in the Matrah bazaar included meat roasting and sword repairs, while there was also an apothecary.[234]

Because Muscat was cut off from the interior by its surrounding hills it depended on Matrah, at over 3 km away by sea, where there was good anchorage for local vessels. "It is here the caravans from the interior concentrate, and where the Arabs chiefly obtain their requirements by exchange for produce.[235] Only from Matrah there was any pass into the interior of the country.[236] Anybody who wanted a cloak of Omani weaving, an Omani made dagger, a carpet of Omani texture and the like had no problem acquiring such items in Matrah. "Every Monday a general rendezvous takes place of the countrymen and villagers from the interior, with fruits and vegetables, sweet potatoes, badinjans [eggplant], melons, gourds, apricots, grapes, peaches, and mangoes, according to the season."[237] Also, there was production of some pottery at Matrah, but commercially it was unimportant.[238] In short, the Matrah bazaar offered a lively and colorful spectacle to the visitor. According to Bartle Frere it was "a thriving labyrinth of fish, meat, cloth, grain and vegetable sellers, shoemakers, cutlers and hardware sellers, and the shops and beads and ornaments."[239] At the other side of town, towards the interior of Oman, lived the "artificers, masons, carpenters, and boat builders."[240]

Given the importance of Matrah for trade, the supply of food and other services to Muscat, there was heavy traffic between the two cities. This inter-city trade was entirely in the hands of the Indian community, which also dominated the pawn business, taking arms, for example, as security.[241] There existed a road or rather footpaths from Muscat via Riyam to Matrah and another to Sidab, but traveling over them was arduous, tortuous and lengthy. Here and there were some houses and traces of forts, but no vegetation. Roberts held that the road was difficult to travel and that there were many villages between Muscat and Matrah. Bent reported that taking the land route could take an entire day. Moreover, the passes were walled, gated and guarded[242] and the intervening hills were so rugged and impassible for laden animals that it was easier to go by water in large canoes.[243]

Therefore, practically all traffic between the two towns was by water.[244] The African and other boatmen ensured transportation between Muscat and Matrah, "passing on

---

233 Wellsted, *Travels*, vol. 1, p. 32.

234 Ruschenberger, *A Voyage*, vol. 1, pp. 76-77.

235 Administration Report 1873-74, p. 78.

236 Stiffe, "Ancient."

237 Palgrave, *Narrative*, vol. 2, p. 363.

238 Administration Report 1873-74, p. 77.

239 Martineau, *The Life*, vol. 2, p. 105.

240 Martineau, *The Life*, vol. 2, p. 106.

241 von Oppenheim, *Vom Mittelmeer*, vol. 2, p. 330; Maurizi, *History*, p. 129.

242 Fontanier, *Voyage*, vol. 1/2, p. 24; Wellsted, *Travels*, vol. 1, p. 32; Roberts, *Embassy*, p. 358; Ruschenberger, *A Voyage*, vol. 1, p. 68; Bent, "Muscat," p. 172; Lorimer. Gazetteer, vol. 2, p. 1180; Maurizi, *History*, pp. 25-26.

243 Stiffe, "Ancient"; Miles, *The Countries*, p. 462; Geary, *Through Asiatic Turkey*, vol. 1, p. 15. For pictures of the difficult mountain path, see Petrson, Historical, photos 165-66.

244 Wellsted, *Travels*, vol. 1, p. 32; Bent, "Muscat," p. 172; Miles, *The Countries*, p. 462.

their way three villages at the mouth of the ravines, Mataira, Riyam, and Kalbuh."[245] They operated "gaily painted canoes, with temporary date-leaf roof, and a mat to sit on."[246] As a result, the harbor of Muscat was always filled with vessels, dhows, and canoes, "propelled by two Arabs, one in the bow and the other in the stern, with a dozen passengers at the bottom." The rowers singing Arabic songs to their passenger during the trip.[247] In the evening many merchants working in Muscat returned to their homes in Matrah or other places.[248] As a port, Matrah had the disadvantage of not being well protected against the wind, so that in case of stormy northern wind (*shomal*) communication by sea with Muscat was discontinued.[249]

As a sign of modern things to come, in 1859 Muscat was connected to Aden via a maritime telegraph cable, thus, connecting it to Bombay, its most important trading partner. Unfortunately, one year later the line was cut by superstitious Arabs. It was only in 1901 that the British connected Muscat via Khasab with the landline between Karachi and Gwadar.[250] This was not the only sign of modernity, for, as of 1864, there was post-office in Muscat (and other Gulf ports), established by the government of India to facilitate contact with its diplomatic representatives in the Persian Gulf. In the 1890s, its postmaster was a "well-educated 'Baboo'-i.e. Bengali."[251] Sultan Faysal (r. 1888-1913) introduced an ice factory, a short-lived novelty, because by the early 1890s it was closed.[252]

DRESS

In 1768, "The dress of the Arab Shaikhs consists of a pair of pyjamas, a shawl or a lungi which covers the head, a coat or cloak (jubbah) and over it a coarse woolen garment." The dress of the Arab soldiers and the common people was a cloth (*lungi*) tied over the head and a *lungi* covering the lower part of the body, with a cloak over it.[253] Some 50 years later, men often were described as being half-naked, only wearing a loincloth and/or headwear.[254] Maurizi, referring to the first two decades of the nineteenth century, stated that "the common dress is a cloak of white linen or fine muslin, with a turban to cover the head; but such expensive article can only be afforded by those in good

---

245   Administration Report 1876-77.

246   Roberts, *Embassy*, p. 358; Sadid al-Saltaneh, *Tarikh*, pp. 57-58, 71 (canoe or *huri*).

247   Ruschenberger, *A Voyage*, vol. 1, p. 68; Keppel, *A Personal Narrative*, vol. 1, p. 32 (the canoes were made from a single tree); Lumsden, *A Journey*, p. 27 (canoes, cut out of a single tree); Palgrave, *Narrative*, vol. 2, p. 363 (a double prowed, hollowed out tree that could be rowed forwards and backwards); Stiffe, "Hot baths," p. 123 (the canoes or *balam*, made out of one tree imported from Malabar, could "be very large, many of them carrying twenty or thirty people comfortably.")

248   Germain, "Quelques mots," p. 346; de Rivoyre, *Obock*, p. 103; Binning, *A Journal*, vol. 1, p. 126 (some slept on board of vessels in the bay); Sadid al-Saltaneh, *Tarikh*, p. 73.

249   Fontanier, *Voyage*, vol. 1/2, p. 24; Aucher-Eloy, *Rélations*, vol. 2, p. 572; Bent, "Muscat," p. 172.

250   Landen, *Oman*, p. 104; Sadid al-Saltaneh, *Tarikh*, p. 145.

251   Lorimer, *Gazetteer*, vol. 1, p. 238; Wilson, *The Persian Gulf*, pp. 264-66; Weeks, *From the Black Sea*, p. 141; the stamps used were British-Indian and the mail was brought and collected by the bi-weekly mail steamer. Allemann, 'Mascate," p. 90.

252   Bent, "Muscat," p. 173.

253   Abdul Qadir, *Waqai*, pp. 27-28. In Oman, the *lungi* worn around the waist is known as *izar*.

254   Fraser, *Narrative*, p. 6; Osgood, *Notes*, p. 93; Roberts, *Embassy*, p. 358; Heude, *A Voyage*, pp. 22 ("half-naked Baluchi"); Shepherd, *From Bombay*, p. 44 ("a crowd of half-clad dirty slaves and natives").

Figure 28, Arab merchant, Dieulafoye

circumstances; the poor here as in the greater part of Arabia, are half naked; and it is a general custom among them to wear a leathern girdle which keeps their rags together; this ligature is so tight that it forms a cicatrice [scar] on the skin of the loins and serves to hold paper, an inkstand, a knife."[255] According to Wellsted, in the mid-1830s, Persians wore a flowing and richly-colored dress; Arabs a coarse cloak of broad alternate stripes, while the Baluchis wore a white garment and had long hair, while Africans wore but a waist cloth. The common people wore a simple white robe, which was buttoned in front. The turbans usually were a woolen or silken fabric; if a man was rich he wore a turban with gold embroidery. Often, an embroidered vest was also worn. The wealthy wore over that a wide camel cloth mantle with sleeves and gold-embroidered hems. They also wore a chiseled silver dagger and for respectability the *neba`* walking-stick.[256] Dieulafoy writes that the native Arabs wore the gandourah of white linen, an embroidered vest, a silken turban or a chintz of gay colors.[257]

Maurizi explicitly states that "The Arabs of this province never cover their heads at any period of the year, excepting only the chiefs, the merchants, and a few of the citizens of Mascat,"[258] however others disagree. Ida Pfeiffer, for example, mentions that "many wear turbans, others a conical cap of black Astrachan, from a foot to one and a half high," while Fraser writes that the negro slaves wore a "scrimp turban."[259] Ruschenberger submitted that "the material of which the turban is made distinguishes the tribes, but none except those of a royal lineage may wear it above a prescribed height."[260] Around 1770, the Imam wore a blue instead of a green turban as in Turkey to indicate that he was a sayyed.[261] Towards the end of the nineteenth century some men also wore a red fez with tassel.[262]

Osgood, referring to the situation in the 1840s submitted that Banyans:

> wore a white calico striped with red, seven or eight feet long, is wound around the waist, passed between the legs and the end secured behind in the folds behind the waist. In cool weather they wear a short of white frock with long sleeves, which is fitted in gathers closely about the neck and the wrists, a high crowned turban and red slippers with pointed turned up toes.[263]

255 Maurizi, *History*, p. 23.
256 Wellsted, *Travels*, vol. 1, p. 28; Roberts, *Embassy*, p. 358; Palgrave, *Narrative*, vol. 2, p. 365; Maindron, "Mascate," pp. 330, 341; Allemann, "Mascate," p. 81; Osgood, *Notes*, p. 94 (Baluchis wore "a waist cloth and over it a long cotton gown with a sash around the waist."); Buckingham, *Travels*, p. 516 ("a shirt and trowsers of fine muslin, slightly girded round the waist, open sandals of worked leather, and a turban of small blue checked cotton, with a silk and cotton border or red and yellow, a manufacture peculiar to the town of Sahar."); Taylor, *A Voyage*, p. 188.
257 Dieulafoye, *A Suse*, p. 206 (a ghandurah is a sleeveless garment resembling a shirt). For a description of the Sultan's dress and that of wealthy notables, see Shepherd, *From Bombay*, pp. 42, 53.
258 Maurizi, *History*, p. 19.
259 Pfeiffer, *A Woman's Journey*, p. 237; Fraser, *Narrative*, p. 6.
260 Ruschenberger, *A Voyage*, vol. 1, p. 136.
261 De Pagès, *Travels*, vol. 2, p. 65.
262 Maindron, "Mascate," p. 335.
263 Osgood, *Notes*, pp. 97-98; Binning, *A Journal*, vol. 1, p. 130; de Rivoyre, *Obock*, p. 64; Maindron, "Mascate," p. 623. The style and color of the turban indicated the merchant's caste. A Bhatia wore a red or maroon turban, a Goswami a saffron colored one, for example. Goswami, *The Call*, p. 92; see also Allen, "The Indian Merchant," p. 48, n. 64.

Contrariwise, Khojas dressed like rich Arabs.[264] The Banyans sitting in the Muscat bazaar wore high red turbans.[265] Parsis wore linen clothes and a tiara of waxed cloth. Jews wore a long robe, had a shaven head and ringlet curls that were hennaed.[266]

Contrary to the men, women did not show much skin, although it happened that African women showed themselves on the roofs naked to the hips or walked in the streets with "bare legs and covered faces."[267] However in 1770, de Pagès observed that no women were seen in the streets or market. The only women he saw were a few African slaves on the block, but these were "wrapped up in large linen cloaks."[268] All women wore half masks made of black cloth or silk," fastened upon springs or wires, which project some distance from the face; a hole is cut in the mask between the forehead and the nose, which allows something more than the eyes to be seen." Women only used them when they would go at some distance from their house.[269] Ruschenberger calls these veils "or rather dominos," which were held in place on the head by a silver chain. However, according to Maurizi, women seldom wore veils, "except the wives of the Sceks."[270] Roberts reported that women dressed in black, blue or dark robe, with trousers of the same or cross-barred silk, Ruschenberger described female dress a sort of silk gauze, generally yellow, made in the form of robe, worn over pantalettes, set close at the ankles, which are ornamented with metal bangles. Their feet in stocking or gay colored pointed slippers, or bare with rings on their toes. On the breast was a jacket with short sleeves.[271] Although women were not often encountered in the streets they usually with interest stared at the European visitor, being "not less amused with our appearance than we were with theirs, many turning round and laughing loudly as we passed them." Stiffe reported seeing suburban women in red and yellow garments, turquoise rings in their ears and noses, look from behind their flimsy doors.[272] In Matrah, all women had their faces uncovered, while their hands were hennaed. Wellsted found them much too free in their behavior. Lumsden reported that when visiting Sidab, he saw women around a large well, "who were very vastly entertained with our appearance, and shouted when we left the place, as if they had seen so many wild beasts."[273] Ruschenberger was even invited into a Baluch hut in Matrah, where the housewife invited him and his party to sit down and clean water brought. The woman in question wore a domino, i.e. a black mantle over her head, a pink silk frock with long loose sleeves over striped pantalettes. Her feet were stained with henna and she wore metal jewelry and rings on her thumbs. After a while she took off her domino, so that he

264 Martineau, *The Life*, vol. 2, p. 105; see also Badger, *History*, vol. 2, p. 163, n. 1.

265 Ruschenberger, *A Voyage*, vol. 1, p. 72.

266 Dieulafoye, *A Suse*, p. 206 (with drawing of an Arab)

267 Allemann, "Mascate," p. 83; Maindron, "Mascate," p. 462; Shepherd, *From Bombay*, pp. 51, 63.

268 De Pagès, *Travels*, vol. 2, pp. 66-67.

269 Pfeiffer, *A Woman's Journey*, p. 237; Fraser, *Narrative*, p. 6; Curzon, *Persia*, vol. 2, p. 443.

270 Maurizi, *History*, p. 24.

271 Roberts, *Embassy*, p. 355; Ruschenberger, *A Voyage*, vol. 1, p. 72; Johnson, *A Journey*, p. 9; Lumsden, *A Journey*, p. 26; Fraser, *Narrative*, pp. 6-7; Keppel, *A Personal Narrative*, vol. 1, p. 18; de Rivoyre, *Obock*, p. 69; von Oppenheimer, *Vom Mittelmeer*, vol. 2, p. 527 (the black masks worn by women were embroidered in various colors); Allemann, "Mascate," pp. 82-84; Dieulafoye, *A Suse*, pp. 206-07 (with drawing); for a photo, see Zwemer, "Notes on Oman," p. 95; Maindron, "Mascate," p. 467.

272 Stiffe, "Ancient"; Maindron, "Mascate," p. 618.

273 Wellsted, *Travels*, vol. 1, pp. 32-33; Lumsden, *A Journey*, p. 27.

Figure 29, Woman and child, Dieulafoye

could see that she wore a ring in her nose.[274] Palgrave goes even so far to say that "severity on what regards maiden virtue or marriage vow is not a distinctive feature of Oman."[275]

It was not only women who stained their limbs with henna. Men did as well. They used henna to dye the soles of their feet, the palms of their hands and and the nails of hands and feet and all of them had mustaches.[276] In addition, men and women applied "a narrow black stripe along the outer edge of one or both eyelashes, with antimony, to give a more pleasing expression, and sparkling effect to the eye."[277] However, old men who hennaed their beards were socially disapproved. They might even be given a pejorative nickname as Maindron observed at the end of the 1890s, when he met Sa`id al-Donyawi or 'the fop' or 'dandy.'[278]

RELIGION

Given the many ethnic groups that lived in Muscat and Matrah it is not surprising that other than Ibadi Moslems, – the main creed adhered to by Omani Arabs, other religious groups inhabited the two cities. In fact, all other religions were allowed to practice their religion and to erect houses of worship in Oman, which was quite exceptional for a Moslem country.[279] In 1862, the Ibadi Arabs together with Africans were estimated to be some 60% of Muscat's population.[280] In theory, the Ibadi Moslems eschewed tobacco, liquor and any kind of ostentation in dress or otherwise. According to Niebuhr and Fontanier, Muscatis did not offer the water pipe and coffee like other Arabs.[281] In 1810, however, coffee was drunk in the presence of Sultan Sa`id, if not by himself as did all his successors.[282] Moreover, by 1862, according to Palgrave, "the market places of Mascat and of the other towns [of Oman] are full of tobacco-shops, and the mouths full of pipes."[283] In 1905, there were two bars (mokhammarah) in Muscat, run by Christians, but where Moslems could drink their choice of liquor without fear for punishment.[284]

However, twice in the nineteenth century this tolerant situation in Muscat came under severe attacks by political movements that adhered to a radical form of Islam. The

274 Ruschenberger, *A Voyage*, vol. 1, p. 77-78; Wellsted, *Travels*, vol. 1, p. 33; Lumsden, *A Journey*, p. 27 ("As we passed a gate, two women unmasked came, having rings in their noses.")
275 Palgrave, *Narrative*, vol. 2, p. 267.
276 Buckingham, *Travels*, p. 516; Osgood, *Notes*, pp. 97-98.
277 Roberts, *Embassy*, p. 355; Johnson, *A Journey*, p. 11; Buckingham, *Travels*, p. 516.
278 Maindron, "Mascate," p. 333.
279 Roberts, *Embassy*, p. 358.
280 Palgrave, *Narrative*, vol. 2, p. 367.
281 Niebuhr, *Reisebeschreibung*, vol. 2, pp. 497, 499; Fontanier, *Voyage*, vol. 1/2, p. 25; Keppel, *A Personal Narrative*, vol. 1, pp. 14, 20. However, Fraser, *Narrative*, p. 20 reported that in 1821, during his audience with the Sultan, who like his vizier wore a plain dress, coffee was served. In the house of the British Jewish agent brandy was offered to European visitors, while the Sultan's interpreter drank wine at home. Shepherd, *From Bombay*, pp. 48, 61.
282 Maurizi, *History*, p. 86; also Ruschenberger, *A Voyage*, vol. 1, pp. 110, 130, 145; Taylor, *A Voyage*, pp. 179, 185; Shepherd, *From Bombay*, p. 54; Martineau, *The Life*, vol. 2, p. 105. Sultan Sa`id and his officers also had a meal with Malcolm and his men. Malcolm, *Sketches*, vol. 1, p. 15
283 Palgrave, *Narrative*, vol. 2, pp. 265, 376; Maindron, "Mascate," p. 467 (woman smoking), 477 (nargileh or water-pipe with a vessel of a coconut); Shepherd, *From Bombay*, pp. 47-48.
284 Sadid al-Saltaneh, *Tarikh*, p. 57.

first such event occured in 1808, when due to the temporary influence of the fanatic Wahabis over the Sultan of Muscat and Oman, "Six Wahabee teachers were in fact at Muskat, compelling the inhabitants by blows to pray in their manner, and forcing the merchants to repair to the mosques."[285] However, in 1809 Sultan Sa`id II (r. 1806-56) was able to oust the Wahabis, although he coninued to be threatened by them and paid an annual tribute.[286] The second time took place between 1868 and 1871, with the establishment of a religious conservative Ibadhi regime under Azzan b. Qays, who, instead of the usual red flag had a white flag flying everywhere, while the use and sale of drugs, alcohol and tobacco was strictly forbidden.[287] A vessel, belonging to a British subject, carrying tobacco was seized at sea and had its cargo of tobacco burnt on the beach of Barkah in June 1869. Also, fanatic religious volunteers (*mutatawwi`a*s) had imprisoned a few British subjects in Sahm, 22 km south of Sohar for having shaved. Moreover, in August 1869 the governor of Muscat asked Lt. Col. Disbrowe, the British political agent, to issue an order to all British subjects in Oman "forbidding them to beat drums or play any kind of musical instruments." Disbrowe was flabbergasted by this request as the practice of music making was one of long standing. He was willing to consider doing so if the governor asked that no music was made after certain hours as this was a reasonable request. However, he protested strongly against asking him to ban all kinds of music and merriment in the homes and temples of British subjects. He absolutely refused to do so and submitted the matter to the government of Bombay. The intolerant atmosphere led to a fall in trade, the threat to life of property of non-Moslems and twice British-Indian traders were ordered to leave Muscat due to disturbances. Merchants, both Asian and European avoided the port and imports were down by more than 50%. Disbrowe even feared that if the intolerant fundamentalist regime would last that trade would plummet and Muscat risked of becoming "a mere fishing village."[288] Fortunately, with the re-establishment of the tolerant Al Bu Sa`id dynasty in February 1871 matters returned to their more relaxed atmosphere. However, become of Sultan's Turki's weak rule the commercial situation of Muscat only slowly recovered due to the continued insecurity in Oman's interior.

Because of their aversion to ostentation, Ibadi mosques were without ornamentation and minarets. In 1764, Muscat had two small and dark mosques, without a minaret.[289] Some 130 years later, Bent characterized the mosques in Muscat as squalid and uninteresting. Moreover, they were difficult to spot as from the street they looked like the courtyard of an ordinary house. In fact, in 1816, Buckingham did not see a single one! Instead of a minaret there was "a 4-feet high bell-shaped cone which is placed above one corner of the enclosing wall."[290] In some villages there was neither mosque nor *musalla* (prayer ground).[291]

---

285 Bombay Records 1856, p. 179.

286 Bombay Records 1856, p. 180, 288 (payment of 20,000 German Crowns as *zakat*).

287 Colomb, *Slave catching*, p. 125

288 Bailey, *Records*, vol. 1, pp. 359-62, 394-97, 428-29 (decrees); Colomb, *Slave catching*, p. 22 (Azzan b. Qays carried on a crusade against silk and tobacco); Goswami, *The Call*, pp. 104-09.

289 Niebuhr, *Reisebeschreibung*, vol. 2, p. 499.

290 Roberts, *Embassy*, p. 358; Buckingham, *Travels*, p. 518; de Gobineau, *Trois Ans*, vol. 1, p. 104; Bent, "Muscat," p. 172. The old mosques were low, without minarets. Lorimer, *Gazetteer*, vol. 2, p. 1182.

291 Palgrave, *Narrative*, vol. 2, p. 377.

There does not seem to have been a public bath and men were often seen bathing in the sea.[292] The Omani Arabs also were very superstitious, feared sorcerers, and wore amulets against a variety of evils.[293] Despite being the capital of Oman, Muscat did not have the right of public celebration or official prayers; only the former capitals of Nizwah, Sohar and Bahilah had that right.[294]

Apart from Ibadi Moslems there were of course various other groups of Moslems. First, given the presence of many Baluchis, who were Sunnis, as well as Arabs from the Persian Gulf area, Bahrain, Arabia and Iraq this form of Islam was rather strongly represented in Muscat. Throughout the year their ranks were reinforced by the passage, long or short, of other Sunnis, such as Afghans, who were on their way to Mecca and returning from there.[295] In 1800, according to Palgrave, Sultan Sa`id II, after having been defeated by the Wahabis, "permitted the erection of mosques of the orthodox fashion in Mascat and elsewhere." It is not clear whether such mosques were ever built in Muscat. However, in 1862, there were three or four mosques in Muscat that had been set aside for Sunni worship.[296] By 1891, Muscat was full of mosques that were fairly well-attended.[297]

Again, apart from Sunnis, there also were Shiites. First, there were the Nizari Isma`ilis or Khojahs as they were known in the Persian Gulf, who mainly lived in Matrah (see above). In addition to the Khojahs, there were Bohras, who were another Ismaili branch. According to Germain, however, the Bohras in Muscat were Twelver Shiites.[298] In addition, Memons are mentioned as living inside the city. These were Thatta Lohannas who had converted to Islam in the early fifteenth century.[299] The Khojahs split due to an internal conflict within the community about the acceptance of the leadership of the Agha Khan. When a minority contested Agha Khan's claim to the communities' assets this resulted in a court case, which the Agha Khan won in November 1866. As a result, the minority split off from the Isma`ili faith, and either became Sunnis or Twelver Shiites. However, most of the woman remained faithful to the Agha Khan.[300] The quarter of the Khojahs in Matrah had its own mosque, or rather an assembly house (jama`at-khaneh), decorated with a dark blue flag with a star or scimitar in white or yellow, while the Arabs flew a plain red flag with a white border, sometimes with a crescent and star or scimitar in white or yellow. After their conversion the assembly house became a Shiite mosque.[301] There

292   Buckingham, *Travels*, p. 518.

293   Maurizi, *History*, pp. 133-34; Germain, "Quelques mots," p. 351; Palgrave, *Narrative*, vol. 2, pp. 267-71. Sultan Turki believed that "his long continued illness was due to sorcery practiced by his Wazir," whom he dismissed. Administration Report 1888-89, p. 23.

294   Palgrave, *Narrative*, vol. 2, p. 263.

295   Osgood, *Notes*, p. 94 (transient Afghans); Palgrave, *Narrative*, vol. 2, pp. 364, 366; Wellsted *Travels*, vol. 1, p. 15.

296   Palgrave, *Narrative*, vol. 2, pp. 41, 265, 366.

297   Birks, *The life*, vol. 2, p. 370.

298   Germain, "Quelques mots," p. 347; Peterson, *Historical*, pp. 55, 81; Idem, "Oman's diverse society," p. 42; Martineau, *The Life*, vol. 2, p. 106 ("they have cast off the supremacy of the Agha Khan"). Bohra from the Gujarati word 'vehru' or 'trade', their chosen livelihood.

299   Administration Report 1899-1900, p. 26. On these groups, see Engineer, *The Muslim communities*; Goswami, *The Call*, pp. 34-37

300   Lorimer, *Gazetteer*, vol. 1, p. 2378; Goswami, *The Call*, p. 94; Sadid al-Saltaneh, *Tarikh*, p. 73; Badger, *History*, vol. 2, p. 163, n. 1.

301   Martineau, *The Life*, vol. 2, p. 106. The Agha Khan claimed ownership of the house of assembly, which resulted in a complicated religious and political conflict as Sultan Azzan b. Qays had confiscated the building and his successor had sold it. Goswami, *The Call*, pp. 94-95.

were two other Twelver Shiite communities in Oman, viz. the Ajam (or Persians) and the Bahrainis (al-Barahinah). Given the long relationship that existed between Persia and Bahrain on the one hand and Oman on the other their presence in Muscat is no surprise. Also, various Bahraini tribal groups were peripatetic and regularly moved from one place to another in the Persian Gulf. In 1905, there were 200 Bahrainis in Muscat. Together, in the 1860s, Sunnis and Shiites may have represented 20% of the population, according to Palgrave.[302] In 1905, there was one Shiite mosque in the walled city of Muscat and five for the Sunnis and Ibadis. In the Muscat suburbs, there was one mosque for the Shiites and two the Baluchis, who followed the Shafi`ite rite. There also was one *takiyeh* a Shiite mourning and prayer hall, which was built by Hajj Mohammad Ali Kebabi, Sadid al-Saltaneh's grandfather with funds from Fath Ali Shah of Persia. Although Sultan Sa`id intially opposed its construction he gave in, because of the great influence the Hajji had locally. As of 1873, Naser al-Din Shah each year sent 200 tumans to organize the Shiite mourning ceremony (*ta`ziyeh*) in Muscat. When in 1909 this subsidy was discontinued Sadid al-Saltaneh financed the mourning ceremony from his own pocket.[303]

The strength of religious feelings of the Moslems was of a varying nature. For example, when in the 1830s a boat capsized and a British naval ship saved 32 passengers of which eight were women, the latter were killed, because Christians had seen them.[304] There is conflicting information about Moslems eating with Christians. According to Fontanier, his host, the French agent, did no eat with him, but sent him food.[305] However, neither Maurizi nor Mignan found the Muscati Moslems to be bigoted, who were quite willing to eat with infidels and in fact, even the Sultan, the Imam or head of the Ibadi Moslems had no compunction drinking coffee or having a meal with Christians.[306] Although they were not supposed to drink alcohol and smoke, when away from Muscat many Moslems did both.[307] By the end of the nineteenth century, Bent observed that the Omanis made and drunk wine from the grapes growing on the Jabal al-Ahdar. Furthermore, the Ibadis freely smoked tobacco. Coffee was also much consumed and no business was done without it. In fact, so important was coffee drinking that the more important the person the bigger the coffeepot, some of which were 0.6 to 0.9 meter high.[308]

In 1835, the very large and economically important group of Banyans had:

> a small temple, are permitted to keep and protect a certain number of cows, to burn the dead, and to follow, in all other respects, the uninterrupted enjoy-ment of their respective religious tenets, without any of that arbitrary distinc-tion of dress which they are compelled to adopt in the cities of Yemen. Here they appear to possess all the privileges of Mussulman subject, with one single

---

302 Palgrave, *Narrative*, vol. 2, p. 367; Sadid al-Saltaneh, *Tarikh*, p. 46.

303 Sadid al-Saltaneh, *Tarikh*, p. 47.

304 Blakeney, *Journal*, p. 202; see also above about the strict and severe religious policy pursued by the movement led by Azzan b. Qays.

305 Fontanier, *Voyage*, vol. 1/2, p. 25.

306 Maurizi, *History*, p. 121; Mignan, *A Winter's Journey*; Taylor, *A Voyage*, p. 168; Allemann, "Mascate," p. 92.

307 Roberts, *Embassy*, p. 358; Sadid al-Saltaneh, *Tarikh*, p. 57.

308 Bent, "Muscat," pp. 171-73.

exception. The relation of a Banian slain by a Mussulman can be compelled to accept a compensation for blood, while with the Arab it is a matter of choice.[309]

There were two Hindu temples in the Banyan quarter in the walled city and two others in the suburbs, one of which was in Zabadiyah.[310] In 1821, there were two public Hindu temples in Muscat devoted to "Calee Devee" (Kali Devi). There also were temples in private houses.[311] In 1858, although according to de Gobineau, the cows owned and venerated by the Banyans walked freely in the streets of Muscat, it would seem that normally they were held in a fenced off area. The cows were not fed fish, of course, as all other animals were in Muscat.[312] Despite their lengthy stay in Muscat, Banyans rarely converted.[313] Because of abhorrence of killing animals, Banyans were sometimes taken advantage. Arab fishermen would bring them a live fish to get money from them, promising to throw the fish back into the sea.[314] In 1862, together with other Indians they allegedly represented some 20% of the population of Muscat.[315]

Although Wellsted reported that Jews, for the first time, came to Muscat in 1835 from Baghdad where they were oppressed by Daud Pasha, this is incorrect. In 1764, Niebuhr reported that Jews were free to live anywhere they wanted, did not have to wear special clothes or to behave in an abject manner towards Moslems, as they had to in, e. g., Persia. According to Rabbi David Beth Hillel, around 1830, there were four Jewish families in Muscat, who had a small synagogue in that year.[316] Muscatis called the Jews Walad Sara, children of Sara. According to Samuel, in 1835 there were at least 12 Jews in Muscat and about 350 in the Batinah coast. In 1857, Hasi Ezekiel was the only Jew in Muscat, apart from the black household whom he has converted to Judaism. He was from Baghdad and had been British agent for 11 years. He had succeeded his father Reuben in this function. Despite this low number of Jews, Muscat had a beautiful synagogue. In its courtyard there was a bath for women, which formerly was used for religious purification.[317]

---

309 Wellsted, *Travels*, vol. 1, pp. 18-20.

310 Peterson, *Historical*, pp. 29, 80-81; Aucher-Eloy, *Rélations* , vol. 2, p. 553 (their crematorium was at Kalbuh); Niebuhr, *Reisebeschreibung*, vol. 2, p. 498; Taylor, *A Voyage*, p. 176-77 ("with sketches of wretchedly drawn houses and ships covering its walls."); Sadid al-Saltaneh, *Tarikh*, p. 57. For a picture of a Hindu temple and the cremation site at Kalbuh, see Peterson, *Historical*, photos 32, 138.

311 Fraser, *Narrative*, p. 7 ("A few of the Jain persuasion occasionally visit this place; as also some individuals of the various religious mendicants of India, as Jogees, Byragees, Synyassees, &c."). For a discussion of the location and role of these two temples and their religous life, see Allen, "The Indian Merchants," pp. 41, n. 23, 48. For the location, burning and/or destruction of Hindu temples, seePeters, *Historical*, pp. 17 n. 47, 29, 39, 47, 74, 80, 100.

312   de Gobineau, *Trois Ans*, vol. 1, p. 113-14; Wellsted, *Travels*, vol. 1, p. 20 (they had a penned area with some 200 cows); Maurizi, *History*, p. 128 ("the environs of Mascat are full of cows pampered with food" at the expense of the Banyans); Osgood, *Notes*, p. 99; Taylor, *A Voyage*, pp. 183-84 (for a description of roofed enclosure where the cows were kept); Helfer, *Travels*, vol. 2, p. 6 (200 cows); Maindron, "Mascate," p. 612. For the religious role of cows, see Goswami, *The Call*, pp. 91-92 and Allen, "The Indian Merchant," p. 48, n. 63.

313 Wellsted, *Travels*, vol. 1, p. 19.

314 Maurizi, *History*, p. 128; see also Taylor, *A Voyage*, p. 184. However, in 1833, Golab, the British Banyan agent supplied a British ship with bullocks and goats. Owen, *Narrative*, vol. 1, p. 337.

315 Palgrave, *Narrative*, vol. 2, p. 367.

316 Wellsted, *Travels*, vol. 1, p. 21-22; Niebuhr, *Reisebeschreibung*, vol. 2, p. 499; Osgood, *Notes*, p. 94; Beth Hillel, *The Travels*, p. 112.

317 Samuel, *Journal*; Beth Hillel, *The Travels*, pp. 111, 113; Benjamin, *Eight Years*, p. 178; Sadid al-Saltaneh, *Tarikh*, p. 143; Peterson, *Historical*, p. 83.

Figure 30, View from Sidab, Allemann

In 1834, there was no Europeans or Christians in Muscat.[318] Their number amounted to two by the mid-1860s, when two Europeans resided in Muscat, viz. the British consul and the agent of British India Steamship Navigation Company. By the end of the nineteenth century this number had doubled, to wit, the British consul and his wife, the American and the French vice-consul.[319] The cove of Sheikh Jabr, between Muscat and Sidab was the site of the Christian cemetery, which was accessible only by boat.[320]

In short, the Omanis were not only very tolerant in religious matters, but the Sultan also protected other religions.[321] According to Maurizi, an Omani "would not bestow a dollar on a Christian to abandon the religion of the gospel."[322] Maurizi further reported that Sultan Sa`id allowed him to buy a Moslem African slave girl, while he further opined that "the prejudices against Christians have so much abated, that at present, the intercourse

318   Ruschenberger, *A Voyage*, vol. 1, p. 70; Maurizi, *History*, p. 23.

319   Germain, "Quelques mots"; Palgrave, *Narrative*, vol. 2, p. 367; Allemann, "Mascate," p. 82; Birks, *The life*, vol. 2, p. 376 (the British consul's wife and three children joined him in 1891).

320   Peterson 2007, p. 81; for a description, see Birks, *The life*, vol. 2, p. 405 (in 1893 there were 36 graves). In 1838, the body of two American sailors were buried in the Takiyah suburb. Taylor, *A Voyage*, p. 174; Murrell, *Cruise*, p. 55; Francklin, *Observations*, p. 38. For a picture, see Peterson, *Historical*, photo 139.

321   Roberts, *Embassy*, p. 358; Niebuhr, *Reisebeschreibung*, vol. 2, p. 498; Germain, "Quelques mots," p. 352; Heude, *A Voyage*, p. 23; Buckingham, *Travels*, pp. 506-07, 519; Taylor, *A Voyage*, p. 176 (no opposition to establishment of a Christian missionary); Helfer, *Travels*, vol. 2, p. 6; Birks, *The life*, vol. 2, p. 371 (Bishop French unhindered preached several times in the bazaar of Muscat in Arabic).

322   Maurizi, *History*, p. 116.

of an European with a native Courtizan would be considered a matter of no consequence at Mascat, while in Turkey it might bring the offenders into great personal danger."[323] Fifty years earlier, Niebuhr made the same observation.[324] In 1851, Khoja Ezekiel, the Jewish British agent in Muscat, to the great surprise of Binning, was shown great respect and called 'Master'; he had never seen this before that "any son of Islam exhibits the least civility to one of his degraded race."[325]

AMUSEMENTS

Ibadi religious precepts urged believers to eschew amusements. In particular, games of chance and theatrical performances were prohibited.[326] Nevertheless, Omani residents, whether Ibadis or those of other persuasions liked to relax and amuse themselves. For example, at an open place on the beach of Muscat, Baluchis were wont to smoke their water pipe.[327] The Tuyan valley was a favorite place where people, including the notables, came in the evening to take a stroll in the cool, shoot the breeze and make music and dance. Stone seats were available to take a rest.[328] Going up the Tuyan valley you saw some gardens and a few comfortable little villas of Banyan merchants, surrounded by gardens, where they retired from the dust and heat of Muscat. The biggest villa was owned by Gawalpjee, a rich Banyan merchant.[329] Going there was made more attractive by the presence of coffee-houses. In 1816, as yet there were no coffee-house in Muscat, but in the 1830s, in the suburbs there were three rudimentary coffee-houses made with bamboo walls and a palm-leaf roof; clients rested on banks to smoke or drink coffee. Behind a stone counter the host was ready to serve. Coffee was drunk in small cups without cream or sugar.[330] Later in the century, there were many coffee-houses outside the city, some leaning against the city walls, with their stone counter covered with coffee boilers and tiny cups.[331] This was allegedly the only form of recreation available to "the higher order of Arabs."[332]

Music was also heard to enliven important events and accompany dances and singing. The basic instruments were a little drum, a guitar with two strings and a bag-pipe. Because, according to Maurizi, "they are fond of singing. ...The nuptial festivity is generally graced

323 Maurizi, *History*, p. 132.

324 Niebuhr, *Reisebeschreibung*, vol. 2, p. 498.

325 Binning, *A Journal*, vol. 1, p. 126.

326 Maurizi, *History*, p. 101.

327 Maurizi, *History*, p. 141-42.

328 Niebuhr, *Reisebeschreibung*, vol. 2, p. 499; Allemann, "Mascate," pp. 86-87; Zwemer, *Arabia*, p. 82; Maindron, "Mascate," pp. 605, 613, 615-16 (description of the impromptu sword dance), 620. For a picture of people enjoying the gardens, see Peterson, *Historical*, photo 11.

329 Bent, "Muscat," p. 174; Allemann, "Mascate," p. 88 (for a description of the interior of the villa); Maindron, "Mascate," p. 464.

330 Buckingham, *Travels*, p. 518; Ruschenberger, *A Voyage*, vol. 1, p. 74; Allemann, "Mascate," p. 87 (with a photo of its interior).

331 Allemann, "Mascate," p. 87.

332 de Rozario, "An Account," vol. 4, p. 238; the gate guards, if they were not sleeping were drinking coffee; they had an enormous coffeepot that allegedly had a capacity of 20 liters. Maindron, "Mascate," pp. 605-06.

Figure 31, A coffee shop, Allemann

with a few drums and bag-pipes."[333] The same happened when ships safely arrived from India, an event that was celebrated with drums and shawms.[334] People also enjoined themselves in the privacy of their homes. After dinner people amused themselves with various games. "Sometimes twelve cups are inverted, and under one is placed a ring, in discovering which consists the art of the game; or they suffer their eyes to be closed by means of a thick bandage, and endeavour to guess who it is that strikes them."[335] In the suburbs, Henshaw saw a juggler with vipers in his hair.[336] According to Palgrave, Oman was "pre-eminently a land of amusement, of diversion, of dance and song, of show and good living."[337]

Matrah had a more liberal reputation than Muscat, perhaps due to the presence of the Sultan in Muscat and of many sailors in Matrah. When Fontanier was in Matrah in 1840, he was the whole night disturbed by the noise of the tam-tam and the cries of the sailors who were enjoying themselves. He commented that the prostitutes, the acrobats, and the tavern keepers preferred to live in Matrah rather than in Muscat.[338] However, in

333   Maurizi, *History*, p. 111.
334   Niebuhr, *Reisebeschreibung*, vol. 2, p. 497.
335   Maurizi, *History*, pp. 107-08.
336   Ward, *Travels*, p. 17.
337   Palgrave, *Narrative*, vol. 2, p. 267.
338   Fontanier, *Voyage*, vol. 1/2, pp. 23-24.

Muscat there were performances by professional dancing (*nautch*) girls. Also, people had house parties where a singer performed, and in the evening, music playing, singing and the noise of dancing was heard from every house, according to Maudroin.[339] Moreover, there were many prostitutes in Muscat, so that city was not as staid as it was reputed to be.[340] According to Niebuhr and some 60 years later Wellsted, there was a separate quarter in Muscat where women offered themselves to those men in desperate need of their services.[341]

Again, there were more public manifestations of amusements. For example, after the annual *Id al-Fitr*, the festivity to celebrate the end of Ramadan, when all the *suqs* were

---

339 Griffiths, *Travels*, p. 395; Maindron, "Mascate," p. 619.
340 Aucher-Eloy, Rélations , vol. 2, p. 547.
341 Niebuhr, *Reisebeschreibung*, vol. 2, p. 498 (*Beiasiten*); Wellsted, *Travels*, vol. 1, pp. 33, 101, 118 also remarked on the great liberty of Omani women.

Figure 32, View of the stables, Dieulafoye

closed, there were fireworks followed by general merriment; soldiers were jousting with swords and people danced.[342] Near Muscat, at Sidab (about 1.5 km south of Muscat), there was a broad tract of land which had been cleared to hold horse races. The beach area at Sidab was, at certain times of the year, very beautiful with the most gorgeous gardens with orange, lemon and pomegranates trees, and rose and jasmine bushes. Lumsden, in 1819, instead of gardens, "only found a little lucerne and some date trees." Here horsemen exercised their horses in the evening.[343] Here the Sultan occasionally organized horse races, where the riders sat on thick padded saddles without stirrups. They carried a four meter long spear in their right hand, "surmounted by two balls of black and white feathers" with which they supported themselves when wheeling around.[344] After the horse race, African slaves started a 'gooma' dance in 10 or more groups of 12-50 men and 2-30 women.

In the first were twelve men in a circle, to whose legs were attached many wooden globes filled with pebbles. They wore the native costume. Two others wore monkey skin waist bands, and head dresses three feet in diameter, made of colored feathers. The singular costume of this doublet was completed, *a tergo* [from behind], by a horse's tail fastened at a small angle with the waist. They balanced within the circle, moving their limbs in lazy gestures for a moment or two, when they dropped upon their hands and knees, and prancing hither and thither like infirm quadrupeds, shook their heads spitefully, and ended by butting them forcibly together, barking like dogs, or bleating like goats during the performance. Meanwhile three masked women were dancing around them, singing wildly and fanning with a diligence becoming Spanish ladies in a fandango. The men kept up a rattling gallop in their outer sphere. The music by which the dance was timed emanated from three huge log drums, whose goat skin heads were beaten with right good will by perspiring negroes squatting like toads beside them.

In another set twelve men, wearing but a waist cloth and wooden balls on their legs, danced with six women to the noise of four drums and a crescent shaped horn.

A third set of fifty men, some carrying swords and others sticks in their hands, ambled round singly in a circle, chanting solemnly like mate-bereaved blackbirds, though not with such graceful sonrouresness. While keeping up their uninterrupted course they dispensed with of musical accompaniments.

---

342 Osgood, *Notes*, pp. 104-05. Palgrave, *Narrative*, vol. 2, p. 378 gave the following description of an Arab dance in the village of Besheyr: Twenty men, "in saffron-stained dresses and long braided hair, each a sword or a buckler in his hand. On entering the K'hawah they divided themselves into two bands of ten and ten, and went through a series of very pretty evolutions, something between a mock combat and a contredanse, beating time on their targets, and animating themselves into wild activity. Nabtee song followed, and then we broke up and returned home."

343 Allemann, "Mascate," p. 94 (The Sultan's open-air stables were at one of the squares in the city); Lumsden, *A Journey*, p. 27; Keppel, *A Personal Narrative*, vol. 1, p. 2126 ("a drunken Persian ... Giaffer, the superintendent of the Imaum's stud"); de Rivoyre, *Obock*, p. 68; Osgood, *Notes*, pp. 104, 106; von Oppenheim, *Vom Mittelmeer*, vol. 2, p. 326 (200 horses); Taylor, *A Voyage*, p. 177 (40-50 horses in an inwalled square partly roofed); Shepherd, *From Bombay*, p. 57 (stables in the form of a square, "three sides of which, have shelving-roofs" with some 200 horses); Maindron, "Mascate," pp. 337-78; Stocqueler, *Fifteen Months*, vol. 1, p. 7.

344 Osgood, *Notes*, p. 106.

In a fourth, a company of twenty men were arranged in a line opposite as many women. Each of the men was provided with two sticks of hard wood, which were repeatedly clashed together, while the happy dancers sang in concert with the din of seven drums. Opposite couples of this set danced forward and back, and then joined hands in a grand swing round.

Other groups were waltzing and dancing fanciful figures, each distinguished by different ear-distracting noise machines, such as single and two headed drums, gourds shells and boxes filled with pebbles, rude harps, wooden whistles, trumpets, cymbals, and notched bamboo canes rubbed upon sticks, while the whole grand symphony was mollified by frequent vociferations from healthy lungs. The zeal and energy of the actors in this amusement were truly amazing. Several women fainted from too violent exercise in so hearted an atmosphere; but they again resumed their toil of pleasure as soon as they were restored by hydropathic treatment, snapping their joints and violent rubbing. The women wore cotton gowns and masks, so that only their eyes, hands and feet were exposed. Such is what they call sport at Muscat.[345]

Similar dances were performed during what was referred to as the so-called *al-hawl hawl* festival, which was a kind of carnival, celebrated once per year. The population of Muscat gathered on the beach to see people dressed up like giraffes, sheep and all kinds of animals. It was a time of general merriment; music was made, drums were beaten, Africans danced and women watched from the terraces of neighboring houses.[346] Normally during festivals people gathered at the "furthest extremity of Tooyan," where they enjoyed themselves greatly. There was also the so-called Devil's dance, which was performed by eunuchs and Sidis of both sexes.

A circle is traced on the ground, and Seedees of both sexes dance around to the music of a drum, and gradually by degrees first one and then another becomes infused as it were by a peculiar spirit of violence, and attracted towards the drum, before which they suddenly fall on their knees, and exhibit a most frantic figure, throwing their heads backward and forward, and contorting their bodies with such violence and into such forms that none but mad men could. At last exhausted and seemingly insensible they fall, when an old woman appears, makes passes with her hands across the face, and restores

345 Osgood, *Notes*, pp. 106-08; see also Aucher-Eloy, *Rélations* , vol. 2, p. 549; Weeks, *From the Black Sea*, pp. 140-41 (was invited to participate in the dance. of which he made a drawing); Keppel, *A Personal Narrative*, vol. 1, p. 24 (dancing and singing in the suburbs). *Goma*, from the Swahili word *ngoma* meaning 'drum' and also 'dance'.

346 Allemann, "Mascate," p. 93 (with a photo). Dr. Mohamed Redha Bhacker was kind enough to send me this explanation of the festival. The "Al hawl hawl" (الحـول حـول) pronounced as in hawk and not hook - is a traditional Omani ceremony celebrated on the first birthday of each child. The event used to start in mid morning with children gathered and the birthday boy or girl dressed in new usually green dishdasha or dress with sweets, pop corn, candy and chocolate distributed and singing and dancing with the accompaniment of drums and at times other musical instruments such as *oud*. Rice and meat used to be cooked in big quantities and distributed to the neighbours at lunch time." See also, for its modern celebration [http://avb.s-oman.net/showthread.php?t=1726247].

Figure 33, Al-hawl hawl festival, Allemann

them to consciousness, to enable them to return to the circle to be similarly affected again and again.[347]

Sword dances were also performed in the streets of Muscat by soldiers or unemployed armed men, who would ask spectators for some money.[348]

With the establishment of the British political agency in Muscat European pastimes were introduced. When in 1886, Jane Dieulafoye arrived in Muscat she was invited at the *Muscat Lawn-tennis club*, which had its court next to the British Agency. Cricket was also played there. Given the limited number of Europeans living in Muscat it must be assumed that the Indian staff of the British Agency also played these games.[349]

347   de Rozario, "An Account," vol. 4, p. 238. This most likely is a dance belonging to the *zar* ceremony, see Adeline Masquelier, "Zar," in Richard C. Martín ed. *Encyclopedia of Islam & the Muslim World*, vol. 1, pp. 746-47.

348   Maindron, "Mascate," pp. 616-17 (for a description). For a picture, see Peterson, *Historical*, photo 206.

349   Dieulafoy, *A Suse*, p. 198.

CRIME AND PUNISHMENT

The administration of Muscat, including the judiciary, was directly superintended by the Sultan. In his absence one of his close confidantes or relatives was charged with this responsibility in their function of *wali*.[350] The Sultan himself, when in town, held court four times per day; at 10 a.m. and 4 p.m. to attend to matters of governance and at 6 p.m. and 9 p.m. to receive visitors.[351] Most European sources are rather quiet about criminal activities and the judiciary. Various European travelers observed and were amazed that people were very honest so that goods were left unguarded.[352] Maurizi's also noted the safety of property in the city, although "the police resembles that of other Oriental cities, in being absolutely despotic, and often directed by superstition and caprice."[353] In the 1830s, according to Ruschenberger, the Sultan spent much time in the divan hearing petitions and administering justice.

> All litigation involving property is decided by four judges. There are no
> lawyers in the place, and the parties only advise and counsel with their
> friends. Theft is not common, but instances of personal quarrel are frequent
> and are often decided on the spot, by an appeal to the khunger [*khanjar*]
> or sword. Murder is a capital offense, unless the relatives o the deceased are
> willing to commute the sentence for money; in which case they usually
> accept of one thousand dollars.[354]

The magistrate or qazi applied the *shari`a* or Islamic law when judging cases brought before him. He sat daily at the gate of the *Graiza*. Commercial conflicts were adjudicated by a committee of merchants, who were guided by mercantile usage or the *salifah*. Capital crimes were tried by the Sultan in person.[355] It also happened in 1848 that the governor of Muscat, Sayyed Thuwayni, did not even bother to consult the court of justice or any form of trial, but sentenced a murderer to death in the presence of the population of Muscat.[356]

Despite the general safety in the city, there was crime nevertheless, although perhaps less than elsewhere.[357] For example, in 1882, a Sindi was robbed in daylight in Matrah by Wahhabis. After pressure by the British political agent, the Sultan forced the Wahhabi chief to pay compensation and he was imprisoned for 10 days.[358] From this incident it is

---

350 Abdul Qadir, *Waqai*, p. 25; Maurizi, *History*, p. 24.

351 de Rozario, "An Account," vol. 4, p. 236.

352 Niebuhr, *Reisebeschreibung*, vol. 2, p. 498; Parsons, *Travels*, p. 207; Buckingham, *Travels*, p. 519.

353 Maurizi, *History*, p. 24. In 1905, there were five Ibadi judges. Sadid al-Saltaneh, *Tarikh*, p. 47.

354 Ruschenberger, *A Voyage*, vol. 1, p. 140.

355 de Rozario, "An Account," vol. 4, p. 238; Stocqueler, *Fifteen Months*, vol. 1, p. 257 (in cases of importance the Sultan presides otherwise a qadi; robbery: mutilation, banishment, prison - murder: death). Properly, speaking the *salifah al-ghows* was the pearl diving court. It was responsible for settling disputes arising out of preparations from the annual diving season and the debts and claims which often followed it. Jerzy Zdanowski, *Slavery and Manumission: British Policy in the Red Sea and the Persian Gulf in the first half of the 20th century.* Reading: Ithaca Press, 2013, pp. 38, 42, 47, 90-91, 94, 104-05; Goswami, *The Call*, p. 86.

356 Bombay Records, p. 226.

357 Maindron, "Mascate," p. 606 (murders were rare, "but if they happened it was always an Afghan who was the culprit.")

358 Administration Report 1882-83, p. 20.

Figure 34, A lion cage, Dieulafoye

clear that the Imam of Muscat was the chief judge, although as Lt. Col. Hamerton, the
British political agent in the 1850s pointed out:

> Nothing like a court house or a court of justice exists in the Imaum's ter-
> ritories. The Koran is the code, and the Shaikhs, assisted by the Kazees and
> Moollas, at once decide all lawsuits, and administer justice, -in criminal cases
> on the instant; and certainly fair justice is generally done. If the Imaum were
> present, or near, anything of importance would be referred to him. In Muskat,
> when cases are tried by the Kazee, the decisions are not so fair,-bribery is
> usual; but an appeal can be made to the Governor, or the Imaum when he
> is present. ... As directed in the Koran,-for murder, death; for theft, the hand
> cut off, or the ears, and sometimes the nose. Torture is not as a general thing
> resorted to; the flogging, when administered, are inflicted with a stick, and
> often the cause of death of the culprit.[359]

This short assessment was borne out by Maurizi's observations about the same subject
some 40 odd years earlier. He submitted that justice in Muscat was summary; civil liti-
gation or criminal prosecutions were infrequent. In fact, he stated that "an advocate or
solicitor would indeed starve at Mascat; the prisons are generally all but empty." ... "I used

---

359 Bombay Records, p. 241; Fontanier, *Voyage*, vol. 1/2, p. 41; Germain, "Quelques mots," p. 353.

sometimes to visit the places of confinement, and never found more than seven prisoners in them ... all punished for disobedience or robbery of their masters."[360] Maurizi further observed that in a case of murder, the rules of *qisas* (*lex talionis*) applied, for the murderer "was delivered up to the relations of the murdered Arab, according to the custom of the Bedu in such cases."[361] According to Bent, writing in the mid-1890s, under Sultan Sa`id crime allegedly was punished in a rather horrible manner. He reported that in those days, after entering the gate of the Sultan's palace, there was an iron cage in which a lion was kept; adjoining this cage was another in which prisoners were put for their first offence. If this offence was repeated the prisoner was lodged in the cage with the lion at the time when his meal was due. Under Sultan Sa`id reign there were also public mutilations on the shore, tying up in sack and drowning them and other horrors. British influence and the death of the lion allegedly changed all that.[362] However, this was a nice story related to amuse visitors. In 1890, Curzon saw that there was still a cage with a lion in the Sultan's palace. "A miserable woman was immured in a similar den upon the other, and was said to have committed a murder. I asked whether this ominous juxtaposition portended the approaching doom of the culprit; but was relieved to hear that murder was no means regarded in Oman as an offence deserving so bloody a retribution."[363] Indeed, justice was practiced in a much milder form, and difficult cases were presided over by the Sultan himself, such as one in which sorcery was the main accusation.[364] Also, the Sultan himself could be summoned to appear in court by any inhabitant of Muscat.[365]

Since 1828, Persian Shiites were allowed to have their civil and criminal cases judged by their own qazi, who sentenced or acquitted them.[366] According to Mme Helfer, Banyans enjoyed equal rights with Moslems, "extending even to revenge for bloodshed," which seems unlikely. However, it seems that Banyans only had some limited judiciary autonomy, at least in cases not involving Moslems. Because, when a Banyan declared bankruptcy he sat in his shop with a candle burning before him. Those Banyans indebted to him came and cursed him, sometimes even beat him, but thereafter he was not further molested and was allowed to start trading again, but the debt obligation remained.[367] Art. 5 of the treaty of 31 May 1839 between Oman and Great Britain, confirmed this practice of non-interference between British subjects, but extended it to differences with subjects of other Christian nations. However, differences between Omani and British subjects were to be heard by the highest Omani court in the presence of the British consul.[368]

---

360 Maurizi, *History*, pp. 112, 114.

361 Maurizi, *History*, p. 113.

362 Bent, "Muscat," p. 173; for a picture of the lion cage, see Dieulafoye, *A Suse*, p. 203.

363 Curzon, *Persia*, vol. 2, p. 442.

364 Palgrave, *Narrative*, vol. 2, pp. 270-71; Roberts, *Embassy*, p. 361.

365 Malcolm, *Sketches*, vol. 1, p. 11.

366 Wellsted, *Travels*, vol. 1, p. 17; Palgrave, *Narrative*, vol. 2, pp. 216, 366; Helfer, *Travels*, vol. 2, p. 6.

367 Wellsted, *Travels*, vol. 1, pp. 19-20; Osgood, *Notes*, pp. 100-01; Helfer, *Travels*, vol. 2, p. 6. For the religious implications, see Goswami, *The Call*, pp. 89-90.

368 MacGregor, *Commercial statistics*, vol. 2, p. 364; a similar treaty was concluded with France on 22 July 1846. For the text of the treaties with Great Britain, France and the USA (21/09/1833), see Bombay Records, pp. 248-71.

WATER SUPPLY

Muscat had a typical Persian Gulf climate, i.e. hot and arid. There was a six-month
'cold' and a very hot season. The not so cold season lasted from October to March and
was characterized by rain and heavy stormy weather accompanied by malarial fevers.[369] In
1834, the temperature fluctuated between 50 degrees Fahrenheit or 10 Celsius (winter)
and 105 degrees Fahrenheit or 40.5 Celsius (summer). Moreover, humidity was very
high in summer and varied between 40 to 60 percent, making it very disagreeable for
the town's residents. Some sailors actually died of heat stroke.[370] If there was no northern
wind it was very hot in Muscat, because the land wind was not cooled by water.[371] Some
called Muscat the hottest place on earth, while the Arabs allegedly called it *al-Jahannam*
or Hell.[372] Therefore, Muscat was considered to be the least desirable post of the Indian
government.[373] In the 1870s, the average annual rainfall was about 150 mm (6 inches),
but sometimes, such as in 1875-76 it was 317 mm (12.5 inches). Rain usually fell in the
middle of July, rarely more than 38 mm (1.5 inches) and in November-February some
100 mm (4 inches) during the monsoon.[374] Sometimes, the rain was torrential such as on
5 June 1890, when in one day 284 mm of rain fell during a cyclone that struck the city
and caused death and destruction. The official number of dead was 727, but Dr. Jayakar
believed that the real number was much higher.[375]

The water supply of Muscat was ensured by a deep well, some 800 meters from the
city up Wadi al-Kabir, which was protected by a square Portuguese fort with machicoulis
called Qal`at al-Rawiyah (irrigation fort).[376] This well was not the only one, because in
the valley of Tuyan, S.W. of town there were 16 wells, hence the name of the valley, which
means 'wells.' They were deep and supplied the city and its neighboring hamlets. The
quantity of water was sufficient both for drinking and domestic purposes. Mostly African
porters brought the water carrying *masuk*s or water skins on their backs or donekys were
used. This water was used for bathing, washing and for the animals. In addition, there were
two or three wells in the city itself; its quality was indifferent and by the 1870s not much
used, but it was the only water source in case of a siege. Rainwater was not preserved
but ran off.[377] For domestic use, groups of women were also seen carrying water jars

---

369   Bailey, *Records*, vol. 4, pp. 231, 244f.; Sadid al-Saltaneh, *Tarikh*, p. 56.

370   Ruschenberger, *A Voyage*, vol. 1, p. 67; see, e.g., Taylor, *A Voyage*, p. 174 (110 degrees); Stocqueler,
      Fifteen Months, vol. 1, p. 254.

371   Roberts, *Embassy*, p. 353; Fraser, *Narrative*, p. 10; Binning, *A Journal*, vol. 1, p. 126.

372   Skinner, *Adventures*, vol. 2, p. 285; Stocqueler, *Fifteen Months*, vol. 1, p. 254; Birks, *The life*, vol. 2, p. 364
      (the climate in summer is an exceptional horror).

373   Bent, "Muscat," p. 172; for a early annual temperature overview of Muscat, see Maurizi, *History*, p. vi
      and de Rozario, "An Account," vol. 4, p. 243.

374   Administration Report 1876-77, p. 99; de Rozario, "An Account," vol. 4, pp. 239-41; Lorimer, *Gazetteer*,
      vol. 2, p. 1186; Niebuhr, *Reisebeschreibung*, vol. 2, p. 499; Osgood, *Notes*, p. 88; Heude, *A Voyage*, pp. 32,
      34; Fraser, *Narrative*, p. 10; Binning, *A Journal*, vol. 1, p. 126; Curzon, *Persia*, vol. 2, p. 442 (3.5 inches of
      rain).

375   Bailey, *Records*, vol. 4, pp. 231, 244f.

376   Lorimer, *Gazetteer*, vol. 2, p. 1181 (machicoulis is a floor opening between the supporting corbels
      of a battlement, through which stones, or other objects, could be dropped on attackers); Buckingham,
      Travels, p. 524; Wellsted, *Travels*, vol. 1, p. 14; de Rozario, "An Account," vol. 4, p. 234; Curzon, *Persia*, vol. 2,
      p. 441; Maindron, "Mascate," p. 609. For a picture, see Peterson, *Historical*, photos 92-94.

377   Administration Report 1876-77, p. 100; Roberts, *Embassy*, p. 360; Allamann, "Mascate," pp. 81-82;
      Sadid al-Saltaneh, *Tarikh*, p. 56. For a map of the location of the wells, see Peterson, *Historical*, photo 10.

Figure 35, Qal`at al-Rawiyah and the wells during a festival, Whigham

on their head, while the wealthy had donkey carry their water vessels.[378] Some distance above Tuyan, the city's washer men did their work in the water pools of Wadi al-Kabir.[379]

Most of the houses in the Baluchi quarter inside the town walls of Matrah were supplied with water from the same well "named Zarrafee" in Jabru, which also supplied that quarter.[380] However, most of the wells were outside the city, "and troops of women and water-carriers thronged the road, with camels and donkeys bringing in produce from without."[381]

One of the reasons why ships called on Muscat was to take in fresh water. Niebuhr, who in 1764 was in Muscat, describes that the water hauled from the well and kept in a water reservoir was conducted to the port through a water pipe, which appeared to date from the Portuguese period.[382] Some 20 years later, this water pipe had been replaced by

378 Allemann, "Mascate," p. 87.
379 Lorimer, *Gazetteer*, vol. 2, 1184.
380 Administration Report 1899-1900, p. 24.
381 Martineau, *The Life*, vol. 2, p. 105.
382 Niebuhr, *Reisebeschreibung*, vol. 2, p. 499.

Figure 36, Wells near Muscat, Dieulafoye

an irrigation canal or *aflaj*, although from the end the canal water was piped through a hose, According to Lt. Potter, "The water, which is dearest article for shipping, from above a mile above the gates is conveyed to the sea side, through a channel made with Chinnams and stones, to a reservoir, from which it is let out by a leather hose into the boat, which may haul close under."[383] However, he is the only one who mentions this contraption. All other sources after him state that the water for ships and most inhabitants of Muscat was hauled up from a deep well outside the walls, by a buffalo. It was then brought in sheep or goatskins, on men's backs, to the landing.[384] Because the road from the well was so stony casks could not be rolled down over it; therefore, water was transported in skins, which were emptied in the boat until it was

383   Potter, "The Eastern Coast, p. 163.
384   Roberts, *Embassy*, p. 360.

nearly full, or deeply laden (which is what seamen call bringing water in bulk); the boat brings off more water in this manner, but it is subject to great a inconvenience, which sometimes occasions the loss of a whole boat of water. At other times it is nearly spoiled, particularly when many ships are watering at the same time; as it happened wit us at present; for not having boats sufficient to bring water to so many ships early in the morning, (when there is little wind) they bring it oftentimes so late, that the sea breeze setting in when the boat is midway between the ship and the shore, the sea washes over the gunwale, and mixes with the fresh water; it is thus either entirely spoiled, or brought on board quite brackish.[385]

Once the water carriers had arrived at the landing they emptied them in casks.[386] In the sailing directions by Horsburgh it is noted that "It is proper to use the ship's casks in watering, otherwise, the natives will bring it off in bulk, sometimes filled into oily boats," in which it started to smell disagreeably, although still very good. Another consideration was that "the men employed on this service, who generally are negro slaves, make no scruple to come from the shore with dirty feet, and to wash them in the boat; they plunge their perspiring bodies also into the water, remain in it to row off to the ship, immersed up to their middle, and even scrub and wash themselves in it, before coming along, so as to leave all the filth and impurities of their skin behind them."[387]

However, in 1835, Wellsted reported that "A newly constructed aqueduct conveys the water to the town."[388] Because this aqueduct was constructed around 1810, it means that the water carriers filled their skins where it ended in the city and from there carried them to the landing place. Throughout the nineteenth century, the water of Muscat continued to be "conducted into town by means of an aqueduct."[389] In time of war, a permanent guard was stationed there to prevent the cutting off of the water supply. According to Wellsted, the water was hard and of an indifferent quality, but Buckingham found it to be "pure, wholesome and agreeable to the taste."[390]

FOOD SUPPLY

Muscat had hardly any vegetation. There was no brushwood in or near Muscat either. Nevertheless, there was no lack of firewood, which, according to Fraser, was even cheaper than in Bombay. It was mainly *babul*, wood of the gum-Arabic tree, which was brought from a distance of some 30 km west of Muscat by land or sea.[391] Herbage and date trees were limited to a few gardens and date trees outside the city, in the Tuyan valley, which

---

385 Parsons, *Travels*, p. 210.

386 Ruschenberger, *A Voyage*, vol. 1, p. 75.

387 Horsburgh 1836, p. 246; Buckingham, *Travels*, p. 524; Milburn, *Oriental Commerce*, vol. 1, p. 117.

388 Wellsted, *Travels*, vol. 1, p. 14. The aqueduct is already mentioned in 1818 by Capt. Taylor, Bombay Records, p. 10. Maurizi, *History*, p. 19 states that "the Sultan has caused a canal to be dug, which conveys it to the beach." This canal or aqueduct was a *falaj*.

389 Administration Report 1876-77, p. 100; Sadid al-Saltaneh, Tarikh, p. 56. For the location and course of the aqueduct, see fig. 11.

390 Lorimer, *Gazetteer*, vol. 2, p. 1181; Buckingham, *Travels*, p. 524; Wellsted, *Travels*, vol. 1, p. 14; Bombay Records, p. 10.

391 Fraser, *Narrative*, p. 8.

were irrigated from wells (*zijrah*) worked by a bullock, who hauled the water from a depth of 10 to 14 meters. In 1764, the rather large plain outside the city had a few gardens with date-palms and other trees. These gardens remained there when this plain was covered with huts. According to Ida Pfeiffer, one of Muscat suburbs (presumably Jabri) had "a little garden with six palms, a fig, and a pomegranate-tree." The other suburb, presumably Tuyan, "had an extensive garden, which, with its date-palms, flowers, vegetables, and plantations, constitutes a true picture of an oasis in the desert."[392] Arabs lived in the Zabadiyah suburb and worked several acres of cultivation; the people were gardeners and grew small quantities of corn, wheat, dates, onions, potatoes, egg plants, parsley and various herbs, according to Osgood. Lorimer only mentioned the cultivation of lucerne, turnips and *jowari* or sorghum, while observing that Banyans were the owners of some of the best gardens in the suburbs. However, all that greenness was covered with an ash-colored dust, according to Maindron.[393] Lucerne was grown for the horses in Muscat, of which the Sultan allegedly had some 1,500 to 2,000, who in addition also fed them dates.[394] The output of these small gardens clearly was not enough to feed the city. In fact, according to Zwemer, they were hardly large enough "to supply a week's food for 100 self-respecting locusts of normal appetite."[395]

The irrigation system used was a waterwheel (*manjur*) with leather bags that automatically, when lifted up, emptied their charge into a cement-coated water tank. According to Fontanier, the circular path around the well was made with an incline, so that the bullock hurried from the sunny part to the shaded part. However, that was not sufficient an incentive, and therefore, a slave saw to it that the bullock continued walking around. These wells had been dug at the expense of private individuals, who had bequeathed them to the community. The Sultan of Oman supplied an oxen and slave for each, who worked from sunrise until sunset; for the use of the water grain had to be paid. However, in 1905, the cost of water was 10 paisas per waterskin.[396]

Although the rocks about Muscat had the most barren appearance, all travelers agreed that very fine beef and mutton, plenty of vegetables and fruits of most kinds were always

392   Niebuhr, *Reisebeschreibung*, vol. 2, p. 499; Fontanier, *Voyage*, vol. 1/2, p. 28; Ruschenberger, *A Voyage*, vol. 1, p. 74; Heude, *A Voyage*, p. 27; Fraser, *Narrative*, p. 8; Pfeiffer, *A Woman's Journey*, p. 237; Shepherd, *From Bombay*, p. 59; Administration Report 1876-77, p. 100; Bent, "Muscat," p. 175; Curzon, *Persia*, vol. 2, p. 441 (the Sultan's garden). For a picture of the wooden superstructure or *turkbah* of a *zajirah* well, see Peterson, *Historical*, photo 144.

393   Osgood, *Notes*, p. 87; Heude, *A Voyage*, p. 32 (melon, pomegranate, grapes); Keppel, *A Personal Narrative*, vol. 1, p. 25 ("we saw a few enclosures, containing date trees, wheat, and a few vegetables"); de Rivoyre, *Obock*, p. 85; Lorimer, *Gazetteer*, vol. 2, pp. 1184-85; de Rozario, "An Account," vol. 4, p. 234 (fresh fodder and "jassamine"); von Oppenheimer, *Vom Mittelmeer*, vol. 2, p. 329; Dieulafoye, *A Suse*, p. 208 (with drawing); Maindron, "Mascate," p. 611.

394   Owen, *Narrative*, vol. 1, p. 338; Osgood, *Notes*, p. 88. Only the Sultan' horses and camels; the only pack-animal was the donkey. Aucher-Eloy, *Relations*, vol. 2, p. 551. The large number of 2,000 horses is not mentioned by other sources. Moreover, to feed that many horses lucerne would require some 1,500 ha of lucerne cultivation, an area that simply was not available in Muscat.

395   Zwemer, *Arabia*, p. 82.

396   Fontanier, *Voyage*, vol. 1/2, p. 28; Ruschenberger, *A Voyage*, vol. 1, p. 74-75; Keppel, *A Personal Narrative*, vol. 1, p. 24; Osgood, *Notes*, p. 87; Sadid al-Saltaneh, *Tarikh*, p. 56; Allemann, "Mascate," pp. 87-88 (for a drawing of the well with bullock); Dieulafoye, *A Suse*, pp. 209-10 (with drawing of a well). For details about the gardens, see Peterson, *Historical*, 99-102, 112; for a photo of the water-wheel, see Zwemer, "Notes on Oman," p. 91; Maindron, "Mascate," pp. 609-10; Ward, *Travels*, p. 55 (as each water-wheel made its own peculiar noise, the owner could tell by a change in the sound that his workers were idling).

Figure 37, Sketch of a water-wheel, Allemann

available there. Muscat had a good well provisioned bazaar; beef, mutton, poultry, and all kinds of fruit were for sale throughout the year as well as vegetables, while the fish bazaar was also well supplied with all kinds of fish.[397] In 1770, apart from fish from the sea, Muscat obtained its provisions from Persia and Sind as well as from the interior of Oman, whence it was transported on donkeys.[398] This situation did not greatly change in the decades thereafter. Throughout the year, apart from imports (including rice from India) dates, fruits and vegetables from the cultivated spots in the interior were abundant and large droves of camels and dromedaries arrived from the interior daily laden with wheat, dates, grapes, etc.[399] There were valleys in the hills which, when irrigated, were quite fertile, which was done with wells, Persian wheels, and *aflaj*. These were situated in the mountain chain at some 16 to 20 km inland, where a large tract called Batna produced fruits, vegetables and dates. Furthermore, there was excellent fish in the coves and many

---

397   Niebuhr, *Reisebeschreibung*, vol. 2, p. 500; Potter, "The Eastern Coast, p. 163; Maurizi, *History*, p. 19; Milburn, *Oriental Commerce*, vol. 1, p. 117; Fraser, *Narrative*, pp. 8-9; Wellsted, *Travels*, vol. 1, p. 14; Owen, *Narrative*, vol. 1, p. 338; Roberts, *Embassy*, p. 359; Blakeney, *Journal*, p. 200; Osgood, *Notes*, p. 84; Binning, *A Journal*, vol. 1, p. 129; de Rivoyre, *Obock*, p. 63; Administration Report 1876-77, p. 100.

398   De Pagès, *Travels*, vol. 2, p. 66.

399   Owen, *Narrative*, vol. 1, p. 338; Roberts, *Embassy*, p. 358; Stiffe, "A visit," p. 125; Idem, "Ancient," p. 609.

flocks and sheep and goats.[400] In particular the mangoes of Oman were well liked, which were better than those in India. Therefore, "these mango stones are an acceptable present to those in India who have large enough gardens to grow them."[401]

Table 8: Prices of provisions in Muscat in 1821

The following prices of certain articles to be had at Muscat, may serve to give an idea of the value of provisions at this port. Everything is sold by the Mahmoodee of 20 to the [Spanish] dollar, and generally the Muscat *maun*, which weighs somewhat more than 9 lbs. English.

Product	Price in *mahmudis*	Product	Price in *mahmudis*
Bread, per man	6.5	Common cow, not milk cow	1.5 to 6 dollars
Butter	40	Milch goat	4 to 6 dollars
Cheese	15	Mangoes, per 100	7 to 8 *mahmudis*
Milk	5	Limes	2
Beef	10	Peaches	4
Goat or sheep mutton	18	Pomegranates without stones	60
Fowls, per dozen	40 to 60	Pomegranates with stones	40
Grapes per *man*, per quality	3 to 12	Plantains, per 100	7
Figs	3.5	Apricots ripen in June	4
Dates, fresh and good	4	Rose apples (in July)	4
Dates indifferent	3	Sweet limes (July&August)	7
Good milch cow from	16 to 17 dollars	Oranges	5 to 6
-		Mulberries, per *man*	4

Source: Fraser, *Narrative*, p. 10, n.; see also Milburn, *Oriental Commerce*, vol. 1, p. 117; Abdul Qadir *Waqai*, p. 29.

Whereas fish was available in great quantity and variety to visiting British ships, to slaughter an animal and bring its meat to the ship required some subterfuge. There was no problem if the animal was in Muscat; it was then simply slaughtered on the beach. However, if the meat for the ships had to come from Matrah this had to be done in a covert manner, "as the compradore (steward) is dependent on the Company's broker, who is a Hindoo, and very desirous of saving the lives of the bullocks, but they have not that

---

400 Binning, *A Journal*, vol. 1, p. 129; Stocqueler, *Fifteen Months*, vol. 1, p. 255; de Rozario, "An Account," vol. 4, p. 233; Bent, "Muscat," p. 171; Palgrave, *Narrative*, vol. 2, p. 376; Administration Report 1876-77, pp. 79-80; Colomb, *Slave catching*, p. 130 ("the valleys, mere clefts in the burnt-up rocks, abound in springs of water... in beds as small as ordinary hot-beds, abundance of melons, grapes, and other fruit, several kinds of table vegetables, barley, some wheat, and a little rice grow.")
401 Parsons, *Travels*, p. 210.

Figure 38, Photo of a water-wheel, Allemann

authority on shore; they manage so as to bring the cattle on board in the night time."[402] In 1775, all provisions were good and cheap in Muscat, according to Parsons:

> Every ship bought sheep and some oxen. The fish are brought on board the ships by men who sit on catamarans, which are three logs of wood, about nine feet long and one wide, fastened together, on which a man sits naked and cross legged; before him is placed a basket with various kinds of fish, which is fastened with a line to the log. The man, with one short paddle, which he dexterously, and with rapidity, applies on both sides alternatively, drives his catamaran along at a quick rate; the water continually washing over and between the logs, so that the fish in the basket, as well as himself, are continually wet.[403]

In short, food was plentiful, cheap and available in great variety. In 1770, the majority of the population lived "chiefly on dates and milk, converted into a very dry substance, with the appearance of little flint stones, which, however, again dissolved, afford a kind of acid, but refreshing liquor."[404] In the early part of the nineteenth century, the poor lived on a diet of dates, fish, and rice in scanty quantities as their food, eating, twice a day. If they were lucky they also could occasionally afford some goat meat kebab.[405] However, although there was plenty of food for sale this did not mean that the poor, who were "all filthy and nearly naked," had enough food to eat, "even of the meanest kind."[406] The situation of the poor may have worsened during the century, because by 1900, the poor lived mainly on bread made from sorgum (jowari), according, to Lorimer.[407] In fact, in the 1890s, if not earlier, the Sultan was in the habit of distributing two meals a day to the indigent poor outside the walls.[408] This food distribution program probably was financed out of a tax on Indian businessmen. For in 1786, it is reported that Indian businessmen in Muscat paid 15 gaz per month; this monthly amount was "distributed among the poor and disabled."[409]

The rich ate wheat-bread, dates, rice and fried fish; dates and fish they ate in abundance and occasionally meat; they were able to easily get all kinds of luxuries such as high quality khalas dates imported from al-Hasa. Fresh limes were common and much used by the natives as sherbet including with their food. They also used much vinegar. In general, the British Agency physician considered their food quite nourishing, including for the laboring class, i.e., the Baluchis and Africans. The latter did all the heavy work, unlike the higher class, which had little exercise and out-door life, "and also to certain habits from

402 Milburn, Oriental Commerce, vol. 1, p. 117.
403 Parsons, Travels, p. 209 (the price of the fish was halfpenny per pound "and is sold not by weight but by tale.")
404 De Pagès, Travels, vol. 2, p. 66.
405 Roberts, Embassy, p. 353; de Rozario, "An Account," vol. 4, p. 239; Johnson, A Journey, p. 11 (fried fish, boiled sweet potatoes, locusts boiled and fried were offered for sale); Keppel, A Personal Narrative, vol. 1, p. 18, 26; Maurizi, History, pp. 100, 135 (they also chewed a piece of "chestnut together with a small piece of a plant called Ashish, or Ascicse, and some slack lime, is wrapped in a leaf, called tambul, about the size of a boy's hand, ad its effects are supposed to be very favorable to the health.")
406 Roberts, Embassy, p. 358.
407 Lorimer, Gazetteer, vol. 2, 1185.
408 Bent, "Muscat," p. 174.
409 Abdul Qadir, Waqai, p. 28. The term gaz, refers to the qaz, short for qazbak, a small copper coin struck in Persia, see Matthee, Floor and Clawson, Monetary History, p. 25.

Figure 39, Garden in Muscat, Dieulafoye

which the working classes are comparatively free."[410] However, whether rich or poor, all of them eagerly sought boiled, salted or fried locusts, because it was believed that this food contained some special virtue.[411]

Not only humans beings, but also animals lived on dates and fish. Cattle were fed with a mixture of dried fish, a little salted, dates, water and a soft kind of earth, which was said to be very fattening. The meat did not taste fishy, while the butter was very good.[412]

410 Abdul Qadir, *Waqai*, p. 28; Owen, *Narrative*, vol. 1, p. 338; Roberts, *Embassy*, p. 353; Maurizi, *History*, p. 99; de Rozario, "An Account," vol. 4, p. 239; Administration Report 1876-77, p. 100; Palgrave, *Narrative*, vol. 2, p. 363 (*khalas* dates).

411 de Rozario, "An Account," vol. 4, p. 239.

412 Potter, "The Eastern Coast, p. 163; Parsons, *Travels*, p. 159 (they grind date stones of which they make oil; the remaining paste is used to feed the cattle); Fraser, *Narrative*, p. 8; Keppel, *A Personal Narrative*, vol. 1, p. 25 ("fed on dates, fish, and the seed of the cotton plant"); Owen, *Narrative*, vol. 1, p. 338; Blakeney, *Journal*, p. 200; de Rivoyre, *Obock*, p. 101 (the Muscat garrison kept goats and rabbits); de Rozario, "An Account," vol. 4, p. 239; Lorimer, *Gazetteer*, vol. 2, 1186 (30 cattle; 200 sheep and goats); Zwemer, *Arabia*, p. 82 (fish was even used as manure); Maindron, "Mascate," p. 611.

SANITATION

Given people's ignorance about hygiene there was no system of public sanitation in Muscat or its neighboring settlements. In fact, every visitor agreed that living conditions were very unhygienic. According to Owen in 1834, Muscat was "the filthiest town in the world" and its people likewise were dirty.[413] However, in 1816, Buckingham reported "the people of Muscat seemed to me to be the cleanest, neatest, best dressed, and most gentlemanly of all the Arabs that I had ever yet seen."[414] All other visitors disagreed with Buckingham. Roberts reported that the streets were "encumbered with filth and rubbish."[415] The air was felt to be unhealthy caused by the large quantity of dead fish lying in the streets.[416] The latter statement seems at odds with Fraser's observations.

> We were informed, that the bazars of Muscat are subject to peculiar regula-
> tions, well calculated to promote health and cleanliness in the town: fish, fruit
> and vegetables, and articles of a like perishable nature, are sold by established
> brokers to the highest bidders, in the morning; and such portions as may be
> left undisposed of in the evening, are carried outside the walls, and sold again
> at another auction for what they may fetch, so that the accumulation of nui-
> sances and filth is prevented.[417]

However, Fraser referred to the practice of whole-sale merchants, while retailers and consumers threw all their garbage into the streets.

In 1877, the British political agent reported that "most streets are clean and free from obnoxious odors, because Arabs in generally are in the habit to clean streets close to their homes both in Muscat and outside. The Baluchis, however, lived in squalid conditions with mounds of dirt around them; their hamlets were all built near large and open grave-yards, "for which they seem to have a particular liking," and as a result the air is putrid and stifling during hot weather.[418] Night soil was another potential health hazard, about which the British Agency physician had the following to say:

> Fortunately the heat dries up the human refuse dumped outside the town
> and did not have a negative effect on people's health. Inside the town use
> was made of cess-pits, the stink of which was excessive and oppressive. They
> are occasionally opened to clean them, in which case common salt and lime
> are thrown into them. In some homes a large quantity of ashes and salt are
> thrown in the pit every or every other morning. Despite this accumula-
> tion of excreta did not have an injurious effect on disease in the town or the
> groundwater, because the ground-floor rooms of most houses are generally

413 Owen, *Narrative*, vol. 1, pp. 336, 338-39; Benjamin, *Eight Years*, p. 197. In 1786, Abdul Qadir, *Waqai*, p. 27, wrote that the inhabitants of Muscat unlike their streets were clean.

414 Buckingham, *Travels*, p. 517.

415 Roberts, *Embassy*, p. 354.

416 Benjamin, *Eight Years*, p. 179.

417 Fraser, *Narrative*, p. 10.

418 Administration Report 1876-77, p. 101; Pfeiffer, *A Woman's Journey*, p. 237; von Oppenheim, *Vom Mittelmeer*, vol. 2, p. 328.

uninhabited and the wells were outside the town. The system of cess-pits did not exist in Matrah; it either dried up in the open or washed away by the sea.[419]

However, twenty years later the British political agent wrote that "Heaps of rubbish and putrefying organic matters" were to be found inside the cities and suburbs of Muscat and Matrah, while Bent opined that Muscat was a most unhealthy place.[420] In particular, the huts of the Baluchis and Jatgals in Matrah, "were mostly in the filthiest localities and themselves most regardless of the commonest rules of personal hygiene." In particular, the situation was bad in the suburbs of Jabru and Tuyan (the Baluchi and Jadgal quarter) and in the city itself, the `Iryaneh quarter.[421] However, it would seem that the inside of the Baluchi huts in Matrah was clean.[422]

DISEASES

Europeans felt that they could not live in Muscat and many crew members died when ships called on the city due the fevers caused by the Muscat climate.[423] In 1817 Capt. Taylor noted that Muscat, because of "the proximity of a swamp, is very unhealthy."[424] All common tropical diseases prevailed such as malaria and other fevers. In 1855, it was reported that yellow fever also occurred, of which several people died, including crew members of British vessels. Gaspar de Rozario, the British Agency apothecary and health official mentioned a special kind of fever that occurred at an ambient temperature between 70 and 85 degrees Fahrenheit and disappeared when the temperature was either below 70 or above 85 degrees; some of its forms could be fatal. However, malaria was the real bane of the residents of Muscat. Common diseases were: Phtisis, which was very common among Khojahs, Abyssinians and Abyssian-Arabs. Bronchitis, colic, catarrh, diarrhea, dyspepsia and hemorrhoids were rather common as were liver diseases. Ophthalmia was very common, in particular among the Baluchis. In 1786, Francklin reported that "you scarcely meet one person out of three who has not visibly suffered from either of the causes abovementioned [small-pox and ophthalmia]." In 1824, Keppel opined that within the walled city of Muscat at least 10% of the people were blind in one eye. Skin diseases were also very common, in particular among the Baluchis, due to lack of personal hygiene. Ulcers were very common among pilgrims and others of the floating population. Chronic forms of muscular rheumatism were very common, but articular rheumatism was almost unknown. Pneumonia only occurred during the cold season.

Uncommon diseases included: dysentery, which was mostly was found among Indian and other pilgrims. Scurvy was mostly seen among pearl divers, who lived most of the

---

419 Administration Report 1876-77, p. 101; see also Geary, *Through Asiatic Turkey*, p. 15. ("The dry-earth system is thoroughly understood; earth and ashes play a great part in keeping Muscat comparatively sweet and wholesome.".

420 Administration Report 1899-1900, p. 23; Bent, "Muscat," p. 174.

421 Administration Report 1899-1900, p. 26-27.

422 Ruschenberger, *A Voyage*, vol. 1, p. 77.

423 Maurizi, *History*, p. 130; Johnson, *A Journey*, p. 9; Wellsted, *Travels*, vol. 1, p. 17-18; Aucher-Eloy, *Rélations*, vol. 2, p. 546; Pfeiffer, *A Woman's Journey*, p. 236; Binning, *A Journal*, vol. 1, p. 126; de Rivoyre, *Obock*, p. 72.

424 Bombay Records, p. 10.

year on dates and dried fish and among Indian pilgrims returning from Mecca. Because local residents ate fruit and used much vinegar in their diet, there was little scurvy and scorbutic diseases. Intestinal worms were quite uncommon, while leprosy occurred among Africans and mixed race cases. Gonorrhea of a mild form was rather common among Africans, but syphilis was very uncommon, mostly among Persians and Indians, who had contracted it in their own country. Interestingly, Dr. Jayakar noted the very uncommon prevalence of organic diseases of the heart and large blood vessels and the rare occurrence of kidney, bladder and brain diseases.

Small-pox, measles, and whooping cough occurred every year from December to April. Occasionally they were epidemics (such as in 1865, 1868, 1871), causing great mortality, in particular among Khojah and Baluchi children. Fortunately, small pox was usually mild, because people had it before and thus, had built up some natural immunity to the disease. However, Bedouins were very vulnerable and it quickly spread among them. In 1855, Dr. Frost, the British Agency medical officer found that vaccination was unknown and that people in the two cities were rather averse to it. De Rozario asserted that vaccination was started for the people of Muscat after nine years of "haranguing and illustration". However, in 1877, Dr. Jayakar reported that the Baluchis practiced inoculation, but he had to conclude that vaccination "has failed due to lack of interest among the population." There was no recollection that plague had occurred in Muscat, but in 1897 there was for the first time plague in Muscat. At Haramil, a small cove accessible only by sea, a small quarantine station was built to screen arriving passengers. In 1872 there was a one-time epidemic of dengue. There was the occasional outbreak of cholera, the worst of which was in July 1821, when it prevailed throughout the Persian Gulf. In Muscat, some 10,000 died; the bodies of the dead were taken out to sea and sunk. In 1865, there was a possible outbreak of cholera. Thereafter cholera sanitary laws were adopted under pressure of the European powers and it was hoped that their application would prevent the recurrence of the disease.[425] The Baluchis, Persians and Africans were disproportionately hit by the cholera epidemic of 1899.[426]

There were few physicians in Muscat and Matrah, and all of them were trained in ancient Islamic-Galenic medicine. Because of the inadequacy of the medical infrastructure and cost considerations, most people relied on folk medicine applying traditional methods transmitted over the generations. These methods included cupping by the barber as well as branding and bathing in cold water to treat cholera, which methods actually led to a higher mortality rate.[427] The British Agency physician who dealt with the outbreak of cholera in 1899, described the following local methods to deal with this epidemic.

Actual cautery, the great Arab panacea, occupies, as may be expected, a
foremost place in the treatment of cholera in the same way as it does now in
the treatment of plague, and the instrument generally used in carrying out this

425 Administration Report 1876-77, pp. 100-09; de Rozario, "An Account," vol. 4, pp. 241-42; Francklin, *Observations*, p. 37; Keppel, *A Personal Narrative*, vol. 1, p. 18; Fraser, *Narrative*, p. 21; Anonymous, "The Cholera", pp. 301-22; *Museum of foreign literature, science and art*, Volume 20, p. 306; Hamerton 1855, p. 242; in 1897 for the first time plague in Muscat. Lorimer, *Gazetteer*, vol. 2, p. 2552; Peterson, *Historical*, p. 35, n. 70
426 Administration Report 1899-1900, p. 31.
427 Administration Report 1899-1900, p. 26.

therapeutic measure is as primitive in its conception as the measure itself. A small sickle, such as gardeners use, is heated in the fire, and with its back two lines, each about two inches in length, are marked out horizontally, one a little above the navel and the other a little below it; a similar line is then marked antero-posteriorly on the top of the head in the middle. It would seem as if the Arabs are practically aware of the beneficial effects of acids in cholera, for soon after the operation of branding, a draught composed of the juice of three of four fresh limes, about two drachms and a half of the power of dried *satar* leaves (*Zataria multiflora*), a pinchful of charcoal ashes and a little water is given to drink; when fresh limes are not procurable, dried limes are pounded with a little water and substituted for them. Following this Arab idea, I found the administration of the juice of fresh limes mixed with a little water and sugar as often as the patient required it, a very agreeable and beneficial remedy for the intense thirst present in the early stage of the disease. The *satar* in the draught acts as an aromatic and carminative, but I fail to see the value of the ashes; in fact I should think that the ashes would partly neutralize the acidity of the juice of limes. This draught is repeated after every evacuation until five or six doses are given. *Sherbet* made with rose-water is given repeatedly and in large quantities to quench thirst, and when at the end of the evacuation stage, great restlessness and sense of burning in the stomach supervene, repeated bathing in cold water, even in the stage of collapse, is resorted to. For suppression of urine the most common remedy is a decoction of the leaves and broken pieces of the stem of *gawzaban* known to the Arabs by the name of *lisan-uththawr* (*Caccinia glauca*) made by boiling about three drachms and a half of the drug in 7 ounces of water, which dose is repeated, if necessary, after two hours. Another common remedy for suppression of urine is a cold poultice made of the fresh bruised leaves and fine branches of the lucerne plant and a little common salt, which is applied over the region of the bladder and kept there for about two hours. Sitting in hot water is also occasionally resorted to for causing the flow of urine, and *arkulkeef* (essence of the male flowers of the date-palm) made by boiling the flowers in water is administered internally in doses of about two ounces and a half, either alone or mixed with water, for relieving the burning sensation in the stomach. During the recent epidemic civet was also employed as a remedy for the suppression of urine, a little of it being applied to the meatus urinarus.[428]

In 1891, there was a small hospital in Matrah which was managed by a Mahratta Brahmin, a surgeon-major of the Indian army and one at Muscat, managed by Dr. Jayakar, according to Birks. It is quite likely that Dr. Jayakar was the same as the Mahratta Brahmin physician mentioned by Birks.[429]

Near Matrah, there was a cascade with several hot baths formed by nature; great quantities of small spotted fish were found in them. The local population believed that a person would die if he would catch one.[430] People probably bathed in these springs as they did elsewhere in Oman as they were believed to be good for skin diseases and "those

428 Administration Report 1899-1900, p. 28.
429 Birks, *The life*, vol. 2, pp. 369, 375, 385.
430 Blakeney, *Journal*, p. 200; Johnson, *A Journey*, p. 11.

who are effected by constitutional complaints, old inveterate sores, &c, &c." People also used the water for culinary purposes.[431]

Vincenzo Maurizio, who claimed to have been Sultan Sa`id's personal physician, had his own private medical practice, which he described as being 'very extensive'.[432] Nevertheless, his treatment was incidental and had no lasting impact on the local medical infrastructure. Modern Western medicine was introduced by the British, after they had established a permanent Agency in Muscat. Gaspar de Rozario, the apothecary attached to this agency since 1863, probably established a so-called civil hospital, meaning public hospital, which in actual fact was but a dispensary. This outpost of modern medical science offered its services to the local population, for both in- and out-patients. Like many others working in Muscat, Dr. Jayakar lived in Matrah, an arrangement that Dr. Cox in 1900 asked to be changed as this was inconvenient, because the dispensary was in Muscat.[433] In 1879, the total number of in-patients treated at the British Agency dispensary was 42, while the number of out-patients was 2,513, with an average daily attendance of 28 patients.[434] In 1899, the British Agency physician was much in demand to deal with the outbreak of the cholera epidemic. The prophylactic measures that the Indian physician recommended were: taking of a dose (m. xx) of dilute sulphuric acid in an ounce of water every morning. He further recommended: "the boiling of all water for domestic purposes, and the addition, if practicable, of a little solution of permanganate of potash to it." Finally, he saw to it that wells were disinfected with permanganate of potash, while a quarantine was imposed.[435] At that time, the Indian community was not affected by the cholera epidemic, because it adopted these proposed prophylactic measures. Moreover, because they lived inside the town of Muscat, they were far away from the greatest centers of infection.[436]

In 1900, the situation as to the medical infrastructure at Muscat was as follows. There was a British Agency dispensary for its employees and British subjects. Many Muscati residents also continued to avail themselves of its services. Furthermore, the Sultan's dispensary was operated by a retired former British Agency hospital assistant, who also was in charge of quarantine arrangements, and finally a plague hospital also managed by a retired former British Agency medical subordinate. The Agency physician had no connection with the other two medical establishments. In 1873, the Agency dispensary was established in a rent-free house in the Moghab quarter, put at the disposition of Lt. Col. Dr. Jayakar. In 1900, Dr. Cox did not consider it to be an adequate building and even

431   Maurizi, *History*, p. 26; Keppel, *A Personal Narrative*, vol. 1, p. 27; Fraser, *Narrative*, p. 25; Stiffe, "A visit," p. 127. For a picture of the village of Bowshar with its sulfur baths, see Peterson, *Historical*, photo 59.

432   Maurizi, *History*, p. xxviii.

433   Saldanha, *The Persian Gulf Précis*, vol. 3, part 1, p. 152; Birks, *The life*, vol. 2, p. 368.

434   Government of India, *Report on the Administration*, pp. cclx-cclxi. For the annual reports concerning the incidence of illness, the number of patients treated and operated, see Administration Report 1898-98, pp. 24-26; Administration Report 1900-1901, pp. 19-22.

435   Administration Report 1899-1900, p. 30-31; Sadid al-Saltaneh, *Tarikh*, p. 46. For the problems as to the formulation and supervision of quarantine rules as well as French interference, see Saldanha, *The Persian Gulf Précis*, vol. 3, part 1, p. 142-43.

436   Administration Report 1899-1900, p. 25.

reconstructing it would not make it fit for a dispensary or hospital.[437] Since 1893, there was a US Presbyterian mission active in Oman. Although, the missionaries distributed medicines, none of them were physicians. It was only in 1904, that the mission established a dispensary in Matrah.[438]

TRADE

After 1749 when Muscat had a new ruling dynasty its commercial situation improved. This was due to a number of factors. First, there was the Dutch and English East Indies Companies' decision to abandon Bandar Abbas, respectively in 1758 and 1763. This decision was based on both political and commercial grounds and the same held for Asian traders based there, who had started to move to Muscat and elsewhere in the Persian Gulf from the mid-1750s. Moreover, both these Companies greatly reduced their trading activities in the Gulf respectively after 1766 and 1773.[439] This vacuum was quickly filled by private merchants of all nationalities, in particular by those based in Muscat. Merchants calling on Muscat did come there, because the Omani market offered very attractive commercial opportunities. According to Parsons in 1775, merchants in Muscat had:

> a large trade with people in the interior, not only Oman but the entire Arabian peninsula. The tribes send large caravans with large quantities of gum, various other drugs, ostrich feathers, hides, sheep and lamb skins, beeswax, honey, live cattle and sheep. In return they send Indian piece-goods, pepper, ginger, rice, tobacco, coffee, and sugar, and other Indian commodities and British products such as cloth, cutlery, toys, and many other goods.[440]

However, it was not these products from the interior of Oman and Arabia that drew merchants to call on Muscat. It was rather, because Muscat was an attractive port of call, i.e. where market information was available about where a merchant might find the best market for his merchandise. Merchants in Muscat supplied the entire Gulf area and some part of the Levant with Batavia sugar and controlled half of the Mokha coffee trade in the same area. Therefore, the second reason, as stated by Abbé Reynal, was that merchants chose Muscat for its location, being an excellent market for the rest of the Gulf. Traders preferred it to Basra, because the voyage was three months shorter. Moreover, they were free from extortion, while customs duties were only 1.5%. Therefore, European country traders went to Muscat,

---

437 Saldanha, *The Persian Gulf Précis*, vol. 3, part 1, p. 151. This was the house of Sayyed Mohammad b. Salem b. Soltan, who had made it into an endowment (*waqf*) for his children. The government had made it available to be used as a dispensary. It had five rooms. In 1905, one was used as examination room, the second as the pharmacy, the third one served as living quarters for the pharmacist, while the remaining two were used as sick wards. The staff consisted of two Indians, one the physician and the other the pharmacist. Sadid al-Saltaneh, *Tarikh*, p. 57; see also Ward, *Travels*, p. 68 (the Bait Graiza); see also above note 168.

438 This dispensary probably was located in the house formerly occupied by Dr. Jayakar, see Peterson, *Historical*, p. 19, n. 53.

439 Floor, *The Rise of the Gulf Arabs*, pp. 72-74; Barendse, *Arabian Seas*, vol. 1, p. 273.

440 Parsons, *Travels*, p. 207.

Figure 40, One of Muscat's city gates, Allemann

because they did not have to pay 5% customs as in Basra. From Muscat, Arab and other native traders carried goods to Basra where 3% was collected. This was no major problem, because these native traders had relatively little overhead and many methods to evade paying duties. Moreover, traders from large European and Asian companies could only sell for prices fixed by their principals.[441]

Of course, the authorities in Basra were aware of this and consequently adjusted their customs rates to make Muscat less attractive as a port. In turn, Sultan Ahmad of Muscat would adjust his rates.[442] Merchants likewise were aware of these changing terms of trade. Their decision to call on Muscat and sell their goods there was tempered by profit considerations. In 1756, the Dutch formulated this as follows: "If the merchants, who are very well informed about the prices of goods in the Gulf, see a good profit they also buy all sorts of other goods and carry these into the Gulf up to Bassora. However, they will buy none other than those with which they see a chance to make a profit of 25 per cent."[443]

441   Amin, *British Interests*, p. 139; Raynal. *A philosophical*, vol. 2, Bk III, p. 78; Mohibbul Hasan, *History*, p. 346; Floor, *The Rise of the Gulf Arabs*, p. 37 ("Mascatte ... is very well situated for the sale of goods."); Barendse, *Arabian Seas*, vol. 1, p. 326 ("as they are not tied to a set price, so they can vend their goods more cheaply.")

442   Risso, *Oman & Muscat*, p. 83. In 1756, Sultan Ahmad asked the Dutch to pay 3% duties, but finally they did not pay any duties at all. Floor 2014, p. 149

443   Floor, *The Rise of the Gulf Arabs*, p. 37.

An additional consideration was security; from Muscat to Basra ships went in convoys because the attacks by Mir Muhanna, the chief of Bandar-e Rig, the Banu Ka`b of Mohammarah and by the Qavasem of Ras al-Khaimah.[444] Despite these drawbacks trade between Basra and Muscat was thriving. In fact, one might argue that because Muscat organized escorted convoys between Yemen and Muscat and then onwards to Basra, just like the Portuguese had done in the early seventeenth century, this boosted and reinforced Muscat's commercial position. Having the strongest fleet in the Persian Gulf further sustained Muscat's preponderant commercial role. Muscat's naval role even included providing naval protection for the Basra area until the late 1820s, paid for by the Ottoman government.[445]

A third reason was the main export of Muscat/Oman, viz. dates. If merchants decided to go to Basra, which was a major exporter of dates, they were certain of a profitable return cargo. This was because the excellent dates of Basra tended to spoil in large slow ships, but in the small fast native vessels they were quickly transported to Malabar and the Red Sea.[446] As a result in 1754, the Dutch commented that Muscat was flourishing quite well.[447]

A fourth reason was Sultan Sa`id active role as a merchant and shipping magnate as well as a promotor of trade.[448] Being a merchant he needed a sufficient number of ships to transport his merchandise and to protect shipping in the Persian Gulf and the Arabian Sea. Therefore, instead of relying on locally built traditional ships he had modern European-type, square-rigged ships built in India. Sultan Sa`id and later his son Sultan Hamad tried to buy ships from the EIC and VOC directly, but these requests were rebuffed. In particular Hamad pursued a policy aimed at ensuring Muscat's dominance of trade in the Persian Gulf. To that end he needed a viable navy to control the entry to the straits of Hormuz as well as the carrying trade of the Gulf. As a result, by 1800 Muscat had a home fleet of some 18 modern European ships and some 250 dhows, many of which were large. The considerable shipping capacity brought trade and security to Muscat, while its ships sailed as far as Indonesia and E. Africa.[449]

Muscati trade policy (low rates, friendly reception, water and food supply) under Sultans Sa`id and Hamad aimed at and succeeded in attracting traders. In consequence, "all came there, because Muscat is a place of very great trade, being possessed of a large number of ships, which trade to Surat, Bombay, Goa, along the whole coast of Malabar and to Mocha and Jedda in the Red Sea. It is the great magazine for goods brought from those parts. All ships from Persia, Basra and other Gulf ports, Mekran as far as the Indus come hither." In fact, trade was so good that in the 1770s goods were piling up in the streets of Muscat, because there were "not warehouses to contain half of them ...Yet there never happens an instance that such goods are robbed or pilfered in the least part."[450] This

---

444 Floor, *The Rise of the Gulf Arabs*, pp. 150-55, 163-66; Idem, *Dutch-Omani*, pp. 255-56; Parsons, *Travels*, p. 208; Abdul Qadir, *Waqai*, p. 35; Bombay Records, pp. 171-72, 175, 180.

445 Parsons, *Travels*, pp. 153, 194; Niebuhr, *Beschreibung*, p. 306.

446 Raynal, *A philosophical*, vol. 2, Bk III, p. 78.

447 VOC 2863, f. 18 (18/09/1754)

448 Niebuhr, *Beschreibung* p. 306.

449 Bombay Records, pp. 282-83 (1834), 631-32; Allen, "The State of Muscat," pp. 117-18; Abdul Qadir, *Waqai*, p. 28.

450 Parsons, *Travels*, p. 207; Niebuhr, *Reisebeschreibung*, vol. 2, p. 498.

Figure 41, The small port of Muscat, Allemann

storing of goods in the open air was partly due to lack of storage capacity and partly due to the rising volume of trade that Muscat handled. Around 1790, two long-time Basra-based British merchants (Manesty and Harford Jones) estimated that more than 50% of the Persian Gulf's long-distance trade passed through Muscat.[451] Most of those goods were destined for Basra and Bushehr and to a lesser extent to ports on the Arabian coast (Bahrain, Kuwait, Zubayra). As a result, "the people of Muscat accumulated unimaginable wealth at the end of the [eighteenth] century."[452]

Raynal's list of Muscat imports and exports in the 1770s does not seem to totally reflect reality. He lists as imports "rice, blue linens, iron, lead, sugar, spices," and as exports: "myrrh, incense, gum-arabic, some silver."[453] Although such goods undoubtedly were traded in Muscat, it is very odd that fish and especially dates are not listed at all, which, until recent times, were Muscat's main export commodities. According to the Dutch, in 1756 the commercial situation of Muscat was as follows:

> The native vessels from this Gulf bring here tammer [sic; *thamr* or dates],
> wheat, liquorice, rosewater, raisins, almonds, tobacco and similar coarse goods,
> which are brought by native vessels from the opposite coast and [from]
> Mallabaar, to wit Kitscheri,[454] rice, coconuts, kapok-wool, bamboos, etc.
> The main trade of Mascatte is the sale of these goods. Into the country itself,

---

451   Saldanha, *The Persian Gulf Précis*, vol. 1, pp. 404-16; Amin, *British Interests*, pp. 139-40.

452   Bhacker, *Trade and Empire*, p. 27.

453   Raynal, *A philosophical*, vol. 2, Bk III, p. 78.

454   Kedgeree or Kitchery, a sort of rice and pulse mixed together.

which is inhabited by Bedouins or Arabs who live under tents almost no
other goods are carried than the necessities of life, apart from a little lead, tin,
iron and coarse, rough brown blue linen such as that from Devil.[455]

The Imam of Mascatte still possesses the fortress on Bombassa [sic; Mombassa]
on the African coast, which they conquered from the Portuguese in the past
to which each year his ships carry tammer, wheat and coarse textiles and in
return again with coconuts, hair,[456] elephant teeth, slaves and amber.[457]

The VOC also decided to test the Muscat market. When in 1755, Jacob Schoonderwoerd,
the chief of the VOC Bandar Abbas factory returned to Batavia, he suggested to the governor-general of the VOC to start trading with Muscat, because he believed that profitable
business might be done there. He noted that merchants would have to be granted a short
period of credit, which at the same time would have an inflationary effect on prices. The
best time for trading in Muscat, Schoonderwoerd believed, would be at the beginning of
October when the so-called Mokha monsoon began. Muscati traders and vessels were
deeply and increasingly involved in the Mokha coffee trade.[458] At that time coffee could
be purchased at six *stuivers* or slightly more per lb.; high quality aloe from Socotra and
other kinds of gums were also procurable. Finally, the cash situation in Muscat was most
favorable then, and as the Dutch had orders to sell for cash this was an important factor.[459]
As a result, the VOC sent two ships in 1756 and 1757. Although, indeed good profits
were made, the chief of the VOC factory on Khark complained that sales in Muscat hurt
his sales. This was due to the fact that the Persian Gulf constituted one market, where all
ports competed with one another. If considerable sales of a particular commodity took
place in one port this had consequences for the price of that same commodity in other
ports. It could even happen that other sellers of the same commodity would have to sell
at a loss.[460] Captain Rood, who made the last VOC voyage to Muscat, did not agree with
the decision to stop trading with Muscat. He pointed out that much rice had always
been carried from Bengal and Malabar to Muscat. In 1757, five small private English
grabs had come from Malabar with rice, pepper, sandalwood and cardamom. They had
bartered these goods for dry and wet dates and other items. Because the trade carried on
by British country traders was not as important as before Rood proposed that one ship
from Batavia (carrying spices, sugar, and metals) and two from Bengal (carrying rice and
textiles) be sent to Muscat each year. However, in that case the second ship from Bengal

455 Diul-Sind or Dewal, etc. was the name by which the major port of Sind was known. For a discussion
     of the name and the location of the port see Monique Kervran, "Le port multiple des bouches de l'Indus:
     Barbariké, Dēb, Daybul, Lāhore Bandar, Diul Sinde," in Rika Gyselen ed., *Sites et monuments disparus
     d'après les témoignages de voyageurs* (Paris, 1996), pp. 45-92.
456 With hair coconut coir is meant.
457 Floor, *The Rise of the Gulf Arabs*, p. 37.
458 Risso, *Oman & Muscat*, pp. 77-79, 84; Parsons, *Travels*, pp. 157 (Mokha coffee was mostly brought in
     Muscati vessels), 283-84. The Mokha monsoon refers to the coffee traders who traveled from Mokha
     (Yemen) to Basra in July to sell their coffee and buy dates and other goods. On their return to the Red
     Sea many stopped at Muscat in the hope of benefiting from lower prices. Muscat's involvement in the
     coffee trade stood out so much that a British traveler bluntly stated that in 1791 'they trade mainly in
     locally-grown coffee and pearls and sail in vessels with no deck except for a small part to cover the
     helmsman and perishable goods.' Ward, *Travels*, p. 9.
459 NA, VOC 2885, Schoonderwoerd (Muscat) to Batavia (24/01/1756), f. 52-56.
460 On this problem, see Floor, *The Economy*, pp. 107-110.

would have to depart three months after the first one. This schedule also would allow the return of such a ship as soon as possible. These goods were to be bartered for pearls, copperware, rosewater, dates, various gums, brimstone, rock salt and drugs in addition to gold ducats. In this way, Rood argued, the VOC could take away business from English country traders by seeing what prices the VOC might obtain for its goods from Batavia, and make short swift voyages.[461]

His proposal was not accepted, but that did not mean that others did not see their advantage in trading with Muscat. There were above all the country traders, both European and Asian. The Sultan of Oman promoted trade with Europeans, but, according to de Pagès, not that they settled there, which was at odds with his efforts to attract Dutch and English traders. In fact, in September 1756, the governor of Muscat told the captain of the VOC ship that had come to trade that he had received a letter from Sultan Ahmad granting the Dutch the right to build a house in Muscat wherever they desired.[462] Not having a factory, the British and French appointed a local Banyan as their agent in Muscat to facilitate their trading activities. As of the 1830s, the British employed a Jew as their local agent, who later was succeeded by his son. He remained in function until 1867, when the British government appointed a consul at Muscat.[463] Dutch country traders also continued doing business with Muscat from Surat and after 1777 directly from Batavia.[464] British traders had become so familiar to the people of Muscat, that "the boys in the street will say as you pass 'God Dammy,' but they, through ignorance of the word, think it is a compliment."[465]

Sultan Ahmad's liberal and trade promotion policy was also extended to Persian merchants, despite the existing enmity between the two nations. For example, there was trade between Bushehr, Bandar Abbas and Muscat. Sultan Ahmad allowed Persians to come to Muscat to trade, but they had to pay with cash. The promise of unmolested trade also applied to the voyage to and from Persia and Muscat. However, Persian trading vessels whose destination was not Muscat were fair game for Omani vessels, who were allowed to take them as prizes, the same as they would do with Persian war vessels.[466] Muscat also

461 NA, VOC 2937, Rood to Mossel (Batavia, 08/03/1758), f. 87 (should be f. 101).

462 Floor, *Dutch-Omani*, pp. 147-49. Amin mistakenly states that the Dutch requested permission to build a factory and hoist the Dutch colors. This also holds for the Imam's alleged reply to this request, viz., "The Imam agreed that the Dutch land their cargo, hire a suitable house, and leave proper persons to carry out the business, but he refused to permit them to build a factory or hoist their colors." Amin, *British Interests*, p. 145, n. 5; Risso, *Oman & Muscat*, p. 84 is also wrong on this issue. In 1799, the Sultan told Malcolm after agreeing to a treaty with Great Britain, that he "would be equally willing if stipulated the establishment of a thousand English gentlemen instead of one at Muscat." Kaye, *The Life*, vol. 1, 110.

463 De Pagès, *Travels*, vol. 2, p. 64; Francklin, *Observations*, p. 37; Parsons, *Travels*, pp. 207-08; Sadleir, *Journey*, p. 141 (the Company's accredited broker was Goolah Anandass in 1819); Fontanier, *Voyage*, vol. 1/2, pp. 24 (Seyd-ben-Calfaun was the French agent), 43 (Ruben was the British agent); Shepherd, *From Bombay*, p. 42. The British had appointed a Resident in September 1840 to Muscat, who remained in office until 1843, see Onley, *The Arabian Frontier*, p. 232. The Dutch also had a Banyan agent in Muscat, at least until 1764, see Floor, *Dutch-Omani*, p. 259.

464 Floor, *Dutch-Omani*, pp. 161-66.

465 J. Macluer, *An Account of Navigation between India and the Gulf of Persia at all Seasons*. London, 1786, p. 11. In the 1750s, people near Hadd on the Batinah coast were also familiar with the presence of Europeans in Oman, see Floor, *Dutch-Omani*, p. 253 ("We continued going through the entire village and the people seeing us there called: *Portugees! Englees! Hollandees! Francees!*")

466 Parsons, *Travels*, pp. 188, 207-08.

Figure 42, Guards at one of the city gates, Allemann

had active trade relations with Bahrain, which in 1775 was still under Bushehr, and thus, nominally under Persian control.[467]

According to Allen, Sultan Hamad b. Sa`id (r. 1789-92) established Muscat as a coastal state that was independent from the rest of Oman, with the development of trade, enforced by naval power, as its single focus. This also meant non-interference in Omani affairs. However, Redha Bhacker takes issue with this point of view. Two of his dynamic successors (Sultan b. Ahmad r. 1792-1804 and Sa`id b. Ahmad II r. 1806-56) pursued a strong commercial policy. However, the rise of and the opposition by the Qavasem and the Utbis made achieving Muscat's policy objectives difficult, which were rendered totally unattainable after 1820, due to Great Britain's enforcement of maritime peace in the Persian Gulf.[468]

Muscat's relations with E. Africa, apart from attacks on Portuguese possessions, were with Omani-controlled Zanzibar and with Mombassa, Melinde and other ports.[469] In the eighteenth century, after peace had been concluded with Portugal, trade was also started with Portuguese ports as well as with Mauritius, which exported sugar. In return

---

467 Parsons, *Travels*, p. 203.
468 Allen, "The State of Muscat."; Bhacker, *Trade and Empire*, pp. 24-25.
469 Floor, "A description," pp. 2-3, 40; annex II.

the French from Mauritius took in return wheat and donkeys.[470] After Muscat had taken possession of Zanzibar the island became its outpost for commercial activities with E. Africa, in particular for the acquisition of slaves, ivory, rice, wood, gums, cowries, wax, and other African products.[471]

Muscat's relations with Sind were centuries old and remained active under Sultan Ahmad. Small Kathiawar Banyan vessels sailed to Oman and Muscati vessels were found in Kathiawar, while many Kathiawari Banyans resided in Muscat. Imports from Sind included cotton, cloth, saltpeter, tallow, butter, grain, oil, hides, indigo. From Mekran: sheep, *jowari* (sorghum), and grain and from Kutch: cotton, oil, silk, and cotton stuffs.[472] There continued to be an active and increasing trade with Malabar, where Omani vessels brought dates, rosewater, pearls and drugs, while purchasing rice, sugar, spices, pepper as well as shipbuilding materials such as timber and cordage from the Dutch, who held Cochin at the time. In 1775, Parsons further noted the presence of 10 Muscati vessels in Cochin.[473] Despite its own shipbuilding activities the Sultan had many of his ships built in Surat. In addition, W. India continued to be important for Muscat as the supplier of rice, cottons and goods it needed for is E. Africa trade (beads, cloth).[474] In Mangalore, which was controlled by Heydar Ali, Tipu Sultan's father and ruler of Mysore, Parsons observed in 1776 that four Muscati vessels bought rice and wheat.[475] When rice supply from Mangalore was disrupted by pirates around 1775, the Muscatis attacked and expelled them. A grateful Tipu Sultan sent a present to Sultan Ahmad to show his gratitude for this action. In return, Sultan Ahmad offered Tipu Sultan a building in Muscat, which became known as the 'Nawwab's house' and which was located to the west of Muscat port. It served as factory and warehouse for Tipu Sultan's trade with Muscat thereafter.[476]

Dutch country traders discontinued their annual voyages from Batavia to Muscat in 1796 or 1797 due to the state of war between Great Britain and the Netherlands, which had been incorporated into the French state in 1795. Moreover, in 1796 the Sultan of Muscat had concluded a treaty with the English East-India Company, in which he promised not to allow Dutch and French vessels in his territory nor allow them to establish trading stations there.[477] Sultan b. Ahmad (1794-1806) was none too happy about this commercial restriction. Although sugar and cloves were available in Western India, prices in Batavia were more competitive. Therefore, in August 1798, the Sultan sent the ship *Sib Badam* under captain Abdol-Rahman, assisted by mate al-Mu'allim Wazir, to buy sugar and other goods in Batavia. Sultan b. Ahmad clearly wanted to renew commercial relations with the Dutch, so that they might continue with their annual voyages, as had been done since 1777, or if that was not possible that Omani ships would make these

470 Griffiths, *Travels*, p. 396.

471 Niebuhr, *Beschreibung*, p. 306; Saldanha, *The Persian Gulf Précis*, vol. 2, p. 26.

472 Barendse, *Arabian Seas*, vol. 1, p. 323; NA, VOC 2863, 04/01/1755, f. 38; Saldanha, *The Persian Gulf Précis*, vol. 2, p. 26.

473 Risso, *Oman & Muscat*, p. 81; Parsons, *Travels*, pp. 229-32; Barendse, *Arabian Seas*, vol. 1, p. 326; Saldanha, *The Persian Gulf Précis*, vol. 1, p. 26.

474 Risso, *Oman & Muscat*, p 82; Parsons, *Travels*, p. 262.

475 Parsons, *Travels*, pp. 238-39.

476 Badger, *History*, pp. 2170-71; Parsons, *Travels*, pp. 239-41; Abdul Qadir, *Waqai*, p. 27. For crops raised in Oman, price list and currency and weights. Idem, p. 29. On Tipu Sultan's factory in Muscat and its operation and trade, see Mohibbul Hasan, *History*, p. 346.

477 For the text, see Risso, *Oman & Muscat*, pp. 218-19 or Bombay Records, pp. 248-49.

voyages. The Omani ship also carried some unnamed cargo and two horses as a present. Sultan b. Ahmad asked the governor-general of the VOC for special treatment given the old existing friendship between the Dutch and Oman. The *Sib Badam* had a successful journey and returned to Muscat with presents and a letter from the governor-general in Batavia. Thereafter, at least until 1806, there were annual voyages from Muscat to Batavia.[478]

What these relations with these various countries shows is that, according to Buckingham, the ships from Muscat

> were then the carriers of India, under a neutral flag, as the Dutch once were, and after them the Americans, in Europe. The wealth which their merchants acquired from the high freights given to their vessels, both by the English and the French, in the time when the India Sea was a theatre of naval war, enabled them to purchase largely of the prize goods which were then to be found in the ports of both nations at a very low rate, and to carry them in their own vessels with security to every part of the Eastern Islands, the coasts of Pegu, and the ports of the Arabian and Persian Gulfs, where their profits were immense. Their own port too, being made, like Malta in the Mediterranean, a magazine or depôt of general merchandize, the smaller vessels of all the surrounding nations who could not procure these goods from the English to French settlements direct, came and bought them here, so that the port was always crowded with shipping.[479]

In 1800, Malcolm estimated the value of the entire Persian Gulf trade at 16 million rupees (1 crore, 60 lac), most of which was trade with India and ports in the Gulf itself. Around that same time, some 68% of the trade of Muscat with British-India was with Bombay/Surat, some 25% was with Bengal and the remaining 7% was with Calcutta (Ft. George) and dependencies.[480] In 1834, Muscat traded with Gujarat, Surat, Bombay, Daman, the Bay of Bengal, and Ceylon.[481] This pattern of the dominating role of trade with India did not significantly change during the nineteenth century.

---

478 Floor, *Dutch-Omani*, pp. 167-69, 274-306.

479 Buckingham, *Travels*, p. 510.

480 Amin, *British Interests*, p. 130; Milburn, *Oriental Commerce*, vol. 1, p. 116. One year later Malcolm revised his estimate to 30,00,000 million rupees, of which 4,00,000 EIC goods the rest being Indian goods. Grummon, *The Rise of the Gulf Arabs*, p. 174, n. 7. The main imports were: coarse piece-goods, silk and cotton fabrics (Surat), oil cotton and grain (Bownaghur), iron, lead and other European goods (Bombay), rice, spars, and timber (Malabar), calicoes and chintz (Coromandel) and rice, muslin, sugar, silks, and piece-goods (Bengal). Saldanha, *The Persian Gulf Précis*, vol. 1, pp. 406-07; vol. 2, p. 26; Buckingham, *Travels*, p. 510.

481 Roberts, *Embassy*, pp. 361-62.

Table 9: Imports from British India

Year	Merchandise	Treasure	Total
	Sicca rupees	Sicca rupees	Sicca rupees
1802	35,32,988	-	5,32,988
1803	41,96,537	2,000	41,98,537
1804	53,61,813	34,075	53,95,888
1805	61,43,978	334	61,44,312
1806	77,09,937	1,215	77,11,152
Total	289,49,253	37,624	289,82,877

Source: Milburn, *Oriental Commerce*, vol. 1, p. 116.

Table 10: Exports from British India

Year	Merchandise	Treasure	Total
	Sicca rupees	Sicca rupees	Sicca rupees
1802	15,29,730	42,16,993	57,46,723
1803	15,43,999	35,81,035	51,25,034
1804	20,15,272	53,02,818	73,18,090
1805	17,02,357	50,84,272	67,86,629
1806	18,77,906	58,39,054	77,16,690
Total	86,69,264	240,24,172	326,94,436

Source: Milburn, *Oriental Commerce*, vol. 1, p. 116.

What also did not change, as Milburn and other contemporary authors pointed out, was that Muscat/Oman was running a deficit on its current account with India. It imported more than it exported, while the difference had to paid for in specie.[482]

Muscat also traded with other markets such as Yemen, Sind, Batavia, Mauritius, Zanzibar, Mekran and the various Persian Gulf Ports. For example, in 1816, some 20-30 Arab ships between 300-600 tons traded in pearls from Bahrain, dates, copper from Basra changing these with India for muslin, spices, timber, rice, pepper, and Chinese goods; with Mauritius for cotton and coffee; and with Zanzibar for gold, slaves, ostrich feathers and ivory.[483]

Like his grandfather Sultan Sa`id II realized that Muscat depended on trade for its daily bread. To encourage trade and traders under his rule "merchants have security of property and person and all creeds are welcome," while customs rates were reasonable. At the same time the Sultan actively participated in trade. In fact, he was called "the chief merchant." He had a significant comparative advantage over other merchants in that he did not pay any customs duties and the Banyans extended loans to him. However, unlike

---

482 Milburn, *Oriental Commerce*, vol. 1, p. 116; Amin, *British Interests*, pp. 130-31. On that problem for the Persian Gulf area in general, see Matthee, Floor and Clawson, *Monetary History*.

483 Buckingham, *Travels*, p. 525.

other rulers he was content with his profits.[484] However, the failure of his and Sultan Hamad's commercial policies, viz. to control access to the Gulf and trade within it, meant a reduced role for Muscat. It also meant a change of policy, which led Sultan Sa`id II seek to extend Muscati power and influence in East Africa. To increase his share in trade Sultan Sa`id II even had some of his warships transformed into commercial vessels.[485]

Despite the lack of trade statistics for Muscat prior to 1873, it is clear that Muscat's commercial situation had deteriorated since the 1800s. According to Palgrave, who visited Muscat in the mid-1860s, its last prosperous period seems to have been in the 1830s, when the city may have had 60,000 inhabitants. "The great Keysareeyah ... is now about one-third deserted; though the Sooks or market-places all around, the resort of the more ordinary shopkeepers and petty business, are still full and crowded."[486] However, the decline started much earlier. In 1816 Buckingham reported that "about twenty years since, the foreign trade of Muscat, in its own vessels, was much more considerable; and the number of ships, under other flags, resorting to its port, much greater than at present."[487] Moreover, in 1826, Sultan Sa`id II came to the realization that Muscat had no great commercial future. He wrote to his agent in Bombay that he was willing to consider "the abolishment of the slave trade if the British Government would agree either to defend him by land and sea against his enemies in Arabia and the Gulf, or to obtain Portuguese Moçambique for him as compensation. Another alternative would be for them to grant him sufficient money to enable him to withdraw from `Oman altogether and settle in Zanzibar."[488] Muscat's decline was clear to Sultan Sa`id II, as indicated by the price that he received for the customs farm of Muscat. Whereas around 1810 he received 180,000 Maria Theresia dollars, in 1835 and in 1854 this amount had dropped to respectively 105,000 and 80,000 dollars.[489] The decline was further reflected in the significant reduction of Indian and Arab merchants, whose number continued to fall throughout the second half of the nineteenth century.[490]

However, the decline was not linear, but rather progressed in fits and starts as is clear from the table below.

---

484   Owen, *Narrative*, vol. 1, p. 339; Fontanier, *Voyage*, vol. 1/2, pp. 27, 42; Bombay Records, p. 632. According to Stocqueler, *Fifteen Months*, vol. 1, p. 256, the Sultan did not so well as a merchant.

485   Fontanier, *Voyage*, vol. 1/2, p. 27. Given the imposition of the Pax Britannica in the Persian Gulf after 1820 and the abandonment of efforts to conquer Bahrain this was but a logical step. See for an analysis, Allen, "The State of Muscat," pp. 123-25. However, whenever there were troubles on the Persian side of the Gulf merchants often preferred to sell their goods in Muscat, even as late as 1838. Fontanier, *Voyage*, vol. 1/2, pp. 40-41.

486   Palgrave, *Narrative*, vol. 2, p. 369.

487   Buckingham, *Travels*, p. 509.

488   Kelly, *Britain and the Persian Gulf*, p. 428; see also Bhacker, *Trade and Empire*, pp.92-100.

489   Maurizi, *History*, p. 29; Osgood, *Notes*, p. 53; Wellsted, *Travels*, vol. 1, p. 22

490   Landen, *Oman*, pp. 138-39.

Table 11: The customs revenues of Muscat (1765-1907) in nominal terms

Year	MT$
1765	47,000
1786	93,000
1802	130,000
1804	180,000
1816	95,000
1821	90,000
1825	188,000
1827	188,000
1834	100,000
1841	180,000
1848	136,000
1854	80,000
1868	115,000
1871	105,000
1875	51,400
1883	125,000
1884	131,000
1892	17,000
1907	140,000

Source: Bhacker, *Trade and Empire*, p. 78

There were several reasons for Muscat's slow but steady decline after 1830, since those more prosperous days. First, in addition to Sultan Sa`id II's failure to achieve the objectives of his commercial policy, there was the rise of rival ports such as Basra, Bushehr, Bandar Abbas, and Bandar-e Lengeh, which, after 1820, increasingly drew more trade and reduced Muscat's importance as an emporium.[491] Second, the unsettled political situation of the country due to internecine problems, conflicts and fighting after 1820, in particular after the death of Sultan Sa`id II in 1856. This meant that the Sultan did not control much of the interior of Oman, had to spend much time and money to deal with the internal problems, while the Al Bu Sa`id were even expelled from Muscat altogether between 1868-71. The result of these conflicts was that the town was falling into ruins. Therefore, merchants preferred to send only small quantities of goods to Muscat to lower their risk. Also, much trade with India gradually was drawn to Sohar and Sur, where no customs were levied. Third, and more importantly, was the reduction and later the abolition of the slave trade in respectively 1845 and 1873,[492] which had been an important source of revenue, while the loss of Bandar Abbas in 1868 and Zanzibar in 1856, also represented a

---

491 Floor, *Lengeh*, Idem, *Bandar Abbas*.

492 Bombay Records, pp. 220, 226, 243 (in August 1822 the Sultan prohibited to sale of slaves to any Christian nation and in September 1822 allowed British warships to seize Omani vessels when sailing beyond a fixed latitude in the India Ocean).

considerable loss to the Sultan's revenues. In the 1830s, the slave trade revenues represented 13% and the Zanzibar revenues 36% of the Sultan's total revenues, or together 47%, hence their loss was a considerable financial blow. Given that the Zanzibar revenues increased considerably after the 1830s the impact must have been much greater than suggested here, because the revenues of Muscat-Matrah instead of increasing fell.[493] Fourth and finally, very important was the advent of steam navigation in the Persian Gulf in 1862. After 1820, when the British enforced security in the Persian Gulf shipping lanes, owners of native ships enjoyed a significant cost advantage over European square-rigged vessels. Therefore, the bulk of goods were transported by native ships and vessels. In 1834, Roberts observed that there were many ships in Muscat, but most were "small craft, having but a few ships and brigs."[494] However, this cost advantage lasted until the arrival of steamships in the Persian Gulf in 1862.[495] In particular, the weekly mail service provided by the British-Indian Steam Navigation Company (BISNC) had a major replacement effect. By the 1870s, the BISNC collected "at the various ports of the Persian Gulf, the produce that formerly concentrated at Muscat before it was distributed to more distant countries."[496]

These changes could not change some of the fundamentals of the trade of Muscat, and indeed of Oman. Because the country was a subsistence economy based on agriculture, incomes rose and fell in harmony with the harvest. If there was a drought or a bad harvest, for whatever reason (heavy rains; locusts), trade fell. It was not just any harvest, but in particular the date harvest that was of vital commercial importance, because dates constituted Muscat's main export commodity. This meant that if there were less dates, there was less export, and, thus, less earnings to pay for imports. Because dates were the people's main food staple, a date shortage led to increased cheap wheat imports from Persia and Basra. Trade increased of course, when there was a bumper date harvest.[497] The growing presence of American traders in the Muscat market not only boosted trade, but also brought an element of risk. For the main US import from Muscat was dates. Not just any date, but the US market demanded so-called *fard* or *fardh* dates. By 1883, the demand for this type of date had increased so much that it value had increased significantly and Omanis were planting this type to the exclusion of others. This looked like a positive development. However, when importers had overestimated US market demand, this led to overstocking in New York and finally to less export of dates by Muscat.[498] At times, date exports, and therefore trade, also suffered from competition from Basra dates.[499] Again, trade suffered when some major trading houses went bankrupt as happened in

---

493 Bombay Records, p. 633. We don't have data on the Sultan's revenues from Bandar Abbas (and from Hormuz salt), but in 1802 he allegedly received 100,000 Maria Theresia dollars from there, representing one-third of his total revenues at that time. Saldanha, *The Persian Gulf Précis*, vol. 2, p. 25.

494 Roberts, *Embassy*, p. 362.

495 On the beginning and development of steam navigation in the Persian Gulf, see Issawi, *The Economic*, pp. 166, 168-70; Landen, *Oman*, pp. 83-92, 98-100, 119.

496 Administration Report 1873-74, p. 77; Administration Report 1874-75, p. 30; Administration Report 1876-77, pp. 80-81; Goswami, *The Call*, p. 116; Sadid al-Saltaneh, *Tarikh*, pp. 52, 55 (non-payment of *zakat*). On the loss of Bandar Abbas, see Floor, *Bandar Abbas*, pp. 94-96.

497 Administration Report 1873-74, p. 77; Administration Report 1874-75, p. 30; Administration Report 1878-79, p. 120; Administration Report 1880-81, p. 207; Administration Report 1882-83, p. 140; Administration Report 1884-85, p. 112.

498 Administration Report 1883-84, p. 148; Administration Report 1884-85, p. 112. *Fard* dates are small, deep dark brown with a tender skin, a sweet flavor, and a small seed.

499 Administration Report 1885-86, p. 96.

Figure 43, Panorama of Muscat, Allemann

1883 in Bombay and Zanzibar. These insolvencies continued to have a downward impact on Muscat's imports in later years.[500] The loss of the slave trade was partly compensated by the sudden increase in arms trade after 1890, with Muscat being the main emporium for arms in the Persian Gulf.[501]

Trade, of course, was influenced by government policy, in particular the level of its customs duties. In 1765, Europeans paid 5% on imports, Moslems 6.5%, Jews and Banyans 9%. On dates, the principal export, 6% were levied in kind.[502] In 1786, there was a tax on tobacco; its revenues were used to repair the forts and government buildings. English, French and Portuguese traders paid 5%, Arabs and Persians 6.5%, Indian merchants generally 8%, but goods from Mysore only 4%.[503] Around 1800 and thereafter, Moslems paid 2.5%, while all other merchants paid 5% on imports. There was no export duty.[504] Because at the beginning of the nineteenth century "every boat going up and coming down the Gulf must touch at Maskat," the Sultan, even as late as 1820, collected 0.5% duties on all merchandise passing up the Persian Gulf in Arab ships.[505] Rates for some non–Moslem merchants were higher. British and French merchants paid 5% *ad valorem*, but other Western merchants, such as American ones, had to pay 7.5% on imports and 7.5% on exports plus presents and anchorage, prior to the treaty of 1834. Thereafter, US traders also paid 5% and even did not have to pay for pilotage.[506] This customs regime of

---

500   Administration Report 1883-84, p. 148; Administration Report 1885-86, p. 96.

501   Goswami, *The Call*, p. 118; Sadid al-Saltaneh, *Tarikh*, pp. 53-54.

502   Niebuhr, *Beschreibung*, p. 306.

503   Abdul Qadir, *Waqai*, p. 28

504   Milburn, *Oriental Commerce*, vol. 1, p. 117; Buckingham, *Travels*, p. 509; Saldanha, *The Persian Gulf Précis*, vol. 2, p. 26.

505   Saldanha, *The Persian Gulf Précis*, vol. 2, p. 26; Fraser, *Narrative*, p. 16. The customs dues were sometimes collected in kind such as in 1824. "At the Custom-House we observed a curious mode of extracting toll. A negro slave, standing on a mat at the gate, had in his hand a long sharp grooved instrument, on the principle of a cooper's bung-tap. With this, he perforated every bag of rice, that was carried past him, and extracted a small portion from each. Keppel, *Personal Narrative*, vol. 1, pp. 20-21.

506   Roberts, *Embassy*, pp. 360, 362; Fontanier, *Voyage*, vol. 1/2, p. 27 (reasonable rates).

5% *ad valorem* on imports (there was no duty on exports) remained in force during the entire nineteenth century. Goods, imported from Europe and India, had to pay a storage fee called *arziyeh* at a rate of four paisa per day per package, respectively after 21 and seven days. In addition, the following duties applied: transshipment duties 5%; dates Rs 1-8 to 2-8 per camel load; and wharfage and weighing half anna per package.[507] In July 1881, Sultan Turki increased the tax on goods coming from the interior from 1.5 or 2.5 to 5%, which increase was included in the customs farm at MT$15,000.[508]

After rice, the main imports were: slaves, British and Indian piece-goods, metals, sugar, sugar-candy, coffee, indigo, spices, dried fruit, dates, salt, pearls, ghee, etc. Most of these goods were sold to the tribal population of Oman or re-exported to the various ports in the Persian Gulf.[509] Imports from Africa in particular consisted of gums, aloes, colombo root, other drugs, ivory, tortoise-shells, rhino horns, hides, beeswax, cocoa-nut oil, rice, millet, and ghee.[510] Muscat's main import commodity was rice; in 1874, rice import was one-third of the normal volume, due to famine in Bengal. The same occurred in 1877, when less of it was imported, due to famine in W. and S. India.[511] Rice was mainly imported by square-rigged vessels from Calcutta, although their number was falling. In 1872, there were 10, while in 1877 there were only six.[512] The main exports, after dry and pressed dates, were: grain, salt and dried fish, salt, shark fins, cotton, pearls, raisins and other dried fruit, a great variety of drugs and donkeys (to Mauritius and Réunion).[513] Dates were mainly exported to the USA, India, Yemen, and Zanzibar.[514] There was also the slave trade, which around 1810 contributed 75,000 Maria Theresia dollars/year in revenue for the Sultan.[515]

From 1873 onwards there are statistics on the trade of Muscat, although these are but approximate values. According to Miles, the British political agent, "It is impossible to obtain correct returns of the trade of this port."[516] There was no change in the quality of these data, because three years later Miles commented on the trade statistics supplied by him as follows:

> It must, however, be repeated that these returns cannot be altogether relied
> upon as correct. The books of the customs' farmer, from whom they are

---

507   Administration Report 1873-74, p. 78; Sadid al-Saltaneh, *Tarikh*, p. 52.

508   Administration Report 1881-82, p. 14. For the cost of freight by local sailing ships, see details at Sadid al-Saltaneh, *Tarikh*, p. 55.

509   Administration Report 1873-74, p. 77; Ruschenberger, *A Voyage*, vol. 1, p. 135; Brucks 1856, pp. 631-32; Sadid al-Saltaneh, *Tarikh*, pp. 50, 61-62.

510   Roberts, *Embassy*, p. 361; Ruschenberger, *A Voyage*, vol. 1, p. 136.

511   Administration Report 1873-74, p. 77; Administration Report 1876-77, p. 82.

512   Administration Report 1876-77, p. 82.

513   Administration Report 1873-74, p. 77; Roberts, *Embassy*, p. 361; Ruschenberger, *A Voyage*, vol. 1, p. 135; Bombay Records, p. 632; Stocqueler, *Fifteen Months*, vol. 1, p. 255 (imports: pitch, tar, rope, hemp plus the main other items mentioned by other sources; exports: matting, pots, almonds, raisins, dry limes, wheat, etc.). In 1791, Captain Matthew Jenous submitted that Muscat traded "mainly in locally-grown coffee sand pearls and sail in vessels with no deck except for a small part to cover the helmsman and perishable goods." Ward, *Travels*, p. 9, Omani dates were prefered to those from Basra and Bushehr. Fraser, *Narrative*, p. 17; Sadid al-Saltaneh, *Tarikh*, pp. 51, 62-63.

514   Administration Report 1880-81, p. 207; Administration Report 1884-85, p. 112.

515   Maurizi, *History*, p. 29; Fontanier, *Voyage*, vol. 1/2, p. 33 (slave trade produced considerable revenues).

516   Administration Report 1873-74, p. 78.

obtained, are not kept in a way to show the exact quantities of goods passing through the Customs-house, and it is to his interest to diminish the apparent trade of the port to keep competitors out of the field. The figures given are undoubtedly much below the actuals, especially of the imports. The exports may be accepted as fairly correct.[517]

Despite the caveat as to the reliability of Muscat trade statistics nevertheless these show that Muscat's position as an entrepôt had declined, while certain characteristics such as trade pattern and partners as well as the trade deficit on the current account showed little change.

From Table IV.1 it is clear that India remained Muscat's dominant trading partner, both for imports and exports. In the first quarter of the nineteenth century, Muscat annually imported 0.4 to 0.5 million *morah*s of rice from Mangalore and the Malabar Coast. In addition, it imported large quantities of timber, pepper and cardamom from there as well as Mysore coffee via Malabar.[518] India usually supplied over 70% of all imports, although in some years its market share dropped to 58%, such as in 1885/86. India held a similar market share in Muscat's exports, for the years that data on export destinations are available. However, there is no reason to assume that this was any different during the earlier part of the nineteenth century. After all, Indian trade dominated trade in all Persian Gulf ports and had done so for centuries.

The second trading partner were the various Persian Gulf ports, including Mekran (see Table IV.1). From Persia, Muscat imported raw silk, carpets, wheat, opium, ghee and various other products in small quantities. Cottons was the major commodity imported from the Mekran. Muscat (re)exported to Bushehr coffee, pepper, sugar, metals, hides, *fathanee* (Kutch leather), rafters, spices, indigo, Kutch lamp-oil and mats (*kafat*) and gunny bags.[519]

The third trading partner was S. Arabia and E. Africa, including Mauritius and Madagascar until about 1890 (see Table IV.1). From E. Africa Muscat imported slaves, cloves, timber, masts, sugar etc.[520] After 1890 Great Britain took over this third place, with the USA and France as runners-up. The USA was only a threat to British market share in some market segments such as cottons and metal sheets. By 1880, a large share of imported cottons came from America. The British consul reported that "The superior quality of the 'Merikanis' is fully appreciated here, and they are driving the adulterated Manchesters out of the market." This trend continued for some time.[521] Although US kerosene imports were increasing this was not a product with many competitors. However, the British consul was happy to report on in 1884, that "Merikani [American] sheetings are now superseded by Bombay products."[522]

---

517 Administration Report 1876-77, p. 81; Fontanier, *Voyage*, vol. 1/2, p. 42.

518 Bombay Records, p. 632. One *morah* = 80 lbs. of rice. According to Pelly 1865, p. 66, Arabs preferred Indian rice, because "it is lighter and swells more in the boiling [than local rice]; hence it is more filling at the price, and takes longer to digest: a sufficiently nutritive substance being granted, the essentials of a poor man's food, the greatest possible bulk at a minimum cost."

519 Taylor, *A Voyage*, p. 178; Administration Report 1873-1905; Goswami, *The Call*, p. 85. For Muscat's trade with Bushehr in the 1860s, see Pelly "Remarks on the Tribes," pp. 97-98

520 Pelly, "Remarks on the Tribes," p. 66.

521 Administration Report 1880-81, p. 207; Administration Report 1881-82, p. 137.

522 Administration Report 1883-84, p. 148.

There was some trade with Java, Sumatra and Singapore.[523] In 1824, the government of the Dutch East Indies sent the vessel *Baron van der Capellen* to the Persian Gulf with a typical eighteenth-century cargo: sugar, tin, copper, spices, steel, nails, iron, and sappanwood with a total value of Dfl. 125,000. The ship not only called on Muscat, but also Bandar Abbas and Bushehr. The captain was able to sell his goods and for his return voyage took on horses, rose water, gallnuts, opium, and especially specie, which accounted for two-thirds of the value of the first return cargo. The profits were attractive enough to encourage merchants to finance four other voyages of a single ship each, between 1828 and 1831. But the fact that the Dutch had no agent representing their interests on the spot was a disadvantage. Moreover, as security on the Persian Gulf coast was uncertain it was decided to discontinue the voyages.[524] However, Armenian merchants based in Batavia continued to sail between Batavia and the Persian Gulf, with a cargo of mainly sugar.[525]

Because of the varied number of trading partners, climatological reasons as well as the use of both sailing and steamships both import and export commodities arrived and departed at different times of the year. According to de Rozario, in the 1860s, rice from Calcutta was imported from April to June. Cotton goods from Bombay came with bi-monthly steamers. Sugar from Mauritius came in August or March and arrived in no more than two ships. Coconuts, rafters and cloves from Zanzibar came in May. Grain from the Persian Gulf ports arrived in native ships. Furthermore, silk, wool, opium, and nuts (almonds etc) from Bushehr and Bandar Abbas arrived from September to March. Native sailing craft brought rice, sugar, oil, condiments, and luxury items from Bombay during the fair season. US vessels brought piece-goods, arms, ammunition, household furniture and ornaments, while Yemeni vessels brought coffee and a kind of coarse sugar. As to exports, dates were shipped from August to January. Salt from Qeshm and Bandar Abbas went to Calcutta, although it usually was used as ballast. The sweet, sticky *fard* date was not well liked in the Gulf area, but Americans loved it. Its durability allowed it to survive long voyages. American ships usually returned to New York in the fall, just in time for the dates to be served at Thanksgiving, which became a tradition. Mauritius imported salt-fish, corn and dates in return. Americans only exported *fard* dates, while Yemeni vessels took in return three to four varieties of dates. Items such as *halwa* and fruit were exported in small quantities to Calcutta, Bombay and the Persian Gulf. Shark fins were exported to China (via Singapore), while fish maws, cotton and mother-of-pearl was exported in small quantities to Europe via Bombay.[526]

By the early twentieth century, despite some arms smuggling, Muscat once again had become a minor port, be it this time a sleepy steamer port. The fall in trade and revenues also resulted in a drop in population, from about 30,000 in the mid-eighteenth century to some 15,000 in the early years of the twentieth century.

523   Roberts, *Embassy*, pp. 361-62 (Sumatra, Java, Comoros, E. Africa, Madagascar, Red Sea);
      Ruschenberger, *A Voyage*, vol. 1, p. 136.

524   N. J. den Tex, "Onze Handel in de Perzische Golf en de Roode Zee," *De Economist* 1 (1871), pp. 23, 28.

525   Floor, *Traditional Crafts*, pp. 332-34, 337-38.

526   de Rozario, "An Account," vol. 4, p. 235.

Figure 44, View of Muscat, Dieulafoye

Afterword

Despite Muscat's political upheavals the morphology of the city basically remained unchanged, be it that its fortifications were much reinforced by the Portuguese, such that these became the city's hallmarks. Also, there was a population inside the wall city and outside in the suburbs. Although data about the changes in the size and composition of the population are scarce for the period prior to the 1800s, it is clear that Muscat's population always had an ethnically mixed population. In fact, it was a population of minorities. Arabs may have dominated in the early period, and, in an a miscegenated form probably remained the largest minority. After the 1670s, Africans grew in number and by the 1800, may have become the second largest minority group. Baluchis and Mekranis, the third largest minority, probably were already living in Muscat before 1500, but they certainly became permanent residents thereafter. Many of them served in the ruler's army and navy and provided unskilled labor. Various Indian traders and craftsmen, most of whom were Hindus, had been residents in Muscat and other Omani ports at least since the 1400s. They certainly were a dominant part of Muscat society after 1500, often dominating many sectors of the economy, in particular in the nineteenth century.

As the population grew so did the city, which meant, given space constraints and economic opportunities, that many had to live in make-shift huts. The suburbs with its *barasti* huts became as emblematic for Muscat as its narrow streets and market lanes. The influx of disparate ethnic, linguistic and religious groups had consequences for public life in the city. The international mixture was enhanced by the presence of other ethnic groups, so that in Muscat's bazaar one could hear up to 14 languages spoken. Some were spoken more than others, while one or two acquired the role of lingua franca among its inhabitants. Although inter-marriage was mainly between Arabs and Africans, both socially and religiously interaction between the various groups was generally one marked by tolerance. This meant that there was cross-cultural fertilization, in particular by Africans, and the relatively free exercise of any religion. There were of course, exceptions to this rule, but these were temporary in nature. Also, be it within traditional clearly set boundaries, there was an atmosphere of political tolerance, in that people were allowed to speak their mind, question their 'betters' and even appeal to the Sultan in public. In particular, French travelers were struck by this seemingly democratic spirit such that Lt. Allemann, even went to so far to write that the spirit of 'Liberty, Equality, and Fraternity' was more in evidence in Muscat than in countries that had this slogan as their official motto.

Although without proper and easy access to the main land, Muscat had a well-organized system to ensure the supply of goods and food and everything its inhabitants, travelers and traders needed was generally available in its market. Water supply was well organized as well, not only to satisfy the needs of its own population, but also for all those ship crews that called on Muscat. Despite the oppressive heat during the summer months, when many moved to cooler locations, and the dense population living in highly unsanitary conditions with no effective medical care, living conditions were not worse than in other ports along the Indian Ocean basin.

Much of the above could be said about other Persian Gulf ports as well. The same holds for their role as ports, because Muscat did not really have a comparative advantage over these other ports. Throughout known history most ports in the Persian Gulf were but sleepy fishing villages, while a few of the more fortunate ones were ports-of-transit, or a caravan terminus for the markets up-country in the interior, which had to compete with each other for business. They were but ports-of-call and merchants chose to land their goods in those markets where customs rates, prices and business climate were the most attractive. Also, none of these ports, whether an emporium or not, had an important hinterland. In fact, Muscat had no hinterland at all, because there was no trade route into Oman's interior, hence its dependence on Matrah, which did have access to the interior. This situation had prevented Muscat from acquiring a role larger than that of the provider of water and provisions to ships coming into and leaving the Persian Gulf. It was only when the role of other ports in the Gulf was severely constrained and Muscat's rulers pursued an aggressive and cohesive trade policy that Muscat acquired some importance, once even acquiring the role of emporium between 1750-1810.

Those ports that held the role of emporium during the Islamic period, i.e. a distribution center to supply other less important ports, such as Siraf, Qish, and Hormuz, did so because they were able to force vessels coming up and down the Gulf to call on its port and pay taxes. After the fall of Hormuz in 1622, this control of access to and egress from the Persian Gulf was impossible due to the supremacy of the Dutch and English shipping. Also, this meant that the Persian Gulf boasted of several smaller emporia, the most important of which were Bandar Abbas and Basra. After 1622, the Portuguese tried in vain to make Muscat the center of their operations in the Persian Gulf. However, it was Bandar-e Kong, with Persia as its hinterland that became more important. In fact, Goa had to heavily subsidize Portuguese presence in Muscat.

The situation changed somewhat after 1650, when the Ya`ariba dynasty established rule over Muscat and Oman. However, despite the build-up of a strong fleet after the 1670s, which made Muscat the strongest local power in the Persian Gulf, the Ya`ariba rulers never were able to translate this power into an enhanced commercial role for Muscat. It was only when conditions in Bandar Abbas temporarily became less attractive for country traders (the Dutch and English East Indies companies had their own arrangements) that Muscat was able to draw a larger market share (1662-67) with competitive customs rates and a friendly welcome. However, the Ya`ariba rulers were never able to make this a lasting situation. Moreover, from 1718 to 1749 Oman was completely sidelined by a dynastic war (1718-47) and an invasion from Persia (1739-47), which meant that Muscat hardly played any commercial role of importance.

With the establishment of the Al Bu Sa`id dynasty in 1749 things changed. This was because its first ruler, Sa`id took advantage of the opportunity offered by the anarchy that reigned in the Persian Gulf. Bandar Abbas had been abandoned by both Asian and European merchants, while many of the former moved to Muscat. Bandar-e Kong had been destroyed, Bushehr was having start-up problems, while Basra was subject to attacks by the Muntafiq and Ka`b Arabs. Furthermore, shipping in the Persian Gulf was attacked by Mir Mohanna of Rig, the Banu Ka`b of Southern Khuzestan as well as by the various Hula groups on the Persian Shibkuh coast. Sultan Sa`id realized that by offering reasonable rates and a friendly welcome plus armed escort to Basra merchants would flock to Muscat, which they did. Also, having no enemies, neutral Muscati mainly state-owned vessels could go where others could not. Also, the wars between e.g. Britain and France resulted in cheap prize goods, which Muscati ships transported and its merchants sold with high profits. Finally, Muscat was the port where all kinds of goods were available that were not available to all, because of hostile relations. The result was that Muscat's political and economic elite became very wealthy.

Hamad b. Sa`id after usurping his father's rule tried to fine-tune his father's policy by developing an aggressive commercial policy aimed at controlling the entrance to the Persian Gulf and the carrying trade in the Gulf. To that end Muscat acquired a modern fleet of European ships and forced vessels to call on Muscat, just like other emporia in the past, and either through direct conquest (Gwadar) or leasing (Bandar Abbas) it controlled both sides of the Straits of Hormuz. However, the policy failed, even though Hamad's successors pursued the same objectives. This was because Muscat's power grab was strongly opposed by the Qavasem of Ra's al-Khaimah and the Utbis of Bahrain. Muscat was unable to subdue these rising powers and it had to give up its dream of controlling the trade of the Persian Gulf when Great Britain imposed a maritime peace after 1820, to which all Arab chiefs signed on. This meant that if Muscat wanted to use its naval power to subdue the Qavasem or Bahrain it had to face British naval power. The Pax Britannica in the Persian Gulf also enabled the growth of Basra, Busher, Bandar Abbas and Bandar-e Lengeh, which soon took over much of Muscat's market share. Therefore, Sultan Sa`id II, seeing that Muscat's trade was declining, changed his commercial policy by virtually abandoning Muscat and concentrating, with much success, to increase Muscati power and influence in E. Africa.

Consequently, Muscat's commercial role was greatly reduced and its trade was completely controlled by Indian traders, who before that time had to share the market with Muscati state-controlled trade. These Indian traders had played an important role in Muscat as well as other Omani ports at least since the fifteenth century. Muscat not only suffered commercial decline after the 1820s, but its ruler lost the revenues of Zanzibar (1856) and Bandar Abbas (1868), while the Sultan's growing interference in Omani affairs sapped the city's strength. Also, the arrival of steam ships supplanted the smaller local vessels that had been the main carriers of its trade until then. As a result, Muscat's trade and prosperity further declined and its once thriving Indian trading community slowly diminished in size. As a result, Muscat became a small port of little significance.

Appendix I

THE CURRENCY OF AL BU SA`ID MUSCAT

In the nineteenth century the Maria Theresia thaler was the most popular coin in the Oman region. However, during the first two decades of that century, the French and German crowns and the Spanish dollar were the most common coins in use in Muscat. But in addition all Persian and Indian coins also circulated in Muscat. The value of these coins changed in accordance with their actual silver content and the market price for silver, rather than their so-called monetary value.[1] Because India was Muscat's main trading partner, the value of, e.g., the German crown was expressed in Bombay rupees. In 1821, 100 German crowns were equal to 217 Bombay rupees. Everything was sold by the *mahmudi*, a copper coin that was locally struck, 20 of which equaled one Maria Theresia dollar. A smaller denomination was the *goz* or *gaz*; five *goz* = 1 *pie* (*paisa*) and 20 *goz* = 4 *pies* = 1 *mahmudi*. Accounts were kept in *goz* and *mahmudds*. The *mahmudi* was unit of account; 11.5 *mahmudi* = 1 French dollar, and 100 *mahmudi* = 1 *tuman*, also a unit of account.[2] Because a large variety of coins freely circulated in Muscat their value usually was expressed in another currency that was legal tender in a country that was one of Muscat's trading partners. For example, in 1834, the US envoy to Muscat noted that: one hundred and forty-two paisa or pesos made one Spanish dollar, but it varied from 120 to 150. Three and quarter of a Persian rupee made one Spanish dollar. The latter in copper coin called a black *mamoodee* = 0.25 EIC anna. 11.5 white *mahmudis* = 1 Spanish dollar, which was a money of account. 2.25 Bombay or Surat rupee minus 5 *paisa*s = 1 Spanish dollar. Spanish doublon = 14-16 dollars.[3] The Indian silver rupee and the bronze quarter anna, as well as silver quarter rupees and bronze twelfth annas (a.k.a. *ghazi*) also circulated. The quarter anna or *paisa* was called *baisa* in Muscat, because of the absence of the 'p' sound in Arabic.

In 1893, the silver currency circulating in Muscat was: (i) the Maria Theresia dollar, which was the only coin accepted in the interior. It might be said that is formed a kind of national currency and (ii) the Indian rupee, which was current with the dollar. The *mahmudi* still was a unit of account at 11.5 *mahmudi*s per dollar, in which all accounts were kept. Muscat's copper currency consisted of: (i) the Indian copper pice; (ii) the Zanzibar copper pice; and (iii) possibly the German East African copper coin. Copper coins were also partly minted by the Sultan at Muscat or for him in London. Because the Bombay

---

1 On the characteristics of the monetary system, such as existed in Muscat, see Matthee, Floor and Clawson, *Monetary History*, chapter one.

2 Fraser, *Narrative*, p. 9, n. ; Osgood, *Notes*, p. 83. Ten years later, 20 *gaz* = 1 *mahmudi* (a unit of account); 14 *mahmudi*s = half a dollar. Stocqueler, *Fifteen Months*, vol. 1, p. 257; Beth Hillel, *The Travels*, p. 112 (the *gaz* coins were made in Muscat, of inferior and much alloyed quality).

3 Roberts, *Embassy*, p. 263.

mint stopped striking copper coins in 1890, this led to a shortage of small coins in Muscat. Therefore in 1893, Sultan Faysal b. Turki began striking copper coins (*baisa*s and *ghazi*s), while coins were also imported from Great Britain. Given the general scarcity of coinage in Muscat, for commercial transactions payments were made by bills of exchange or *hundi*s, or *kundi*s as they were called in Muscat.[4]

Weights were peculiar to Muscat and Matrah and differed from those used elsewhere in Oman. Even in these cities there was a large variety and for example a customs house *man* differed from a *man* used in the market. They even differed per kind of product sold. Therefore, I refer the reader to Lorimer and Sadid al-Saltaneh, who provide detailed information on this subject.[5]

---

4 Saldanha, *The Persian Gulf Précis*, vol. 3, part 1, p. 139. In 1898 the mint was closed to the free coinage of silver (for the problems resulting see Idem); Lorimer, *Gazetteer*, vol. 2, pp. 1188, 1414. For a detailed discussion for the currency used, see Sadid al-Saltaneh, *Tarikh*, pp. 49-50. For Muscat's currency crisis after 1870, see Landen, *Oman*, pp. 127-31.

5 Lorimer, *Gazetteer*, vol. 2, 1188; Sadid al-Saltaneh, *Tarikh*, pp. 48-49; Roberts, *Embassy*, p. 263 (bazaar *man* = 8, 8.25 and 8.5 lbs.)

Annex II

The Trade of Muscat in 1673

Muscat.[1] To analyze the trade of Muscat to the best of our meagre ability, we first will mention all things brought from other countries in the year 1673, and after that what we have further observed.

We therefore, begin with **Sind** (Sindy).

Fourteen barques came here, to wit: four on 16 February, seven on 17 February, one on 20 February, one on the 1 March, one on 4 March, or in total fourteen small and large barques. They have brought the following items:

770	packages with various kinds of textiles (*cleeden*).
250	*candis* (*candijs*)[2] *borborrij*[3]
6	*candis* putchok (*petsjock*)[4]
108	*candis* lamp-oil
50	*candis* salammoniac
50	*candis* saltpeter
40	*candis* lack called *tockte*[5]
4,000	pieces of hides
30	*candis* cumin

Kutch (Ketsi).[6] Four small ships came here to wit: one on 8 May, one on 13 May, one of 14 May, one of 15 May; they brought the following to the market:

350	*candis* lamp-oil

---

1 This annex is taken from merchant Georg Wilmson's report (VOC 1305, f. 473-91vs) as published in Floor, "The Description," pp. 37-50.

2 *Candi* is weight used in South-India, which is roughly about 500 lbs, but varying much in different parts. It was generally equivalent to 20 *man*. In Tamil the word is *kandi*; the Portuguese write the word as *candil*.

3 *Borborrij* a word derived from Javanese *boreh*, is a yellow ointment prepared from coconut oil, sandalwood and curcuma.

4 *Poetsjoek* or putchock is the trade name for a fragrant root, a product of the Himalayas. It is used as a chief ingredient of Chinese pastille rods commonly called jostick.

5 *Lack* or lacca from the Hindi word *lakhi*, the resinous incrustation produced on certain trees by the puncture of the lac insect (*Coccus lacca*). The term tochte maybe the Persian word takhteh, meaning among other things 'a board, plank, or a sheet of paper.'

6 Ketsi may be identified with Kutch (Gujarat), the home base of the Sanganian pirates.

1/2	*candi* silk *t'sjadder*[7]
115	packages of cotton
60	*candi*s of *cajang*[8]
60	*candi*s of cotton yarn
57	*candi*s of peas
240	*corges*[9] of red and white *sjoerij*[10]
15	*candi*s of *milij*[11]
5	*corges* of *kad aewasije*[12]
1	*corge* of silk *longis*[13]

Patan.[14] Two small ships came here, to wit: one of 23 April, one on 6 June, which brought the following to the market:

40	packages of *bhaer*[15] of cotton
90	*candi*s of lamp-oil
23	*candi*s of ground-nuts
17	*candi*s of *milij*
42	*candi*s of peas
16	*candi*s of sesamium
50	*corges* of *zjoerijsen*[16]
12	*candi*s of cotton-yarn

From the sea ports in the **domain of the Shivaji** (Sewagie)[17] fourteen ships came here, both large, such as grabs (*goerab*)[18] and small ones, to wit:

Two from Sangameshwar (Songmeijser)[19] on 6 February.

---

7   *Tsjadder* from *chador* (Persian) meaning 'veil, tent.' Here undoubtedly fabrics are meant that were used as veils.

8   This was a Malay term for groundnut, but was also used in VOC records as the generic name for pulses.

9   A term of Indian origin meaning 'a score,' or a unit of 20.

10 I have been unable to identify this term; it may be the same fabric referred to as *jurries* by Hamilton, vol. 1, p. 77.

11 *Milij* from the Portuguese *milha*, meaning millet, but in Dutch mostly used to refer to maize or so-called Turkish wheat.

12 *Kad* from *qadak*, meaning "of a person's size" (*be andazeh-ye qad*), was a tightly woven Persian cotton fabric which is also referred to as *nankeen* in European sources.

13 *Longijs* from the Persian *longi*, a cloth worn around the loins and passed between the legs. Here is refers to the kind of textile used for that purpose.

14 Patan (Maharashtra State) in India.

15 A *bahar* is a unit of weight used in India and Persia, whose weight varies per location and per product, see Willem Floor, "Weights and Measures in Qajar Iran," *Studia* Iranica, 37/1 (2008), pp. 57-115.

16 *Zjoerijsen* or *sjoerij*, I have been unable to identify this term; it may be the same fabric referred to as *jurries* by Hamilton, vol. 1, p. 77.

17 Shivaji Bhosale (r. 1674-1680), the founder of the Maratha Empire.

18 *Goerab* or *grab* (English) from Arabic *ghurab*, meaning 'raven,' was a galley, a two or three-masted square-rigged vessel, sometimes with and sometimes without a bowsprit.

19 Sangameshwar (Maharashtra State) in India.

One from Killiesie[20] on 6 February.

Two from Hardtsjerie,[21] one of 7 March, one of 9 April.

Five from Rajapur (Ragiapour),[22] one of 20 April, one on 9 May, one on 12 May, one of 18 May, one on 19 May.

One from Harapatnam[23] on 12 May.

One from Aatsjerek[24] on 10 May.

Two from Vengurla (Wingurla),[25] one of 20 January, one of 6 April.

Altogether fourteen ships and *grab*s came, which brought a variety of goods that we therefore, have tabulated and which consisted of the following:

1358	packages of various kinds of textiles
73.5	*candi*s of cardamom
243.5	*candi*s of *borborij*
117.5	*candi*s of sandalwood
83.5	*candi*s of ginger
70	*candi*s of black sugar[26]
271	*candi*s of hemp
123.5	*candi*s of white and cooked areca[27]
140	*candi*s of tamarind
110	*candi*s of *helileh*[28]
8	*candi*s of *Cassia fistula*[29]
26	*candi*s of *goony*[30]
66	*candi*s of *coetlij*[31]
293	*corge*s of white rice *dengie*[32]
500	packages of ordinary rice

20 Killesie, probably Kelashi or Kelshi, now a village on the west coast of India (Maharashtra State).
21 Hardtsjerie, unidentified place on the west coast of India (Maharashtra State).
22 Rajapur (Maharashtra State) in India.
23 Harapatnam, unidentified place on the west coast of India (Maharashtra State).
24 Aatsjerek, unidentified place on the west coast of India (Maharashtra State).
25 Vengurla is a town in Sindhudurg district of Maharashtra, India just north of Goa.
26 *Jaggery* or *gurh*, traditionally produced sugar from date, cane juice or palm sap, mixed with a variety of other ingredients; it is brown in color.
27 This refers to the areca nuts from the areca nut palm of the Malabar coast, which, fresh or dried, were used for chewing.
28 *Terminalia chebula*, known under various vernacular names, but in Persian as *halileh-ye siyah*, or *myrobalan nigrae*, a dye.
29 Its root was used as a purgative,
30 *Goony* from Hindi *goni*, a sack, sacking. It was the popular and trading name of the coarse sacking and sacks made from the fiber of jute.
31 *Coetlij* or properly *sutli* means 'yarn, string.'
32 *Dengie* rice, perhaps refers to the Gujarati word for 'unmilled rice,' *dangar*.

83   *candis* of coir (*caijer*)

23   *candis* of lamp-oil

50   packages of glass beads

100,000 coconuts

From **Surat** and **Broach** (Brootchia)[33] two small ships called here, which brought the following to the market:

200   packages of textiles

122   *candis* of lamp-oil

104   *bahars* of 640 lbs. each of cotton

20   *candis* of *borborrij*

45   *candis* of white rice *dengie*

3   *candis* of zinc

1/2   *candi* of aguilwood.[34]

From **Karwar** (Karwaar)[35] a small ship called on 14 April that brought the following:

300   packages of textiles

83   *candis* of white rice

22   *candis* of hemp

14   *candis* of ginger

18   *candis* of areca

45   *corges* of *goony*

19   *candis* of *soetlij*

From the **Cannarese coast**, from ports such as Bhatkal (Batticale),[36] Basrur (Bassalore),[37] and Mangalore (Mangaloor)[38] twenty-seven ships and *grab*s came here with cargos of rice from 1 December of last year until the end of May, some of which made two voyages. These, according to a rough estimate, have brought here, both in packages and in bulk, more than 7,000 *lasts*.[39]

From the **Malabar coast**, seven small ships came here fully laden, to wit:

One from Calicut[40] on 10 March.

One from the same on 22 March.

---

33 Broach a port at the mouth of the Narabada, north of Surat.

34 Aguilwood or eagle-wood is the name of an aromatic wood from Cambodia and some Indian regions. It is also another name for aloes-wood, It is derived from Tamil, *agil*.

35 Karwar in Mysore, India.

36 Bhatkal on the isthmus connecting Karwar Head in Kanara with the land is situated close to Karwar.

37 Basrur is a port on the Malabar Coast (Kerala State).

38 Mangalore a port in Mysore.

39 One *last* is 2 tons.

40 Kozhikode, also known as Calicut, is a city in the state of Kerala in southern India on the Malabar Coast.

One from Ponnani (Pannanij)[41] on 23 March.

Two from Dharmapatam (Dermenepatan)[42] on 22 March.

One from Cannanore (Cannanoor)[43] on the same date.

One from the same place on 14 April, or in total seven small ships from the Malabar coast, which brought the following to the market here:

1,300	*candis* of copra or kokospit
555	*candis* of pepper
97	*candis* of red areca
276	*candis* of *borborrij*
135	*candis* of fried ginger
120	*candis* of cardamom
154	*candis* of iron
113	*candis* of sappanwood
146	*candis* of *trehiel*[44]
170	*candis* of coir
50	*candis* of *soetlij*
210	planks
123,000	coconuts

195 bundles of reeds plus bamboo, conifers and other timber.

From **Mokha** and **Aden** (Adon), three small ships arrived here between 28 May and 4 October, two belonging to the Imam and the third one to Alaur Aga.[45] These ships take most of their cargo to Persia and other parts of the Gulf. In addition fifteen to sixteen barques arrived; all of them carried the following from there to Persia and beyond:

3,000	*candis* of coffee
345	packs of pepper
53	large packs of *ruinas*[46]
22	packs of cardamom
22	packs of dried ginger
22.5	*candis* of wax
4	*candis* of camphor

---

41 Ponnani is situated south of entrance to Bharathpuzha River on the Malabar coast (Kerala).

42 Dharmapatam town is situated on an island formed by the mouths of the river of the same name on the Malabar Coast, 5 km north of Tellicherri.

43 Kannur, also known as Cannanore (Kerala).

44 I have not been able to identify this term.

45 I have not been able to identify this person.

46 *Ruinas* is a corruption of the Persian word *runas*, meaning madder, a red dye.

2.5   *candis* of benzoïn.

From **Patta** (Pate),[47] situated on the Melinde coast,[48] two small ships arrived here, one belonging to the Imam, which left thither mid-February and returned on 4 October, one vessel from Pata also arriving on 4 October. These two small ships brought the following:

570   slaves, 450 for the Imam's account and 120 for that of those of Pate

250   planks for the Imam's account

8   masts

Further, some amber and civet [skins?].

From the **Maldives** two vessels called here, which only brought coir, coconuts and chanks.

All goods that are brought here from foreign parts have to be unloaded at the bankshall (*bankschael*)[49] and have to be recorded there.

Weighed goods are mainly packed according to a standard weight and are taken to the merchants' houses after having been counted and recorded. If part of them is sold, the goods have to be taken to the weigh-house to be weighed; here the buyer's and seller's names, the date and the price of the transaction are also recorded to calculate the amount of tolls to be paid at the end of the monsoon or on departure of each ship. If the year has expired and some goods are still unsold, no toll is demanded until they are sold or transported elsewhere.

Textiles (*cleeden*) that are taken to the weigh-house are recorded and on each pack a seal is affixed, so that they cannot be changed. Nobody is allowed to open any pack in his house without the presence of an official. The settling of the account of toll to be paid is done in the same manner as with the weight goods.

Having discussed the trade of various foreign parts carried on here, Your Honor may observe next the following, to wit:

Sindh. From the textiles that are brought here, Muscat consumes 800 packs or a little more than one quarter; the remainder is taken to Bahrain, al-Qatif (Katijf), Qatar, Basra, and Persia in the following manner. Those [traders] from Sind have their agents here to whom they send their goods each year. These keep all that is consumed in Muscat and send the rest to the above places to other agents, who mostly reside there on their behalf to sell these goods. Mostly, they send the proceeds via Bandar-e Kong (Congo) back to Sind.

The fabrics (*lijwaten*) and materials that Muscat consumes have been reported to us to consist of the following varieties and quantities:

---

47 Patta Island is situated on the coast of Kenya, north of Witu. Hamilton, *A New Account*, vol. 1, p. 18 states that "Patta is now in the hands of the Musqat Arabs, and affords good Store of Teeth [tusks] and slaves for Musqat."

48 The Malindi coast is situated in Kenya.

49 Bankshall (Bengali *banksala*) a term used to denote a warehouse or the office of the Harbor Master.

		length	width	
500	*corges* of *goeries*[50]		24	1.25 *cobido*[51]
200	*corges* of *goeries*, coarse	24	1.25	
50	*corges* of black *baftas*[52]	28	1.50	
20	*corges* silk *alegia lackij*[53]	25	1.50	
40	*corges* long *loebieij*[54] 6 of which			
	make one piece	24	2	
50	*corges mawijs*[55]	4	2	
15	*corges* *mawijs* of which 2 make			
	one piece	12	1.50	
25	*corges tsiadder 'tsjonnie*[56]	12	1.50	
80	*corges* *kad kenaiedaar*[57]	24	1.25	
15	*corges* *longijs sabonie*[58]	12	2	
200	*corges paleng peosj moltony*[59] per pair	11	4	

Further, many small goods of various kinds of silk as well as cotton materials, but only a little of each.

The fabrics (*lijwaten*) of which a large quantity is transported to other parts are the following:

	length	width	
White *goeries*	24	1.25	Bahrain, Basra, Persia
Idem	32	1.50	idem
Idem	32	2	idem
Idem, coarse	24	1.50	idem
Kadmiersay[60]	20	1.25	idem
Black *baftas*	28	1.50	Mokha, Hasa, Basra, Persia

---

50 I have not been able to identify this fabric.

51 Cubit or ell.

52 *Baftas* from Persian *bafteh* or woven; these are fine cotton fabrics.

53 *Alegia* are fine fabrics made of so-called *legi* silk; they were five yards long with a wavy pattern running in the length of either side. I have been unable to identify the word *lackij*.

54 *Long* probably is *longi* (see above) and *loebieij* perhaps the place of origin.

55 I have not been able to identify this fabric.

56 Probably a corruption of the word *chador-e chaneh*, or face veil from the Persian words *chador* (veil) and *chaneh* (chin, jaw).

57 For the term *qad* see above. The word *kenaredaer* is from Persian *kenarehdar*, meaning 'having a hem, bordered.'

58 *Longi*, bath cloth; *sabonie* perhaps from Persian *sabuni*, meaning 'soap.'

59 Properly *palang-push-e Moltani*, or a cloth cover (Persian *push*) for a palanquin made in or of the design of Moltan (a region in Sind).

60 I have not been able to identify this fabric.

Alledzja molla abrahunnij[61]	24	1.50	Persia
Alledzja mioneh[62]	24	1.25	idem
Alledzja kalberga[63]	24	1.25	idem
Alledzja zjome waar[64]	11.50	1.25	idem
Alledzja zjome shah[65]	11.50	1	idem
Chitsware	18	1.50	idem
Sole-leather			
Indigo [to] Basra, al-Hasa and Persia			
Salammoniac, mostly to Persia			

Irias,[66] *putchok* in the Hindi fashion on lead (*op loot*)[67] is made in Sindh and has been brought here by the English for two consecutive years.

Kutch. All goods coming from there are sold in Muscat. Afterwards, part of it is taken by buyers from al-Hasa, Bahrain, etc. Trade from those parts does not amount to much value. If the Sanganians (Sanganers)[68] have taken vessels coming from Sind they take the goods in those vessels to their [own] vessel here to which are added other goods from Kutch.

Patan. Trade from those parts is of no importance, it mostly consists of all kinds of grains, lamp-oil, *Cassia fistula*, and cotton. It is all sold in Muscat and it is shipped from there to other parts.

Konkan (Conken).[69] This is the popular name for all sea-ports in the possession of the Shivaji. It also includes Karwar. From there, a considerable quantity of textiles and other merchandise is brought here. The weighed goods are mostly sold here and then taken elsewhere by the buyers, who then sell these goods to Arab and Persian merchants. Of the 1,500 to 1,600 packs, Muscat consumes little more than 300 to 400 consisting mostly in dongrys with black and red heads, *chador*s of all kinds, coarse *chilla*s named *cahonie* of an inferior quality,[70] common *parcallen*,[71] long 24, wide 1.5 [cubits], cotton yarns, etc.

All weighed goods are sent from here to Persia and the Arabian coast.

---

61 *Alledzja*, see above. Mullah Ibrahimi refers to the original designer or manufacturer of this special variety of this silken fabric.

62 *Miyaneh*, a Persian word meaning 'middle,' here referring to a special quality of this silken fabric.

63 Kalberga refers to the place of production, i.e. Gulbarga a city in the Indian state of Karnataka, which formerly part of Nizam's Hyderabad state. Gulbarga is 200 km from Hyderabad.

64 *Jamehvar*, a Persian word referring to a kind chintz or flowered sheet or shawl; here it indicates a quality of fabric.

65 Royal *jamehvar*, refers to a special quality or pattern of this silken fabric.

66 From the root of the iris (orris root) an oil was made, known as irias, used as a medicine.

67 I have been unable to understand the meaning of this part of the text. "*Poetjoek op sijn Hindies op loot valt in Sindij,*" where the words *op loot* don't make sense to me, unless the meaning is that the jostics rods were made of lead (*loot*).

68 The Sanganians inhabited the coast of Kathiawar and Kutch, Bayt being their principal center, see Ovington, *Voyage*, pp. 99, note 2 and 254f.

69 Konkan, the low country of Western India between the Ghauts and the sea, extending roughly from Goa northward to Gujarat.

70 *Chilla* (from Sanskrit *chela*) refers to a fine cotton fabric. *Cahonie*, probably a copyist's error for *catoni*, derived from the Arabic *qutni* (also atlas) referring to a mixed silken-cotton fabric. For the various textile terms, see Willem Floor, *The Persian Textile Industry in historical perspective 1500-1925* (Paris, 1999), chapter 2.

71 This word already occurs in Middle Dutch as *perkaal*. It is probably derived from Persian *pargaleh* and referred to a plain, un-patterned cotton fabric. For other possible meanings, see Hobson-Johnson q.v. *percaulas*.

The remainder of the textiles (*cleeden*) consisting of various kinds bought by Persian merchants at Golconda are taken here and then shipped to the small sea-ports of Persia, because they pay lower imposts, so that Muscat only serves as a transit station.

Surat. From there little trade is carried on here. The only ships that come here in the bay do so out of necessity or out of fear of the Portuguese. The goods taken here by two small ships have already been sold. The textiles consisting of two kinds, namely *kahonie* and *patha*,[72] which for the greater part is taken by Muscat, only a small quantity was taken to Basra.

Kanara. This is the store-room of Persia and Arabia. Its rice is sold here and then transported in small lots, mostly by barques, except that consumed in Muscat itself.

Malabar. All that is brought from to Muscat is for the greater part reserved by the Imam's agent, for he considers this to be the most profitable trade. He keeps the goods until the end of the year and will not sell them if he cannot make a considerable profit. These goods are transported to the surrounding Arabian and Persian sea-ports, which trade he increases or decreases, depending on the state of the market in Persia or elsewhere.

Mokha. Coffee is the main item from Mokha, all of which is taken to Basra and Persia. Only a little is stored and brought here by Arab merchants; the greater part is transshipped or forwarded by the same barques. The fact that this year pepper, cardamom, and ginger were brought here was caused by the abundant import and low prices of these goods in Mokha. Formerly, they used to sell better there.

Patta, situated on the Melinde coast. This trade is carried on by the Imam. He only takes cash, rice and dates when he sails thither. From Patta 400 to 500 slaves, masts, planks and other construction timber are taken. The annual trade carried on by the citizens [of Patta] with a small vessel is of little importance. They bring more or less 150 to 200 slaves, some ambergris, some tortoise shell, further conifers and other construction timber.[73]

Maldives. We have already mentioned what is brought from there, which only consists of trifling goods.

The prices of weighed goods fluctuated during the trading season. We have noted it every month and recorded it at the end of the *Dagregister* (Journal) to which we humbly refer. The same holds for the list of fabrics (*lijwaten*), which we have already sent.

The abovementioned places take various goods from Muscat and are reported to consist of the following:

Sind annually imports around 1,400 to 1,500 great *bahars* of 1,600 lbs of dry as well as wet (*pakdadel*) dates; 400 to 500 candis of copra; 300 to 400 candis of white areca depending on the size of the imports [into Muscat]. Furthermore, *ruinas*, pepper, cardamom, lead, tin, sandalwood, is taken depending on the market situation there [i.e. Sind].

---

72 I have not been able to identify the term *patha*. Possibly, *patha* just refers to the Sanskrit word *patta*, meaning 'fabric, strip of cloth,' or to the famous *patola* fabrics from Gujarat, which are colorful silken *ikats*. For the term *cahonie*, see note 590.

73 Robert Padbrugge suggested in his report (VOC 1288, f. 437r-vs) that it would be worthwhile to investigate the slave trade of the island situated on the coast of Sofala (Caffala/Mozambique) where many castrated negroes (*caffers*) were offered for sale. Here they were bought with prices ranging from 10 to 14 Spanish reals (*Spaanse matten*) and sold at 25 to 36 *rijksdaalders* (the Dutch base unit of account) equal to 2.5 Dutch guilders) per slave. The slave dealers refused to sell slaves to Padbrugge, because they feared that the negroes might become violent [?] (*voor den droos hebben*).

Kutch annually imports 600 to 700 *bahars* of dried and wet dates; 100 to 150 candis of copra; 40 to 50 candis of white areca; 35 to 40 candies of *tebhiel*,[74] *hing*,[75] pepper, etc., depending on whether the Malabar spices are expensive or cheap in Patan.

Patan annually imports 200 to 300 *bahars* of dry and wet dates.

Konkan imports nearly 1,000 *bahars* of dry and wet dates; 100 candis of *ruinas*; 100 corges of *japancij*;[76] 400 candis of *hing*; 100 to 150 horses; some rosewater and fruits; and cash.

Surat imports. Depending on whether ships call here, 200 to 300 *bahars* of dry and wet dates per ship in exchange for cash.

Kanara only imports cash, but sometimes also 30 to 40 horses for the *Neijk* [77] or ruler of their land.

Malabar. Little else is taken back to their country other than cash, except for some saltpeter, rose-water, Persian earthenware, and fruits.

Mokha. If spices such as cloves and nutmegs had a willing market there, they take some of these goods from Kong, sometimes also from Muscat. Furthermore, native loaf-sugar, textiles from Sind and great quantities of wet dates.

Patta imports the following from Muscat: [blank] *bahars* of dates; Spanish reals called *foulerie*;[78] some Persian porcelain, some 10 to 20 chests of Muscat loaf-sugar; black coarse *longi* from Vengurla; *chador daboelij*[79] of poor quality; *paatsjehaer* called *chonne*[80] produded in Masulipatnam; Surat textiles (*cleeden*); blue *baftas*; some chintzes; *patha*; *chador cambatij*,[81] black *cannekijns*.[82]

Bahrain, **Qatar** and **al-Hasa** buy from the merchandise that comes here from all parts in such large quantities as will not be seen anywhere else.[83]

There are a few goods of which they only take a small share. They only enter the market for cash.

The trade of Abdollah. We can hardly say anything definite about trade in general, because the Imam's agent, without whose prior permission no foreigner may buy or sell anything, daily issues new trade regulations. During our stay here, we observed that he sometimes acquired a whole ship's cargo, sometimes half, and also a quarter [of a cargo]. He allowed himself to be guided by his expectation of the profit likely to be earned from the imported goods. All this is done under the guise of an honest sale, and they [the importers] are hardly allowed to show that they feel wronged in some way, or else prison is their future. The *nakhoda* (*nachoda*) or commissioner of any ship that arrives from abroad has to submit the bill of lading. He is then ordered to provide samples of each good ashore. Then he has to go to Abdollah's house, who is there with a company of Banyans and others, to contract a sale.

---

74 I have been unable to identify this product.

75 Asafetida, a fetid smelling spice, much used in Indian cooking. It is made from the dried latex exuded from the living underground tap root of several species of Ferula, which is a perennial herb.

76 *Yapanji*, a felt cloak or great coat used to protect the wearer against the cold and rain.

77 *Neijk*, from Hindi *nayak*, meaning 'leader, chief, general.'

78 I have not been able to identify this term, which is not known to numismatists.

79 Referring to a *chador* coming from Dabhol, a famous Konkan port.

80 *Paatsjehaer* or patchery, were so-called Coromandel textiles (*doeken*), which usually were two in one piece of double width. The term *chonne* I am unable to explain, unless the Persian word *khaneh* (house) is meant, which is unlikely.

81 The *Cambatij chadors* are those coming from Cambay, the famous port of Gujarat, which Arab authors usually rendered as Kanbayat.

82 Fine cotton fabrics; the word is derived from the Portuguese *canequim*.

83 According to Robert Padbrugge (NA, VOC 1288, f. 437), each year 1,000 *last* (a Dutch measure equivalent to two tons) of pepper were imported from Malabar. The greater part of this pepper was re-exported with caravans to/from Mecca. He also reported that the best-selling products were those of inferior quality.

But only he [i.e. Abdollah] is allowed to make a bid, which is rather unsettling, for it is so low that the seller is taken aback. However, whatever the market situation is, he is obliged to part with his goods- the one more, the other less-, at a difference of 1.5, 2, 3, 4 to 5 *laris* per *man* of 24 lbs. or per *candi* of 480 lbs. with the current rate.

The goods, which Abdollah wants to buy and to have sole possession of, are taken ashore and via the weigh-house taken to the Imam's warehouses. The remainder is stored in the seller's house, where they may be sold to the highest bidder, provided Abdollah has given permission and that it is sold with a considerable profit. In case of a sale at higher prices than at first was fixed, the first transaction automatically becomes null and void, without any further ado [by Abdollah]. When these people are about to leave, and he still may have a liking for some goods, he then again concludes a transaction with them, but as has been stated above, [at a price] lower than the market rate. This mostly happens with weighed goods, for he seldom takes an interest in textiles (*cleeden*). Several goods such as anchors, coir, and coir ropes, planks and masts, cannons and iron are mostly bought on the account of the Imam. He, after having taken from these goods what he needs, then sells the remaining coir, iron, etc. to others.

If one of the arriving merchants wants to be exempt from these servitudes, he settles with him [Abdollah] for a certain amount, or he only profits from a share of their goods in order to be allowed to sell the rest of them to their own liking. All this having been done, nothing may be sold [nevertheless] before the broker has obtained his prior permission to do so after having informed him that there might be something to his liking. In that case, when the goods have already been put on the scales, and he pereives a profit for himself, the purchaser has to withdraw. Or if Abdollah allows him [the purchase], it has happened that he will take half of it. Thus, hardly anything is sold by foreigners that he does not have a share in it. Yes, it even happened that at a time that rice in bulk (*stort rijst*) yielded more profit than rice in straw packages, he ordered those traders [with the packaged rice], for which they had already paid 0.25 *mahmudi* per package or less, depending on whether they were big or small, to unpack it to be allowed to market it freely. When they sold it by measure again they had to pay a certain amount for each *candi*. This is the way trading practices of the Imam's agent were carried out during our stay. What else he will think of is as yet unknown. The majority of the Basrur voyagers [*vaarders*] have left almost bankrupt from here, because of the extraordinary imposts and the assignations with which they have been paid, from which they may expect little merchandise or money. [For example,] there was a Brahmin (*Bramene*) whom they forced to buy more than 40 horses at an unusual high price, in addition to another from whom they took his ship half by force. Those people thought that they could pay with an assignation after deduction of 17.5 per cent tolls on the price agreed upon. [The Basrur voyagers] were not prepared to accept this and lodged a complaint with the Imam, but found little consolation. For as soon as the latter had turned his back, they were put in prison for quite some time. However, they could not be persuaded to agree to the unreasonable transaction and were released. Because the monsoon had long since come to an end, they [the Arabs] suggested that the [Basrur voyagers] took the ship back. Nevertheless, they were held liable for a mere 1,000 *laris*, which the Arabs thought they could claim from their fellow-countrymen. The *nakhoda* again refused to give in and was again put in prison, where he finally died. In this way and the previously mentioned manner, foreigners are treated here.

The **tolls** that were levied on the merchandise coming from the various parts and which were traded here during the year 1673 are reported to be as follows:

Sind, Moorish goods brought here from there paid 2.5 [per] 100; Banyans: 5 per 100.

Kutch, both Moors[84] and Banyans, because they are ruled by a heathen[85] government: 8 per 100.

Patan, Moors: 2.5 per 100; Banyans 8 per 100.

Surat, Moorish goods: 2.5 per 100; Banyans: 5 per 100.

Rajapur, both Moorish and Banyan goods, because the ports are in the dominion of the *Shivaji*: 8 per 100.

Vengurla, the ame: 8 per 100.

Karwar, Moors: 2.5 per 100; Banyans: 5 per 100.

Basrur, **Mangalore**, and **Bhatkal**, because they took so much from the Imam's men: 17.5 per 100.[86]

Basra, Moors: 21/2 per 100; Banyans: 5 per 100.

Persia, the same; idem.

Mokha, the same; idem.

The inhabitants [of Muscat/Oman] being Arabs used to stay there once a year, and pay 2.5 per cent of their property (*middelen*). If they go on a voyage and return with cargo, nothing is collected, when they showed a document stating that they had paid their taxes. However, they have to make so many voyages with their merchandise that they have to pay tolls every time, and to show documentary proof thereof at the place of their residence.

The Banyans living or residing in Muscat did not pay anything on their imported goods in former times. However, on our arrival, a toll was levied for the very first time. Those who possessed a house (*landshuis*) in the country had to pay 5 and others 10 percent. Therefore, everybody was forced to take a house in the country, even though it was only a shop. Similarly, nothing was taken, be he Moor or Banyan (even when the goods were taken ashore), when the goods were sent to other parts. However, this also changed during our stay, for now both Moors and Banyans have to pay the legal toll on all goods that are taken ashore. However, if a ship continues is journey, only toll is levied on that which was taken ashore or that which was transshipped; in case of Moors sometimes allowances are made.

From exports nothing was levied during our stay, when the importer had already paid tolls on them.

Similarly, nothing is paid on exports of dates and loaf-sugar and everything that may be produced in the country itself.

The brokerage (*makalardij*). The brokerage of all coming and going ships in addition to the city's weigh-house and thirty to forty houses have been farmed out to a Banyan, called Thewil, for

---

84 Meaning Moslems.

85 Heathen meaning a non-Moslem government.

86 Those of the Indian coast retaliated by coming with a few ships only, which created a scarcity of rice and other products in Oman. In 1674, the Imam, therefore, tried to attract merchants from the Kanara and Malabar coast by lowering the customs duties for them to 2.5 percent only, see NA, VOC 1297, Bent to XVII, Gamron 1 April 1675, f. 1015. In 1674 rice was hardly obtainable in Muscat and it was one of the best-selling goods, because during the last monsoon only four vessels from Cannanore had come with pepper, ginger, cardamom, coir, etc., see NA, VOC 1304, Ritsert to Maetsuycker, Mascate, 19 September 1674, f. 523.

an amount of 30,000 *lari*s.[87] He appoints a broker for each ship to whom they are obliged to pay 1.5 percent of all goods sold. One percent is for the main broker and 0.5 percent for his deputy brokers, yes even for the freight goods, which a ship takes from here on its return journey.

Similarly, this broker allots to each ship or its crew one of the said houses, for which he gets 5, 6 to 8 *abbasi*s,[88] depending on their size or location, until the day they leave. Someone who stays here until the end of the monsoon makes a contract with him for the second journey from the end of May or till the last of September or October for that whole period.

The weigh-house. The sum that is paid for each pack, be it two or up to 50 *man* of 8 lbs. amounts to: 1/16 *mahmudi*[89]

apart from cloves, each pack	0.25
rompen,[90] each pack	idem
cinnamon, each pack	idem
one *bahar* of cotton of 640 lbs.	5/8
tin or lead per *schuit*[91]	1/16
silk per pack	2
elephants tusks per candi	idem
for the measurable products (*meetwaren*), the buyer pays for each candi	0.5
in case of *parren*,[92] insufficient to make up one candi each	1/32

The weights that are used are as follows:

the great *bahar* is	200 *man* of 8 lbs or	1,600 lbs.
the small *bahar* is	80 *man* of 8 lbs. or	640 lbs.
the candi is	60 *man* of 8 lbs. or	480 lbs.
ferasileh (*farsaleh*)[93]	10 *man* of 8 lbs. or	80 lbs.
mandilij	3 *man* of 8 lbs. or	24 lbs.
man Muscat	1 *man* of 8 lb.	8 lbs.

20 *parren* equals one candi of rice, wheat, etc.

---

87 A *lari*, meaning [coined in] Lar, a town in southern Persia, is a coin shaped like a bent hairpin. They were struck with circular or rectangular dies in Persia, Ottoman Empire, Arabia, India, Sri Lanka and the Maldives and a popular coin for international trade.

88 A Persian silver coin first issued in the late 16th century.

89 A Persian silver coin first struck in the 1580s.

90 A kind of inferior nutmeg.

91 Metal was cast in the mould of a *schuit* or boat. In Japan, for example, *schuitzilver* (boat silver) was the base unit of account. In British records tin is usually recorded in a number of 'pigs.'

92 I have been unable to identify this product.

93 *Feraseleh* a weight of 10.5 kg.

The horse trade is also of great interest to the Imam's agent. Every year he sends a factor to Persia who buys twenty to thirty ordinary horses on the account of the Imam. In addition 200 to 300 horses, one year more, the other less-, are marketed here and sold to Indian merchants. Those that remain unsold, the [horse] traders take them to Vengurla, Rajapur and other Indian seaports. No Indian merchant is permitted to buy any horse, before he has bought one, two or three from the Imam's agent, so cheap that he has to scratch his head. Sometimes, they have to buy all his horses without being permitted to buy [horses] from anybody else. He himself has no stables, but on learning that there are some prospective buyers, he goes to the Persian horse traders and chooses from their herd those he likes best. He then holds on to them and is unwilling to sell them at civil prices. One may well think that they will almost have to eat through their fodder, [for] he will have to keep them until the end of the monsoon, or through lack of keep, let them go free. These people are afraid that they have to be accommodating by buying at least two, three or four and as long as he still has some animals; the brokers are not allowed to take buyers elsewhere.

The toll on the sale of horses is paid by the seller and amounts to 2.5 percent for one.

Its brokerage has been farmed out this year for 1,600 *mahmudi*s and its farmer was Chelliel,[94] for which he in turn enjoyed the following:

Rent for the area where the horses are kept, which amounts to two *mahmudi*s per head per month.

Similarly for the preparation of the transportation of each horse, ten *mahmudi*s of which the merchant and the *nakhoda* each pay half.

Freight. The rate of freight to all parts is paid as follows, but there are no fixed rates, for they fluctuate depending on the number of ships or vessels moored.

Sind. During our stay freight was paid in a ship

For each *bahar* of 1,600 lbs.	15	R a/s[95]
Later on another ship	11.5	R a/s
Similarly on barques	25, 30	laris
Mostly it is stipulated to pay there the return voyage:		
weighed goods per candi	12	*laris*
piece goods or packs, each pack	36-40	*laris*
Idem, on barques, weighed goods, per candi	7	*laris*
each pack	25	*laris*

Kutch. Per *bahar* of dates to be paid there | 25, 30 | *laris*
Other products per *candi* | idem |

Vengurla. Each great *bahar* of dates | 26 | *laris*
each horse | 20 | *pagodas*[96]
each chest | 8 | *mahmudi*s
on these brokerage has to be paid, *ruinas* etc. per candi | 20-25 | *laris*

94 Khalil, who was the special advisor to Abdollah, the Imam's agent.
95 Short for Indian rupee.
96 The *pagoda* or *pardao* was a coin long current in South India, see Hobson-Jobson, s.v.

Rajapur. The great *bahar* of dates   33–35   *laris*

    ruinas per *candi*   32   *laris*

    each horse   idem as above

    If thereafter, another voyage is made 400 *mahmudis*.

Mokha. From here:

    each great *bahar* to be paid there   40   *laris*

    one pair of chests of loaf sugar   9–12 *mahmudis*

    big pack of textiles   20   *mahmudis*

    small ditto   14–16   *mahmudis*

    The return voyage:

    one *bahar* or candi to Muscat   2   Rsd.[97]

    to Basra   3   Rsd.

Basra. each pack of textiles   10   *mahmudis*

    weighed goods per candi   10   *mahmudis*

    loaf-sugar, pair of chests taken as one   4–5   *mahmudis*

Gamron and **Kong**. textiles, each pack   2.5–3   *mahmudis*

    loaf-sugar, pair of chests   2.5   *mahmudis*

    weighed products per *candi*   4   *mahmudis*

    One pack of cotton of one *bahar* of 680 lbs.   8   *mahmudis*

Ships. All private vessels have to lower their sails (*inkorten*) on arrival in the inner-bay between the water passage-ways. Immediately a guardsman is put on board, who stays on the vessel until it leaves. All goods in it have to be unloaded, unless the ship's crew have stipulated otherwise prior to their entrance into the inner-bay. Nobody is allowed to leave or come aboard after sunset. No ship is allowed to depart before having shown a pass to the western water passageways.

As far as we have been able to learn and observe from the coming and going ships are as follows:

The monsoon from here to **Sind**: the barque usually leaves the first time in mid-May and the second time in mid-September and return again in mid-November until mid-February. Those who want to come from Sind to here after these dates have to sail out of the Gulf to gain the East[ern winds] and may then smoothly run back.

Ships from all other Indian parts come here for the first of December until the end of May. They return home again until 8 to 10 May. Those who have not left by then have to stay until mid-September, when the monsoon to India is good again.

Mokha. From here to Mokha, barques and ships leave from the first of October until the last of February of the next year. They return from there when the monsoon starts at the end of February

---

97 Short for *rijksdaalder* the first coin issued by the Republic of the Seven United Provinces ofthe Netherlands; it was equal to 48 or 50 *stuivers*.

until the end of April, or at the latest 10 May. Those who have not left by then remain until mid-August, when they can come hither until the end of September.

Patta. From Muscat to Patta one can go from mid-November until 20 February. To return from Patta the first time is from the end of March until mid-April, which is the latest date. Those who have not left by then have to stay until the end of July when they can sail again from there until 20 or 25 August. The Imam's vessel mostly is out at sea for 9 to 10 months.

A n n e x   I I I

PRICES IN MUSCAT, 1672-1675

Hereunder are prices for some goods offered from the year 1671 until 1674 as they were found in VOC documents.[1] From merchant Georg Wilmson's report (VOC 1304, f. 479vs) it is clear that selling goods in Muscat was a time consuming affair. Apart from having business flair, a merchant needed patience. Goods were both sold in large and small quantities, both by the merchants and shopkeepers. Sales in Muscat depended very much on the information on prices elsewhere in the Persian Gulf and on information of the prices in Surat (this held especially true for the merchants from Mokha). If the level of imports was high this had a downward effect on the price level. This was due to the fact that the absorption capacity of the Muscat market was not considerable. Muscat was a transit port and the prices of the Muscat market, therefore, had to compete with those of other markets in the Persian Gulf. For example, the consumption of cloves and *rompen* in Muscat itself was not more than two to three hundred pounds yearly for each product. Depending on prices elsewhere merchants from Bahrain, al-Hasa, or Mokha would or would not buy the rest. Wilmson observed that for a great range of goods, prices in Muscat in 1673 (pepper, ginger, sandalwood, sappanwood, *borborrij*, textiles) were lower than in Persia or Basra. Therefore, he advised against VOC trade in Muscat, for its sales there would have a negative impact in sales in Persia and Basra. Because it would be dangerous to draw conlusions from these prices given below other than that what has been said above, I just offer these prices as a piece of tentative information. More such information will be needed before analytical conclusions for the Muscat economy are drawn.

Prices in Muscat (VOC 1279, f. 467vs-468; Harckz report)

500 *bahar* pepper [from Malabar]	per *bahar*	38.5	*rijksdaalders*
35 *bahar* Cochin cinnamon	per *bahar* of 400 lbs.	100-115	"
Kanara rice	per *last*	65-70	"
sold in April–May 1671			

Prices in Muscat in 1672 based on Dutch trade information (VOC 1279, f. 1030).

Japanese copper (*staafcoper*)	per 24 lbs.	44	*laris*

---

1   This is a reproduction from Floor, "The Description," pp. 50-53.

Rompen (inferior nutmeg)	per 8 lbs.	33–35	"
Japanese camphor	per 8 lbs.	30–32	"

Prices of goods sold by Wilmson in 1762–73 in Muscat (VOC 1304, f. 497vs–480).

Japanese copper (*staafcoper*)	per 24 lbs.	42–44.5 *laris*	
Tin	per 24 lbs.	38–40.5 "	
Japanese camphor	per 8 lbs.	29–30	"
Rompen	per 8 lbs.	33–34	"
Cloves	per 8 lbs.	93.5–95 "	
retail	120	"	
Radix china	per 8 lbs.	2.5–21	"
Cinnamon	per 8 lbs.	52	"

Goods sold by others

Wild Kanara and Malabar cinnamon		per 480 lbs.	
ordinary		40–70	"
middle		150	"
best		320–400	"

Prices in Muscat (VOC 1285, Wilmson to de Haze, Mascate 10 July 1673, f.418).

Pepper	per *bahar* of 400 lbs.	25	Rupees
Dried ginger	"	20	"
Borborrij	"	10	"
Red areca	"	12	"
Benzoïn	per *farsala* of 24 lbs.	16	"
Cloves	"	81	"
Rompen	"	20	"
Cardamom	"	10	"
Copper	"	8	"
Lead	"	3.5	"
Zinc	"	9	"
Loaf sugar	"	5	"
White Surat sugar	"	3.5	"
Tin	"	10	"
Coffee	per *bahar*	45	"

These prices were considered to be high, due to the fact that during the season only eleven vessels came to Muscat: Surat 2; Diu 3; Cambay 3; Daman 1; Malabar 1; Bombay 1.

Some merchants from Mokha wanted to buy cloves at 100 Rs., but did not come, because of lack of money (f. 516).

Prices of goods sold by the VOC trading station mid-1674 (VOC 1297, f. 1014vs).

		Profit in %
200 Ps. *chiadder cangij*[2]	at 100 *mahmudi*s per 40 Ps	25.5
240 Ps. *pancerangijs*[3] "		23 13/18
200 Ps. *foppelij*[4]	"	30
70 lbs. eagle-wood	at 65 *mahmudi*s per 6 lbs.	11 3/8
1,890 lbs. Japanese copper	at 40 *lari*s per 24 lbs.	136 13/16

Prices of goods sold by the VOC trading station in August 1674 (VOC 1304, f. 523).

Vengurla textiles were sold to Arab merchants from the interior (*bovenlandse Arabieren*) at 50 *abbasi*s per corge of 40 Ps. The normal price was 35 to 38 *abbasi*s. The profit was only 20 percent due to the high cost-price and expenses. At a price of 38 *abbasi*s the annual turnover was estimated to be 150 packages, if nobody else imported them.

---

2 I have not been able to identify the term *cangij*.
3 Probably *panj rangi* (Persian), meaning 'five colored.'
4 I have not been able to identify the term *foppelij*.

Appendix IV

IMPORTS INTO AND EXPORTS FROM MUSCAT 1872-1900

Table IV.1: Imports into Muscat (in Maria Theresia dollars)

From	1872/3	1873/4	1874-5	1875-6	1876-7	1877-8	1878-9
India	13,88,900	10,05,930	9,36,195	1,124,390	864,630	1,030,800	914,757
Persian Gulf	3,04,900	3,41,785	4,51,320	478,750	325,950	505,650	189,070
S. Arabia Africa	44,600	38,800	48,800	61,700	107,340	152,050	104,240
Mauritius Batavia	-	25,000	6,000	7,300	14,000	-	5,000
Singapore	1,500	600	24,200	4,140	1,890	-	8,450
Total	17,39,900	14,12,115	14,66,515	16,76,280	1,313,810	1,688,500	1,221,335

Source: Administration Report 1873-74, pp. 80-89; Administration Report 1874-75, pp.31-41; Administration Report 1875-76, pp.79-91; Administration Report 1876-77, pp.84-93; Administration Report 1877-78, pp.131-42; Administration Report 1878-79, pp.123-34;

Table IV.2: Exports from Muscat (in Maria Theresia dollars)

From	1872/3	1873/4	1874-5	1875-6	1876-7	1877-8	1878-9
India							
Specie						200,000	150,000
Total	12,59,000	6,77,975	7,51,400	1,032,450	1,161,750	1,379,400	890,975

Administration Report 1873-74, pp. 80-89; Administration Report 1874-75, pp.31-41; Administration Report 1875-76, pp.79-91; Administration Report 1876-77, pp.84-93; Administration Report 1877-78, pp.131-42; Administration Report 1878-79, pp.123-34;

Table IV.1: Imports into Muscat (in Maria Theresia dollars)

From	1879/80	1880/1	1881-2	1882-3	1883-4	1884-5	1885-6
India	12,22,940	12,85,237	1,175,090	12,62,728	1,341,568	1,320,955	991,857
Persian Gulf	3,01,610	2,08,645	350,845	4,01,305	413,393	433,880	391,690
S. Arabia Africa	1,85,300	1,48,640	144,920	2,10,025	153,285	130,990	187,350
Mauritius Batavia	18,100	-	-	-	-	-	-
Singapore	8,350	9,850*	13,150*	23,215*	-	-	-
US - Mauritius					74,735	77,200	126,400
Total	17,36,300	16,52,372	1,684,005	18,97,273	1,983,981	1,963,025	1,697,297

Administration Report 1879-80, pp.136-48; Administration Report 1880-81, pp.209-25; Administration Report 1881-82, pp.139-54; Administration Report 1882-83, pp.142-57; Administration Report 1883-84, pp.149-61; Administration Report 1884-85, pp.113-25;
Administration Report 1885-86, pp.97-109;
* = Singapore and Mauritius

Table IV.2: Exports from Muscat (in Maria Theresia dollars)

From	1879/80	1880/1	1881-2	1882-3	1883-4	1884-5	1885-6
Specie	2,00,000	2,20,000	250,000	2,00,000	225,000	400,000	350,000
Total	15,22,175	14,70,990	1,332,040	14,78,254	1,604,575	1,641,555	1,392,535

Administration Report 1879-80, pp.136-48; Administration Report 1880-81, pp.209-25; Administration Report 1881-82, pp.139-54; Administration Report 1882-83, pp.142-57; Administration Report 1883-84, pp.149-61; Administration Report 1884-85, pp.113-25; Administration Report 1885-86, pp. 97-109.

Table IV.1: Imports into Muscat (in Maria Theresia dollars)

From	1886/7	1887/8	1888-9	1889-90	1890-1	1891-2	1892-3
India	1,137,350	1,175,830	1,193,080	1,388,403	1,438,610	1,318,582	1,438,340
Persian Gulf	367,475	416,840	401,560	373,004	341,470	326,980	345,640
S. Arabia Africa	180,885	208,525	210,030	194,394	162,340	189,120	184,710
Mauritius Batavia	-	-	-	-	-	-	-
Singapore	-	-	-	-	-	-	-
	92,100	61,200	52,600	41,925	40,850	31,550	13,150
Total	1,777,810	1,862,395	1,857,270	1,997,725	1,983,270	1,866,232	1,981,840

Administration Report 1886-87, pp. 44-55; Administration Report 1887-88, pp. 57-67; Administration Report 1888-89, pp. 48-58; Administration Report 1889-90, pp. 50-60 Administration Report 1890-91, pp. 36-46; Administration Report 1891-92, pp. 38-48; Administration Report 1892-93, pp. 44-54

Table IV.2: Exports from Muscat (in Maria Theresia dollars)

From	1886/7	1887/8	1888-9	1889-90	1890-1	1891-2	1892-3
Specie	355,000	300,000	320,000	300,000	400,000	5,00,000	400,000
Total	1,447,480	1,440,685	1,403,100	14,06,605	1,432,690	15,83,280	1,054,595

Administration Report 1886-87, pp. 44-55; Administration Report 1887-88, pp. 57-67;
Administration Report 1888-89, pp. 48-58; Administration Report 1889-90, pp. 50-60
Administration Report 1890-91, pp. 36-46; Administration Report 1891-92, pp. 38-48;
Administration Report 1892-93, pp. 44-54

Table IV.1: Imports into Muscat (in Maria Theresia dollars)

From	1893/4	1894/5	1895-6	1896-97	1897-8	1898-9	1899-1900
India	1,498,905	1,535,600	1,651,930	1,640,000	2,226,500	1,962,200	1,657,900
Persian Gulf	313,141	335,030	359,005	243,000 Iran	145,000	165,500	297,560
S. Arabia Africa	227,180	191,700	198,125	67,500 Turkey	69,000	71,500	108,110
UK	-	-	-	800,000	900,000	200,000	383,600
France	-	-	-	50,000	100,000	60,000	61,550
US, UK, Mauritius; Singapore	15,780	17,200	174,700	29,000	27,000	48,000	40,000
Other	-	-	-	50,000	70,000	85,000	52,000
Total	2,055,006	2,079,600	2,288,760	2,879,500	3,537,500	2,592,200	2,600,720

Administration Report 1893-94, pp. 44-54; Administration Report 1894-95, pp. 43-53; Administration Report 1895-96, pp.53-73; Administration Report 1898-99, pp. 114-15, Administration Report 1898-1900, pp. 124-25.

Table IV.2: Exports from Muscat (in Maria Theresia dollars)

From	1893/4	1894/5	1895-6	1896-97	1897-8	1898-9	1899-1900
India	-	-	-	1,225,800	1,311,200	1,227,200	1,117,700
USA	-	-	-	110,000	70,000	60,000	48,000
Turkey Asia	-	-	-	135,000	152,000	135,000	119,000
Iran	-	-	-	116,000	43,000	42,000	61,000
Zanzibar/E. Africa	-	-	-	161,500	161,500	137,600	104,300
Other	6,00,000	500,000	75,000	61,000	96,800	95,000	83,300
Total	17,20,320	1,628,580	1,419,450	1,903,300	1,834,500	1,679,400	1,533,300

Administration Report 1893-94, pp. 44-54; Administration Report 1894-95, pp. 44-53; Administration Report 1895-96, pp.53-73; Administration Report 1898-99, pp. 114-15, Administration Report 1898-1900, pp. 124-25.

Table IV.3: Comparison of imports and exports 1873-1900 (in Maria Theresia dollars)

Year	Imports	Exports	Difference
1873-74	14,12,115	6,77,975	734,140
1874-75	14,66,515	7,51,400	715,115
1875-76	16,76,280	1,032,450	643,830
1876-77	1,313,810	1,161,750	152,060
1877-78	1,688,500	1,379,400	309,100
1878-79	1,221,335	890,975	330,360
1879-80	17,36,300	12,59,000	477,300
1889-81	16,52,372	6,77,975	974,397
1881-82	1,684,005	7,51,400	932,605
1882-83	18,97,273	1,032,450	864,823
1883-84	1,983,981	1,161,750	822,231
1884-85	1,963,025	1,379,400	583,625
1885-86	1,697,297	890,975	806,322
1886-87	1,777,810	1,447,480	330,330
1887-88	1,862,395	1,440,685	421,710
1888-89	1,857,270	1,403,100	454,170
1889-90	1,997,725	14,06,605	591,120
1890-91	1,983,270	1,432,690	550,580
1891-92	1,866,232	15,83,280	282,952
1892-93	1,981,840	1,054,595	927,245
1893-94	2,055,006	17,20,320	334,686
1894-95	2,079,600	1,628,580	451,020
1895-96	2,288,760	1,419,450	869,310
1896-97	2,879,500	1,903,300	976,200
1897-98	3,537,500	1,834,500	1,703,000
1898-99	2,592,200	1,679,400	912,800
1899-1900	2,600,720	1,533,300	1,067,420

For a similar table with values in Rupees and Pound sterling, see Landen 1967, p. 125.

Bibliography

ARCHIVES

AHU - Arquivo Histórico Ultramarino, Lisbon
   C.I.: Caixas da India
ANNT -Arquivo Nacional da Torre do Tombo, Lisbon
HAG -Historical Archives, Panaji, Goa [see *BFUP*]
NA - Nationaal Archief (the Hague, the Netherlands).
 VOC - Records of the Verenigde Oostindische Compagnie (VOC) (Dutch East Indies Company)

- VOC 1103, 1106, 1113, 1134, 1135, 1143, 1188, 1240, 1242, 1252, 1259, 1273, 1288, 1304, 1305, 1354, 1379, 1732, 1747, 2416, 2417, 2448, 2449, 2476, 2510, 2593, 2863, 2885, 2973.
- KA 1071, 1071 bis, 1072 bis, 1077, 1086.
- Collectie Sweers/Manis 9

BOOKS AND ARTICLES.

Abdul Qadir, Khwaja. *Waqai-i manazil-i Rum: Tipu Sultan's mission to Constantinople.* tr. Mohibbul Hasan. Delhi, 2005.

Administration Report = *Administration Report on the Persian Gulf Political Residency for the year (1873 to 1940)* in Government of India. *The Persian Gulf Administration Reports 1873-1947*, 10 vols., Gerrards Cross, Archives Editions, 1986.

Albuquerque, Brás Afonso de. *Comentários do grande Afonso de Albuquerque, capitão geral que foi das Indias orientais em tempo do muito poderoso Rey D. Manuel, o primeiro deste nome* 4 vols. (Lisbon, 1774), translated into English by Walter de Gray Birch as *The Commentaries of the Great Afonso DAlboquerque, second viceroy of India.* 4 vols. London, 1875.

Albuquerque, Afonso. *Cartas de Afonso de Albuquerque, seguidas de documentos que as elucidam* 7 vols. eds. Raimundo António de Bulhão Pato and Henrique Lopes de Mendoça. Lisbon, 1884-1935.

Allemann, Emile. "Mascate," *Le Tour du Monde* vii and viii, 16 and 23 February 1901, pp. 73-84 and 85-96.

Allen, Calvin H., Jr., "The Indian Merchant Community of Muscat," *BSOAS* XLIV/1 (1981), pp. 39-53.

___, "The State of Muscat in the Gulf and East Africa, 1785-1829", *International Journal of Middle East Studies*, 14 (1982), pp. 117-127.

Anonymous. *Epistolae Indicae et Iapanicae de mvltarum gentivm ad Christi fidem per Societatem Iesu conversione.* n.p., 1570.

Anonymous, "The Cholera", *Museum of foreign literature, science and art*, Volume 20, pp. 301-22.

Anonymous, *Relãçao das plantas e descripção de todas as fortelezas, cidades e povoações que os Portugueses têm no Estado da India* ed. A. Botelho da Cousa Veiga. Lisbon, 1936.

APO = *Arquivo Português Oriental* ed. Joaquim Heliodoro da Cunha Rivara 6 vols. [Nova Goa, 1857-76] reprint New Delhi, 1992.

al-Ashban, A. A. "The Foundation of the Omani Trading Empire under the Ya`arubah Dynasty 1642-1719," *Arab Studies Quarterly* I/4 (1979), pp. 354-71.

ACE = *Assentos do Conselho do Estado 1618-1750 (Proceedings of the State Council at Goa)*, edited by Panduronga S. S. Pissurlencar/ Vithal T. Gune, 5 vols. (Bastorá/Goa: Rangel, 1953-57).

Assentos do Conselho da Fazenda (1613-1621). Gune, V. T. ed. (Panaji/Goa, 1979).

Aubin, Jean. "Les princes d'Ormuz du XIIIe au XVe siècle," *Journal Asiatique* CCXLI (1953), pp. 77-137.

___, "Le <Orçamento do estado da Índia> de António de Abreu (1574)," *Studia* 4 (1959), pp. 169-289.

___, "Documents," *Mare Luso-Indicum* I (1971), pp. 137-68.

___, "Merces manuelinas de 1519-1520 para a India," in *A Abertura do Mundo. Homenagem a Luís de Albuquerque* 2 vols. (Lisbon, 1987), vol. 2, pp. 123-37.

Aucher-Eloy, Rémy. *Rélations de Voyages en Orient de 1830 à 1838*. 2 vols. Paris; de Roret, 1843.

Badger, George Percy. *Imams and Sayyids of Oman*, 2 vols. London: Hakluyt Society, 1871.

Bailey, R. W. *Records of Oman*. 8 vols. Buckinghamshire: Archive Editions, 1988.

Baladouni, Vahe and Makepeace, Margaret. *Armenian Merchants of the Seventeenth and Early Eighteenth Centuries. English East India Company Sources*. Philadelphia, 1998.

Barbosa, Duarte. *The Book of Duarte Barbosa* translated by M. Longworth Dames, 2 vols. London, 1918-21.

Barendse, R. J. *The Arabian Seas*. New York/London: M.E. Sharpe, 2002.

___, *Arabian Seas 1700-1763*. 4 vols. Leiden: Brill, 2009.

Barros, João de. *Da Ásia*. de João de Barros e de Diogo de Couto. Nova ed. 24 vols. (Lisboa, Na Regia Officina Typografica, 1777-1788) reprint: Livraria S. Carlos, 1973-1975.

Bathhurst, R.D. *The Ya`rubi Dynasty of Oman*. unpublished dissertation Oxford University, 1967.

___, "Maritime Trade and Imamite Government: Two Principal Themes in the History of Oman to 1729," in: D. Hopwood, *The Arab Peninsula. Society and Politics*. London, 1972, pp. 89-106.

Benjamin, Israel Joseph. *Eight Years in Asia and Africa from 1846-1855*. Hanover, 1859.

Bent, J. Theodore, "Muscat," *The Living Age*, sixth series, vol. ix, Jan-March 1896, 169-77.

Beth Hillel, David. *The Travels of Rabbi David D'Beth Hillel; from Jerusalem, through Arabia, Koordistan, part of Persia and India*. London, 1832.

BFUP = *Boletim da Filmoteca Ultramarina Portuguesa* 50 vols. Lisbon, Centro de Estudos Históricos Ultramarinos, 1955-1989.

Bhacker, Mohammed Reda. *Trade and empire in Muscat and Zanzibar: roots of British domination*. Exeter, 1992.

Binning, R.B. M. *A Journal of Two Years' Travel in Persia, Ceylon, etc*. 2 vols. London, 1857.

Birks, Herbert. *The life and correspondence of Thomas Valpy French*. 2 vols. London; Murray, 1895.

Blakeney, Richard. *Journal of an Oriental Voyage*. London, 1841.

Bocarro, António. *Década 13 da Historia da India*, edited by Rodrigo José de Lima

Felner, 2 vols. Lisbon, Academia Real das Ciências, 1876.

___, *Livro das plantas de todas as fortalezas, cidades e povoações do estado da India Oriental*. 3 vols. Lisbon, 1992.

Bombay Records, see Government of Bombay.

Botelho, Simão. *Tombo do Estado da India* in Rodrigo José de Lima Felner ed. *Subsidios para a historia da India portugueza* (Lisbon, 1868).

Boussac, Marie-Françoise and Salles, Jean- François. *Athens, Aden, Arikamedu*. New Delhi: Manohar, 2005.

Buckingham, James. *Travels in Assyria, Media and Persia*. London, 1970.

Carré, Abbé. *The travels of Abbé Carré in India and the Near East (1672-74)*, 3 vols. London: Hakluyt, 1947.

Castanheda, Fernão Lopes. *História do descobrimento e conquista da Índia pelos Portugueses*. 2 vols. Porto, 1979.

Castro, D. João de, Obras Completas de D. João de Castro, eds. Armando Cortesão e Luís de Albuquerque. Coimbra, Academia Internacional de Cultura Portuguesa, 1976.

Colomb, Philip Howard. *Slave catching in the Indian Ocean*. London: Longmans, 1873.

Coolhaas, W. Ph., *Generale Missieven van Gouverneurs-Generaal en Raden aan Heren XVII der Verenigde Oostindische Compagnie*, 6 vols. (The Hague, 1960-1980).

Cordeiro, Luciano. *Como se perdeu Ormuz*. Lisbon, 1896.

___, *Dois Capitães da India*. Lisbon, 1898.

___, *Questões Histórico-Colonais* 3 vols. Lisbon, 1936.

Cordeiro, Luciano and Stiffe, A.W. "Correspondence," *Geographical Journal* 11 (1898), pp. 187-90, 305-06.

Correia, Gaspar. *Lendas da India* ed. Rodrigo José de Lima Felner 4. vols. in 8 parts. Coimbra, 1860-66.

Couto, Diogo de. *Décadas* see Barros.

Curzon, G. N. *Persia and the Persian Question*, 2 vols., London, 1892.

da Silva, José-Gentil. "Une image de l'*Estado da Índia* au debut du XVIIe siècle et ses enseignements", in *Arquivos do Centro Cultural Português* 4 (1972), p. 271.

de Gobineau, Arthur. *Trois Ans en Asie*. 2 vols. Paris: Bernard Grasset, 1922.

Della Valle, Pietro. *Les Fameux Voyages de Pietro della Valle*. 4 vols. Paris: Gervais Clovzier, 1664.

Den Tex, N.J. "Onze Handel in de Perzische Golf en de Roode Zee," *De Economist* 1 (1971), pp. 1-41.

de Pagès, Monsieur Pierre Marie François, *Travels Round the World: In the Years 1767, 1768, 1769, 1770, 1771*, 3 vols. London: J. Murray, 1793.

de Rivoyre, Barthélemy Louis Denis. *Obock, Mascate, Bouchire, Bassorah*. Paris: E. Plon, 1883.

de Rozario G. "An account of Muscat," in: Bailey R, editor. *Records of Oman 1867–1947*, 8 vols. N.p.: Archive Editions, 1988, vol. 4, pp. 231-43.

Diario do terceiro conde de Linhares 2 vols. Lisbon, 1937-43.

Dieulafoy, Jane. *A Suse. Journal des fouilles 1884-1886*. Paris: Hachette & Cie, 1888.

DRI = *Documentos Remetidos da India ou Livros das Monções* eds. R.A. Bulhão Pata and A. da Silva Rego 12 vols. Lisbon, 1880-1972.

DUP = *Documentação Ultramarina Portuguesa* 8 vols. A. da Silva Rego et al. eds. Lisbon, 1960-83.

Engineer, Asghar Ali. *The Muslim communities of Gujarat: an exploratory study of Bohras, Kholas, and Memons*. New Delhi: Ajanti, 1989.

Filippo della S. Trinita, *Viaggi Orientali*. Venice, 1670.

Floor, Willem. "A Description of Muscat and Oman anno 1673/1084 H," *Moyen Orient & Océan Indien*, vol. 2 (1985), pp. 1-69.

___, *The Afghan Occupation of Iran*. Paris: Etudes Iraniennes, 1998a.

___, *Traditional Crafts in Qajar Iran (1800-1925)*. Costa Mesa: MAZDA, 2003.

___, *A Political and Economic History of Five Port Cities, 1500-1730*. Washington DC: MAGE, 2006.

___, *The Rise of the Gulf Arabs. The Politics of trade on the northern Persian littoral 1730-1792*. Washington DC: MAGE, 2007.

___, "The First Dutch Voyage to Thatta (1631). The Journal of Gregorij Cornelisz." *Anais de Historia de Alem-Mar* IX (2008), pp. 381-421.

___, *The Rise and Fall of Nader Shah*. Washington DC: MAGE, 2009.

___, *The Rise and Fall of Bandar-e Lengeh. The Distribution Center for the Arabian Coast, 1750-1930*. Washington DC: MAGE, 2010.

___, *Bandar Abbas, The Natural Trade Gateway to Southeast Iran*. Washington DC: MAGE, 2011.

___, *Dutch-Omani Relations. A Commercial & Political History, 1651-1806*. Washington DC: MAGE, 2014.

Fogg, Wm. Percy. *The Land of Arabian Nights*. Chicago, 1875.

Fontanier, Victor. *Voyage dans l'Inde et dans le golfe Persique par l'Égypte et la mer Rouge*. 2 vols. Paris: Paulin, 1841.

Foster, William ed. *The English Factories in India 1618-1669*. 13 vols. London, 1906-27.

Francklin, William. *Observations made on a tour from Bengal to Persia in the years 1786-7* [London, 1790], repr. Tehran, 1976.

Fraser, J. B. *Narrative of a Journey into Khorasan*. [London, 1821], reprint Karachi, 1984.

Gavetas = *As Gavetas da Torre do Tombo, Gavetas I-XXIII* (henceforth *Gavetas*) 12 vols., edited by A. Silva Rego. Lisbon: Centro de Estudos Históricos Ultramarinos, 1960-77.

Germain, A. "Quelques mots sur l'Oman et le Sultan de Maskate," *Bulletin de la Societe Geographique de Paris* 5 (1868), pp. 339-64.

Geary, Gratan 1878. *Through Asiatic Turkey. Narrative of a Journey from Bombay to the Bosporus*. 2 vols. London: Sampson Low, Marston, Searle & Rivington.

Gosvami, CChaya 2011.The Call of the Sea. *Kachchi Traders in Muscat and Zanzibar, c. 1800-1880*. Hyderabad: Orient Blackswan Private.

Gouvea, António de, *Relaçam em que se tratam as guerras e grandes vito,rias que alcançou o grande Rey de Persia Xa, Abbas, do grão Turco Mahometo, e seu filho Amethe as quaes resultarão das Embaxadas que por mandado da Catholica Real Majestade de Rey D. Felippe II de Portugal fizerão alguns Religiosas da Ordem dos Ermitas de Santo Agostinho aà Persia* (Lisbon, 1611) translated into the French by A. de Meneses as *Relation des grandes guerres et victoires obtenues par le roy de Perse Cha Abbas contre les empereurs de Turquie Mahomet et Achmet son fils, ensuite du voyage de quelques religieux de l'ordre des Hermites de Saint-Augustin envoye,s en Perse par le Roy catholique Don Philippe second roy de Portugal*. Rouen, 1646.

Government of Bombay. *Selections from the records of the Bombay Government No. XXIV- New Series*. Bombay, 1856. reprint Cambridge: Oleander Press, 1985, cited as Bombay Records.

Government of India, *Report on the Administration of the Bombay Presidency for the year 1879-80*, Bombay: Government Press, 1882.

___, *Gazetteer of the Bombay Presidency, History of Gujarat*, Bombay: Government Press, 1896.

Graves, Philip. *The life of Sir Percy Cox*. London: Hutchinson, 1941.

Grey, W.G. "Trades and Races of Oman," *Quarterly Journal of the Mythic Society*, vol. 2, no. 2 (January 1911), pp. 60-61.

Griffiths, John. *Travels in Europe, Asia Minor and Arabia*. London, 1805.

Gune, V. T. ed. *Assentos do Conselho da Fazenda (1613-1621)*. Panaji/Goa, 1979.

Habibi, Hasan and Vothuqi, Mohammad Baqer. *Barrasi-ye tarikhi-ye siyasi va ejtema`i-ye asnad-e Bandar `Abbas*. Tehran: Bonyad-e Iranshenasi, 1387/2008.

Hamerton, Lt. Col. Atkins. "Brief Notes containing information on various points connected with His Highness the Imaum of Muskat" (1855), in Bombay Records, pp. 235-45.

Hamilton, Alexander. *A New Account of the East Indies*. 2 vols. in one. (London, 1930) reprint Amsterdam 1970.

Hamilton, Walter *The East Indian Gazetteer: containing particular descriptions of ... Hindostan*. 2 vols. London: Parbury, Allen and Co., 1828.

Helfer, Pauline. *Travels of Doctor and Madame Helfer in Syria, Mesopotamia and Burmah*. 2 vols. London: Bentley, 1878.

Henshaw, Joshua. *Around the World*. New York, 1840 [not available to me].

Heude, William. *A Voyage up the Persian Gulf, and a Journey Overland from India to England in 1817*. London, 1819.

Ibn Majid, *Arab Navigation in the Indian Ocean before the coming of the Portuguese*. Translated by G.R. Tibbets. London, 1971.

Johnson, Col. John. *A Journey from India to England through Persia, Georgia, Russia, Poland and Prussia in the Year 1817*. London: Longman, 1818.

Kaempfer, Engelbert. *Amoenitatum Exoticarum. Fasciculi V, Variae Relationes, Observationes & Descriptiones Rerum Persicarum* (Lemgo, 1712) reprint Tehran: Imp. Org. f. Soc. Services, 1976.

___, *Die Reisetagebücher* ed. K. Meier-Lemgo. Wiesbaden, 1968.

Kaye, John William. *The Life and Correspondence of Major-General Sir John Malcolm*. 2 vols. London: Smith, Elder & Co, 1856.

Keppel, George Thomas. *A Personal Narrative of a Journey from India to England* London, 1827.

Landen, Robert G. *Oman Since 1856: Disruptive Modernization in a Traditional Arab Society*. Princeton: Princeton University Press, 1967.

Le Gouz, Francois. *Les Voyages et Observations du Sieur de la Boullaye-Le Gouz*. Paris 1653.

Lockyer, Charles. *An account of the trade in India*. London, 1711.

Lorimer, J. G.. *Gazetteer of the Persian Gulf, Oman, and Central Arabia*, 2 vols., Calcutta, 1908-15.

Lumsden, Th. *A Journey from Merut in India to London*. London, 1822 [reprint Memphis: General Books, 2010.

Luz, Francisco Paulo Mendes da, *Livro das cidades e fortalezas que a coroa de Portugal tem nas partes da India e das capitanias e mais cargos que nelas e da importancia delles* [1581] in *Studia* 6 (1960) and as separate off-print.

Macgregor, John. *Commercial statistics: A digest of the productive resources, commercial legislation*. 5 vols. London: Whittaker & Co., 1850.

MacGregor, C. M. *Narrative of a Journey through the province of Khorassan* 2 vols. London: Wm. Allen & Co, 1879.

Maindron, Maurice "Mascate," *La revue hebdomadaire* vol. 5/April 1898, pp. 321-46, 461-77, 605-27.

Malcolm, John. *Sketches of Persia*. 2 vols. London: John Murray, 1828.

Markovits, Claude 2000. *The Global World of Indian Merchants 1750-1947. Traders of Sind from Bokhara to Panama*. Cambridhe: Cambridge UP.

John Martineau, *The Life and Correspondence of Sir Bartle Frere*. London, 1895.

Matos, Luís ed. *Das relações entre Portugal e a Pérsia 1500-1758. Catálogo bibliográfico da exposição comemorativa do XXV centenário da monarquia no Irão* Lisbon: Fundação Calouste Gulbenkian, 1972.

___, *Imagens do Oriente no século XVI: reprodução do códice português da Biblioteca casanatense*. Lisbon, 1985.

Maurizi, Vincenzo. *History of Seyd Said, Sultan of Muscat*. [London, 1819] reprint Cambridge: Oleander Press, 1984.

Membré, Michele. *Relazione*, ed. G.C. Scarcia (Rome, 1969), p. 54 translated by Morton, A.H. as *Mission to the Lord Sophy of Persia (1539-1542)* London, 1993.

Mignan, R.A. *A Winter's Journey through Russia, the Caucasian Alps, and Georgia* London, 1839.

Milburn, William. *Oriental Commerce*. 2 vols. London: Black, Parry, and Co, 1813.

Miles, F.B. *The countries and tribes of the Persian Gulf*. 2 vols. in one. London: Frank Cass & Co, 1966.

Minorsky, Vladimir. *Hudud al-`Alam. "The Regions of the World" A Persian geography 372 A.H.-982 A.D.* London, 1937.

Murrell, William Meacham. *Cruise of the Frigate Columbia around the world*. Boston: B. Mussey, 1840.

al-Naboodah, H.M. "The commercial activity of Bahrain and Oman in the early Middle Ages," *Seminar for Arabian Studies* 22 (1982), p. 81-96.

Nadri, Ghulam A. *Eighteenth-Century Gujarat: The Dynamics of Its Political Economy, 1750-1800*. Leiden: Brill, 2009.

Niebuhr, Carsten. *Beschreibung von Arabien aus eigenen Beobachtungen und im lande selbst gesammelten Nachrichten*. Copenhaguen: Nicolaus Möller, 1772.

___, *Reisebeschreibung nach Arabien und andern umliegenden Ländern*. 3 vols. in one Zürich, 1997.

Osgood, Joseph Barlow Felt. *Notes of Travel: Or, Recollections of Majunga, Zanzibar, Muscat, Aden, Mocha, and Other Eastern Ports*. Salem: George Creamer, 1854.

Ovington, John. *A Voyage to Suratt: In the Year 1689*. London, 1696.

Owen, W.F.W. *Narrative of Voyages to Explore the Shores of Africa, Arabia, and Madagascar* 2 vols. London: Richard Bentley, 1833.

Özbaran, Salih 1994, *The Ottoman Response to European Expansion. Studies on Ottoman-Portuguese Relations in the Indian Ocean and Ottoman Administration in the Arab Lands During the Sixteenth Century.* Istanbul: Isis.

Palgrave, William Gifford. *Narrative of a Year' Journey Through Central and Eastern Arabia (1862-63).* 2 vols. London: MacMillan & Co, 1866.

Parsons, Abraham. *Travels in Asia and Africa.* London, 1808.

Pelly, Lewis. "Remarks on the Tribes, Trade, and Resources around the shore line of the Persian Gulf," *Bombay Geographical Society* XVII (1865), pp. 32-112.

Peterson, J. E. "Oman's diverse society: Northern Oman, "*Middle East Journal*, vol. 58/1 (2004), pp. 31-51.

___, *Historical Muscat: An Illustrated Guide and Gazetteer.* Leiden: Brill, 2007.

Pfeiffer, Ida 1852. *A Woman's Journey Around the World.* London

Pires, Tomé. *The Suma Oriental of Tomé Pires, an account of the East, from the Red Sea to Japan, written in Malacca and India in 1511-1515* translated and edited by Armando Cortesão 2 vols. London, 1944.

Potter, John. "The Eastern Coast of Arabia from Cape Rosalgat to Muscat ... from the remarks made by Lieutenant John Potter," in: Joseph Huddart, *The Oriental Navigator, Or, New Directions for Sailing to and from the East Indies, China, New Holland.* London 1801, pp. 158-64.

Potts, D. T. *The Arabian Gulf in Antiquity.* 2 vols. Oxford: Clarendon Press, 1990.

Ratnagar, Shereen. *Trading Encounters. From the Euphrates to the Indus in the Bronze Age.* New Delhi: Oxford UP, 2004.

Raynal, Guillaume-Thomas-François abbé, *A philosophical and political history of the settlements and trade ...,* 8 vols. London: W. Strahan and T. Cadell, 1783.

Rego, António da Silva ed., *Documentação para a história das missões do padroado português do Oriente* 12 vols. Lisbon, 1947-58.

Risso, Patricia. *Oman & Muscat, an early modern history.* New York: St. Martin's Press, 1986.

Robert, Edmund. *Embassy to Eastern Courts.* New York, 1837.

Rodrigues, Francisco. *The Book of Francisco Rodrigues, Rutter of a Voyage in the Red Sea, Nautical Rules, Almanack, and Maps, written and Drawn in the East before 1515,* ed. Armando Cortesão. Nendelm/ Liechtenstein, 1967.

Ross. E.C. ed. *Annals of Oman from Early Times to the Year 1728 AD.* Cambridge: Oleander Press, 1984.

Ruschenberger, S. W. *A Voyage round the World; Including an Embassy to Muscat and Siam, in 1835, 1836, and 1837 ...* George C. Read, by an Officer of the U. S. Navy, 2 vols., New York: Charles S. Francis; Boston: Joseph H. Francis, 1840.

Sadid al-Saltaneh, Mohammad `Ali Khan. *Tarikh-e Muscat va `Oman, Bahrain va Qatar.* ed. by Ahmad Eqtedari. Tehran: Donya-ye Ketab, 1370/1991.

Saldanha, J. A. *The Persian Gulf Précis* 8 vols. Gerrards Cross, 1986.

Samarqandi, Abdol-Razzaq. *Matla` al-Sa`deyn* 2 vols. ed. M. Shafi`. Lahore, 1949.

Samuel, Jacob. *Journal of a Missionary Tour through the Deserts of Arabia to Bagdad.* Edinburgh, 1844.

Sanceau, Elaine ed. *Cartas de D. João de Castro.* Lisbon, 1954.

Scholz, F. *Muscat, Sultanat Oman. Geographische Skizze einer einmaligen arabischen Stadt* 2 vols. Berlin, 1990.

Schürhammer, G. *Die zeitgenössischen Quellen zur Geschichte Portugiesische-asiens und seiner Nachbarländer, 1538-1552.* Rome, 1962.

Serjeant, R. B. *The Portuguese off the South Arabian Coast.* Oxford, Oxford UP, 1974.

Skinner, Thomas. *Adventures during a Journey Overland to India.* 2 vols. London: Bentley, 1837.

Smith, Gerald Rex. "Muscat in the Arab Lexicographers and Geographers," *Journal of Oman Studies* 6/1, 1983, pp.145-48.

Sousa, Fr. Luís. *Anais de D. João III.* 2nd ed. by M. Rodrigues Lapa 2 vols. Lisbon, 1951-54.

Stack, Edward. *Six Months in Persia.* 2 vols. New York: G.P. Putnam's Sons, 1882.

Stiffe, A.W, "Ancient Trading Centres of the Persian Gulf. IV. Maskat. *Geographic Journal* X (1897), pp. 608-18.

___ , "A visit to the hot springs of Bosher, near Muscat, with a route map," *The Transactions of the Bombay Geographical Society*, Volume 15 (1860), pp. 123-27.

Stocqueler, J. H. *Fifteen Months' Pilgrimage through untrodden tracts of Khuzistan and Persia*. 2 vols. London: Saunders & Otley, 1832.

Straussens, Johan J. *Reisen durch Griechenland, Moscau, Tartarey, Persien, Ost-Indien, Japan und unterschiedliche andere Länder*. Amsterdam: Jacob von Meurs und Johannes von Sommern, 1678.

Taylor, Fitch. *A voyage round the world*. 2 vols. New Haven/New York: Mansfield/Appleton, 1846.

Teles y Cunha, João Manuel de Almeida. *Economia de um império. Economia política do Estado da Índia em torno do mar Arábico e golfo Pérsico. Elementos conjuncturais: 1595-1635*. Universidade Nova de Lisboa, 1995.

van der Chijs, Jacobus Anne et alii eds. *Dagh Register gehouden in't Casteel Batavia vant passerende daer ter plaetse als over geheel Nederlandts India* 1642-1684, 31 vols. Batavia-`s-Gravenhage, 1887-1931.

von Oppenheim, Max. *Vom Mittelmeer zum Persischen Golf*, 2 vols. Berlin: D. Reimer, 1899.

Ward, Philip. *Travels in Oman*. Cambridge: Oleander Press, 1987.

Wellsted, James Raymond. *Travels in Arabia*, 2 vols. (London: John Murray, 1838; reprinted Graz: Akademische Drucke, 1978.

___ , *Travels to the City of the Caliphs, along the shore of the Persian Gulf*. 2 vols. London: H. Colburn, 1840.

Weeks, Edwin Lord. *From the Black Sea Through Persia and India*. London: Harper & Brothers, 1896.

Wicki, Joseph. *Documenta Indica* 16 vols. Rome, 1948-84.

Wilkinson, J. C. "Bayasirah and Bayadir," *Arabian Studies* vol. 1 (1974), pp. 75-85.

___ , *Water and Tribal Settlement in South-East Arabia*. Oxford, 1977.

___ , *The Imamate Tradition of Oman*. Cambridge, 1987.

___ , "Maskat," *Encyclopedia of Islam*2, vol. VI, p. 734.

Zwemer, S. M. *Arabia: The Cradle of Islam*. New York: Fleming H. Revel, 1900.

___ , "Notes on Oman," *National Geographic Magazine* 22/1 (January 1911), pp. 89-98.

Index

CPSIA information can be obtained at www.ICGtesting.com
Printed in the USA
LVOW09s1351091114

412004LV00012B/2/P

9 781933 823768